JUST AN AVERAGE KID FROM IOWA
A JOURNEY OF FAITH

Gordon Sorenson

Just an Average Kid from Iowa
—A Journey of Faith—

Inquiries should be made to:
hummerrv@comcast.net

Published by Gordon Sorenson
12 Rolling Glen
Tomball TX, 77375

Library of Congress Catalog-in-Publication Data
available upon request

ISBN 978-1-60725-425-6

Cover and Book design by: Sherry Paavola, Paavola Design

Printed in the United States of America
at MGB Printing Services, Inc.
Cottage Grove, MN

Printed, November 2008

ACKNOWLEDGEMENTS

My first acknowledgements are to my parents, Harold and Carol Sorenson, who provided the genes, the stable home environment, and moral integrity that shaped my formative years. Then, to my wife Betty and our three daughters, Cynthia Buehler, Sherry Paavola and Shannon Farrier for their love and support and the bulk of my "fond memories". Beyond these precious ones, the list is endless! It would include my brother, Gary Sorenson; my sister, Margaret McPhearson; my grandparents, George and Nina Steig, and Helmer Sorenson; my great grandparents, Jens and Ellen Marie Peterson; my aunt, Bonnie Davis, who has, in recent years, researched much of our family genealogy. There were uncles, aunts, neighbors, teachers, coaches, ministers and Bible school teachers...who encouraged and mentored me. There were employers, fellow high school and college students, ministry colleagues, and a multitude of fellow church members past and present, from all around the country, who had a part in shaping my life, and ultimately the writing of this book. And of course most important, and above all, is my acknowledgement to God, and His son Jesus, and the Holy Spirit, for saving Grace, and for the purpose and direction they have given my life!

I want to especially thank our church friends from Cyfair Christian Church in Texas, who were willing to read and critique the original manuscript; Larry and Molly Metcalf, Al Cosart, Gene and June Black, Mark Bouchard, and in particular, Carol Stanley, who, with her writing expertise, took the time to not only critique it, but check it for grammar and punctuation errors. For their time and kind words, I will be forever grateful.

A special thanks goes to our daughter, Sherry Paavola and her graphic design expertise, for designing and producing this book.

Gordon Sorenson

PREFACE

Psalm 71 was probably written by David, approaching his later, "old and gray" years, wanting to make one last contribution in his service to God in a way that would benefit the next generation:

9 "Do not cast me away when I am old; do not forsake me when my strength is gone."

17, 18 "Since my youth, O God, you have taught me, and to this day I declare your marvelous deeds. Even when I am old and gray, do not forsake me, O God, till I declare your power to the next generation, your might to all who are to come."

I couldn't have said it better myself! It is my reason for writing this book. For the last several years, my wife and three daughters have urged me to do a family history so they, and our grandchildren, would know something of their "history". But as I began to seriously think about my childhood, my experiences in the "halls of learning", and my years involved in church ministry and mission, I realized I had so many fond memories and amazing experiences, I could not write just a family history or genealogy. I decided to write a memoir of all the ways God made himself present in my life, guiding, leading and sustaining me and my family in His mission and service. Perhaps this memoir, "declaring His power and might to the next generation" will not only inform the next generation, but inspire them.

Where some may find their life and work boring, predictable and tame, I did not! From the time I decided to follow God when He called me at age fourteen with my public confession of faith and baptism, and later, to go where He called me, my life and work has been a "kaleidoscope" of every imaginable experience one could dream of. I have had an amazing variety of employment experiences, chief of which was pastoral ministry and mission, where God consistently demonstrated that "He was there all the time!" There were many exciting times, and exhilarating victories but also some low, discouraging, and meager times. Life was much like a "roller-coaster" ride, sometimes with lots of adrenaline rush! From early on, I found that by freeing myself to walk by faith, there would never really be a "dull moment", an insignificant event, person, or place!

CONTENTS

GORDON & BETTY, 2008

CHAPTER 1

ORIGINS

How far back should I go? My Aunt Bonnie Davis has researched our family genealogy for several years. I think she's traced us all the way back to the Mayflower. I'll pick up our history in 1800 in Northern Europe on the German French border, the German Denmark border, Norway, England, and early America.

There were quite an assortment of names: the Sorensons and Petersons and the Steigs, Martzs, Randalls, Fairfields and Billings. They came by ship to America in 1800 and early 1900. They were processed through Ellis Island and Baltimore, Maryland and then traveled by train to Chicago. From Chicago they traveled by train to the Storm Lake, Iowa area, to Montana, South Dakota, and even to Tacoma, Washington. They were mostly farmers, along with some butchers, some carpenters, housewives, telephone operators, and shopkeepers.

DAD'S FAMILY

Jens and Ellen Marie Peterson with their family: Anne Margaret, my grandmother, born June 25, 1893, in Ravsted, Denmark, along with her sister Bena (Jacobena), and brothers Fred, Peter, and little Jake, immigrated to America from Ravsted, Denmark, sailing from Bremehaven, Germany on March 31, 1900. Their oldest son, Soren, stayed in Denmark. They arrived in the port of Baltimore, on April 19, 1900. Anne was seven years old when they came to America. The family's faith was Baptist, which was unusual, since the state church of Denmark was Lutheran. Their main quest in coming to America was to have the freedom to worship as Baptists. They settled on a farm between Alta and Linn Grove, Iowa. They attended the Elk Baptist Church south of Linn Grove and were later buried in the Elk Grove cemetery.

The Sorenson's, Marcus and Mary and their family: Anna, Selma, Mabel, Josephine, John Karl, and Oscar, came to America from Oslo, Norway, sometime in late 1800 before 1890. They settled first around Baker and Ekalaka, Montana. They apparently moved east a few miles to Faulkton, South Dakota, where my grandfather Helmer Ludwig was born on October 18, 1890. After two years in Faulkton, they moved far west to Tacoma Washington, and then after another short time, to the Alta, Iowa area.

There in the Alta, Linn Grove neighborhoods, Anne Margaret Peterson and Helmer Ludwig Sorenson met and married in 1909 or 1910. On May 7, 1911 my dad, little Harold Sorenson, was born in Alta, Iowa. But then a real tragedy struck the family. Approximately two weeks after delivering baby Harold, at age 17, due to the stress and complications of the birth, Anne died. Having lost his wife, the mother of his new son, Helmer didn't feel capable of caring for Harold, so took him to Anne's parents, the Petersons, to care for and raise him. Harold was raised with his Aunt Bena and his uncles, Fred and Pete. As Harold's son , I knew the Petersons, and seeing them interact through the years, saw it was obvious they were closer than most brothers and sisters. My memories are filled with lots of wonderful moments at their homes hearing them tell stories of growing up together, playing cards together, sharing Thanksgivings and Christmases, birthdays and anniversaries, pulling shenanigans, and celebrating life!

Some of their high jinks I witnessed for myself as a youngster. The men would be sitting around, playing cards while the women were in the kitchen having women talk. The men would suddenly be chattering away in Danish, laughing and having a hilarious time. One of the women would poke her head out of the kitchen and reprimand the men for telling dirty jokes. Obviously, the sudden switch to Danish was so all the kids listening wouldn't understand their dirty jokes.

His grandmother Ellen was a wonderful and Godly "mother" to dad and his aunt and uncles. She took them all to church every Sunday at the little Elk Baptist Church down the road. That Bible education at their young age stayed with them throughout their many years. Although they would not consider themselves as religious or devoted Christians, they nevertheless were all hard-working, honest, kindhearted and morally responsible citizens.

In 1917, approximately five or six years after Anne's death, Helmer enlisted in the Army and was assigned to Security Guard duty in New Orleans, Madisonville, and camp Logan, all in Louisiana. He was mustered out on January 21, 1919, and returned to Alta, Iowa, where he lived alone for several years in a small one-room cabin until he suffered a stroke. The stroke left him disabled to the degree that he had to be admitted to the VA Hospital in Des Moines, Iowa. I do remember going with Mom and Dad and my brother Gary to visit him at his little cabin in Alta. We also made trips to the VA Hospital in Des Moines on several occasions to visit him. We would wait in a large visitor's lounge while Dad would wheel him from his room to meet us in the lounge. Finally, in 1950, I remember attending his funeral at a funeral home in Alta.

MOM'S FAMILY

The Steig family had also immigrated to America and the Storm Lake area in 1872, from Alsace Lorraine on the often-contested French German border. Great-grandfather Fred Steig was born there July 9, 1863, to George and Christine Steig, which meant he was nine when they came to America. He met Mary Martz, originally from Illinois, and they married on April 28, 1887. He was 24, she was 18. Their children were George Owen, my grandfather, born November 12, 1887 in Storm Lake, Iowa, Walter, Elizabeth, Elmer, and Leonard.

My Grandmother Steig's family, the Randalls, had long-established ties in America, mostly in New York and Connecticut, as did the Fairfields, her mother's family. But these families also "looked west" and moved to the Aurelia, Iowa, area about 16 miles west of Storm Lake. On January 21, 1880, George O. Randall married Martha E. Fairfield at Cherokee, Iowa, with Rev. John Scott officiating. The children born to the Randalls were Ethel, who died at ten, Fern, Erma, and Nina Emogene Randall, my grandmother, born on June 3, 1891, in Aurelia, Iowa. In November, just before Thanksgiving in 1902, George and Martha and three daughters, Fern, Erma, and Nina moved to Cornell, Iowa, from Aurelia. Albert

3

Reng, who lived southeast of Cornell, had built a store building with living quarters in the rear. The Randall's lived in the store building (which they later owned) until their new house, being built across the street, was finished the following spring.

George Randall was the first postmaster. He had applied for the post office to be located in his store as soon as he opened for business. His store handled general merchandise, where most anything of necessity a farmer and his family would need was sold: overalls, mittens, gloves, tools, and all kinds of groceries. George was a very busy man and worked hard at a number of tasks such as meeting trains to ship the farm products such as cream, eggs, poultry, as well as sort and ship the incoming and outgoing mail. Besides, there was waiting on customers in the post office, testing the cream for butterfat and many other jobs.

Amidst all of this, he also found time for music. He played the violin with his daughter Nina accompanying him on the piano. They went for miles in horse and buggy to play for dances. He was also the leader of an orchestra. There were lots of fond memories of farmers from around the area coming into the store where Mr. Randall would be tuning up his violin with Nina accompanying him in impromptu ho-downs! The first time they played together, since the piano was not yet unpacked from the crate, they just took the front panel off the crate and she played it sitting in the crate!!! What a sight that was! What a great time they had!

Having worked for the Aurelia Telephone Co. before coming to Cornell, George Randall also organized the first Cornell Telephone Co. and supervised the installation of the telephones and system there. The first house built in Cornell was built and occupied by the Randalls and was across the street from the store. The telephone exchange grew, and before long a new and bigger board was needed to accommodate the growing number of customers. The telephone board was located in the Randall home and remained in operation there for 16 to 17 years.

George Randall passed away after a lingering illness September 17, 1916 with Martha following him in death seven years later in 1923. Their daughter Nina Steig and son-in-law George Owen Steig took over the business and post office, making George Owen the second postmaster in Cornell.

So, George Owen Steig, from Storm Lake, Iowa, and Nina Emogene Randall, from Aurelia, Iowa, met and were married on May 16, 1910 in

Sioux Falls, South Dakota, at City Temple Baptist Church. The Steigs moved to Cornell in 1911, then to Alton, Iowa, for a few months, then back to Cornell in the early spring of 1912. From that union were born Milo, while they lived in Alton, Iowa, for a short time, Carol Ruth, my mother, born on December 21, 1912, and her brother Eugene, while they were living in Cornell, Iowa, and later Bonnie, after moving to Storm Lake. Carol was the first girl born in Cornell and later married Harold Sorenson, my father.

While living in Cornell, George and Nina operated the grocery and sundries store and also an outdoor roller skating rink located next door, which later burned to the ground. There were suspicions that the fire had been set, with evidence of gasoline, and someone seen running from that location, but no one was ever charged with arson. They also continued operating the area post office located in their store. Nina was then the Cornell-area telephone switchboard operator. Having lived in Cornell almost continuously from 1902 to 1925, she witnessed almost all of the early history of Cornell, Iowa. They later moved to 711 Hudson Street in Storm Lake, about 30 miles south of Cornell. George operated butcher shops there and in nearby Alta. He later moved the family to San Gabriel, California. Years later, Grandfather George Owen died suddenly of a blood clot following a car accident in El Monte, California, on October 3, 1950. He had been recovering well from a few broken ribs, when suddenly, a few days later, he was gone. Grandmother Nina passed away on November 9, 1977 in a care center in Montery Park, California after a bout with her failing heart.

HAROLD AND CAROL MARRY

The Peterson's and family, along with their grandson Harold Sorenson, also moved to Storm Lake, having retired from their farm north of Alta. They lived at several locations in Storm Lake, one on West 7th and then later, at the corner of East 7th and Hudson known as "the old Cooley place" which was across the street from the Steig's home at 711 Hudson. There, in that neighborhood and in the schools of Storm Lake, Harold Sorenson and Carol Ruth Steig met and dated. It was inevitable that a marriage would happen, but when? It was depression times. There was no money for a wedding. So the Steigs took Harold and Carol aside and urged them to elope! ELOPE? Yes, elope! They would even "furnish the ladder"! So they did. They drove out to Sioux Falls, South Dakota, where they were married on November 23, 1935, by a Justice of the Peace. Mom and Dad often joked about their "Honeymoon". They came back to Storm Lake to a little rental house, with a bed and a cook stove and an old rocking chair with the cane seat broken out and $1.00 in their pocket. Dad had a job with Paul Parks construction in Storm Lake doing carpenter work, so he went to work building things and Mom went to work making a home. Two years and 24 days later, my life began. I was born at Swallum's Hospital on the sunny north shore of Storm Lake on December 16, 1937.

Now, at the time of this writing 2007, as I look back on that date and on the years and events of my life, it seems that an odyssey was beginning, an odyssey of a good life, and of a destiny of faith in God. It was an odyssey of six wonderful years of bible college and college friends. An odyssey of 45 years of missions and ministry with churches in Wisconsin, Minnesota, Iowa, Arizona, and the Upper Peninsula of Michigan. An odyssey of 48 years of marriage to the same good woman, and 46 wonderful years seeing three beautiful and talented daughters grow up, marry three great sons-in-law and raise eight exceptional grand-children! I consider that an odyssey! Like at mythical Lake Woe-Be-Gone, Minnesota "the women are strong, and the men are good looking and all the children are above average"...Now I'll tell you how it all unfolded.

Jens and Ellen Marie Peterson family
Top Row: Ellen Marie, Anne Margaret (my grandmother) Fred and Jens
Bottom Row: Peter, and Bena (Jacobena)

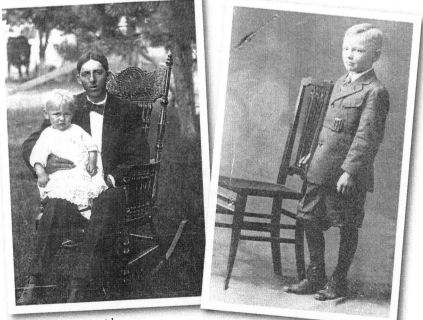

Helmer Sorenson, with
Harold on his lap

Harold Sorenson as a boy

My father, Harold Sorenson

My mother, Carol (Steig) Sorenson

Downtown Storm Lake, IA

Great Grandfather: Fred Steig

Nina Steig holding mom

Great Grandmother:
Mary (Martz) Steig

Milo Carol & Harold

Grandmother:
Nina (Randall) Steig

Grandfather:
George Owen

Grandpa Steig's General Store
& Post Office in Cornell, IA.
Early 1900's

Great Grandmother
Ellen Marie and me

Our "starter home", 604 Superior

CHAPTER 2

MEMORIES BEGIN AT
711 HUDSON STREET

The year before I was born, the Steigs, who lived at 711 Hudson Street in Storm Lake, Iowa, moved to San Gabriel, California. I never heard why they moved to California except I often heard them complain about the cold winters, icy roads, and shoveling sidewalks back in Iowa. They seemed to be relieved to be in sunny California. After the Steigs moved out, we moved into to the house at 711 Hudson. My first memories of "home" were there. I don't know if we were renting from the Steigs or if we were buying the house from them. All I knew was that it was home!

BIRTH 1937 TO AGE FOUR: STORM LAKE, IOWA

I guess at ages one to four a kid is not expected to remember much, but maybe I was the exception, as I have many memories of that period. I remember the milk being delivered to our house by horse and wagon, in one quart glass milk bottles sealed with foil lids with the cream at the top. I remember ice for the ice box being delivered also by horse and wagon, and in singles or multiples of 12 inch square blocks. On "ice day" we would put our "need ice sign" in the front window, indicating how many blocks we needed, and the ice man would carry the blocks with his ice tongs to the kitchen, and place them in our ice box. Of course, the water bucket under the ice pan had to be emptied everyday, as the ice blocks would gradually melt.

WHERE DOES THE ICE COME FROM

All the ice for the season for the city residents was harvested from the lake in the middle of the winter. The ice workers would use a motorized sawmill-type saw on skids and crosscut saws to cut and score the ice in manageable multiple blocks, to be stored in large insulated ice houses located around Storm Lake. On one particular day I witnessed this whole operation. My uncle, Bob Peterson, happened to be hauling loads of ice blocks to one of the ice houses using his used military six-by-six army truck. My brother Gary and I were standing along East 5th Street watching the trucks go back and forth to Cuppy's Ice House. Uncle Bob stopped to pick us up and take us with him on a few rounds from the lake where the ice was being harvested, to the ice house. We got to see both ends of the operation.

TRAINS, TRAINS, TRAINS

We lived just a block south of the Milwaukee Railroad tracks. This gave me my first exposure to huge black, live-steam locomotives, belching smoke, tooting their whistles, clanging their bells, thrashing their side rods, and tugging strings of railroad cars with little cabooses on the tail end. Trains were later to become a big deal to my brother Gary and Dad and me, and even Mom! Our fascination for trains grew as the years went by. And I can honestly say that I still have a romance with the rails at age 70. Whenever I hear a train whistle, my ears perk up, and I have the strong urge to hop in the car and dash down to the nearest crossing to watch it rumble by.

Jumping ahead a few years on the subject of trains, I remember almost weekly going downtown to the Illinois Central depot with Mom and Dad and my brother Gary to watch the Hawkeye Limited passenger train make its daily stop for water, mail, passengers and train orders. We became well acquainted with the firemen and engineers. At the holidays, Mom would bake individual cherry or apple or pumpkin pies, and we would meet the train and deliver them hot to the guys in the engine cab. They really appreciated these fresh-baked treats! To reciprocate the favor, on a few occasions they asked if someone could pick us up at Newell, Iowa, 15 miles east of Storm Lake. Mom said, "You bet I can!" They would invite Dad, Gary and me into the engine cab for a ride in a real live steam passenger engine. The fireman would open the door to the fire box so we could see the inferno inside. He would begin shoveling coal into the fire until the black smoke was rolling out the stack. After the conductor gave the "all aboard" the engineer would "high ball" with the whistle. He would pull the reverse lever, gently crack the throttle to "back up the slack" in the couplers, then move the lever to forward position and gently crack the throttle again. Bump, bump, bump, bump...you could feel each car, as the forward slack let out, and ever so slowly, so gently, we would start rolling. One by one we would pass the crossing gates with the waiting cars. At each one the engineer would blow the whistle with two long blasts, then two short ones. If the next crossing was near, he would just lay on the horn! It was amazing to look out the fireman's narrow window and see the two silver steel rails being eaten up by the gigantic locomotive we were riding in. We marveled at how it stayed on those two silver threads. When we passed the east edge of Storm Lake, he opened the throttle and the speed picked up. Soon we were thrashing down the rails at 60 miles per hour, smoke and cinders filtering in through the cracks and openings around the cab. The giant engine would rock gently from side to side in time to the movement of the side rods. What an experience for a grade school kid! It even turned Dad into a kid! We seldom saw him this excited!

RIDING ON THE "CHALLENGER"

But, that was not the last of riding trains. It was during these early years that Mom and Dad planned a visit to the Steigs in California. To fly by commercial airplane was hardly possible for the average person. So, it was either drive your car, ride a Greyhound bus for two days or, RIDE THE TRAIN! Yeah! Ride the train! To get to the train we had to take the Greyhound bus to Omaha, Nebraska. We then took a taxi from the bus terminal to the huge Union Station. The cavernous station was itself a feast to the senses of a young boy. It was so big it echoed! Even whispers seemed to echo off the walls and marble floors. While we waited for Dad to purchase the tickets, Gary and I would gawk at the giant murals on the walls of scenes from around America and study all the thousands of cut-glass facets of the huge chandeliers. And we waited and waited and waited with Mom.

Finally, it was time to walk down to the train platform and board our car. We went by the Union Pacific's train, The Challenger and found it to be agonizingly slow. It was also the mail train and the milk train and stopped for every whistle stop from Omaha, Nebraska, to Los Angeles, California. Other than that, for two little boys it was an amazing odyssey! We saw all kinds of other trains and engines along the way. Some were 120-car freight trains being pulled by the famous 4-8-8-4 compound mallets called *The Big Boys*! These were the largest and most powerful locomotives in the world. They were actually two steam locomotives built on one chassis. The 4-8-8-4 designation was the wheel arrangement, with a four wheel lead truck, two sets of eight drive wheels and a four wheel trailing truck.

We passed other freights laboring up mountain grades with double engines on the lead, double engines in the middle, and double engines in the rear, with the caboose tagging along behind. The trains stopped in North Platt, Nebraska, Ogden, Utah and Las Vegas, Nevada, to take on water, coal, passengers, and to service the engines. They would disconnect, pull the engine into the service area to grease all the running gear with high-pressure steam grease guns. Dad would get permission from the conductor to take Gary and me closer to the action, to watch all the activity of getting the engine serviced and ready to go again. We would watch as they gently rolled her back for the re-couple. Then we knew it was time to run back to our car, get on board and wait for the high-ball, which was an up and down wave of the lantern by the head conductor, and a quick double toot of the whistle. The engine stack would slowly begin to belch smoke, cinders, and ear-splitting roars. Powerful blasts of steam would shoot from the cylinder bleeder valves, and down the tracks we rolled! Dad would ask the conductor if we could stand in the car entrance area with the open "split" or "dutch" door to watch and listen, as we leaned out into the open air. This was an especially great place to view the train while going around curves. Wow! What a rush, as they say today! For a pair of young boys, "it doesn't get any better than that."

THE RUNAWAY

I made an attempt at "running away" from that house on Hudson Street. Mom and I got crossways of each other, so I decided, "I just ain't gonna take it here anymore. I'm runnin' away!" Mom reminded me that it was cold—ten below zero outside and asked, "Don't you think you ought to wear your coat?" My response was an indignant, "NO!" She opened the door and out I went into the big cold world to "seek my fortune". Years later, in retelling the story, she confessed she hoped the neighbors were not watching right then. They would probably think her an irresponsible mother. But mom knew me pretty well and this "trip" wouldn't take very long. Brave, strong headed, "little Gordie" got to the corner just south of the house, and stood for a few minutes trying to figure which way to go. He had never traveled that far before. With absolutely no idea of which way to go, hardly knowing where I was and freezing to death, I grudgingly returned to the warmth and safety of home! I remember Mom's reply, as I sheepishly came through the front door..."Back so soon?"

A SNIPPY LITTLE BULL DOG

I will not forget one very painful incident at that tender age. Two houses to the north lived a family with a snippy little dog. If the dog was outside, and I happened to be playing too close to his territory, he would chase me home. I hated that little dog. I am sure his bark was much larger than his bite, but he had me terrorized. One day I forgot how far I had strayed up the walk, and here he came at a sprint, barking his head off! I happened to have a Tinker Toy stick in my mouth when I turned tail and ran for the house as fast as my legs go. My first experience with Murphy's Law happened on this race with the dog. At full stride I stubbed my toe on an uneven crack in the sidewalk, and fell face down with that stick in my mouth. OUCH! After the initial gagging and pain in the roof of my mouth had subsided, Mom decided no serious damage had been done, and in a little while I was back to playing in my yard with a very sore mouth! I never did that again—run with a stick or anything else in my mouth. Lesson learned!

PLAYING WITH FIRE

This was also the period in my young life that I decided to become a pyro-maniac! On one occasion, Mother had put me down for an afternoon nap upstairs in their bedroom in their big double bed. Beside the bed, and in front of their bedroom window was a night stand upon which was a small lamp. I wasn't very sleepy, and looking for something to do, I began playing with the lamp. I found I could turn the lamp on and off with the little black switch that moved in and out. I also discovered I could take the lamp shade off and could make the bulb go off and on by putting the lamp under the pillow! Pull it out, the light would go on. Put it back under the pillow, the light would go off! Neat! But, sleep began to fill my eyes in the midst of this neat little experiment. I dozed off with the light bulb on under the pillow. Mom happened to be next door visiting with Cleta Thomas when she caught the unmistakable foul smell of burning feathers. It must have been divine providence that she decided to run back to the house to check on me, when she found the house full of smoke... the smoke of burning feathers coming out the open bedroom window and down the staircase. I don't remember waking up right away, but I do remember suddenly a lot of commotion with water flying and pillows and feathers and bedding being flung out the open upstairs window. Needless to say, that one went down in the family history. I remember whenever people would compliment my folks on how well-behaved my brother and I were, they would break out this bit of "history" to let folks know we were not always that perfect.

And along with that little piece of history, came another similar to it. It was me again. This time it had to do with the old *Warm Morning* coal space heater near the kitchen. Next to it was the coal bucket with a full load of coal. Next to the coal bucket was a one gallon kerosene can which had a significant amount of kerosene still in it. Dad used it to quickly start the fire in the morning, had it gone out the night before. Sometime during the course of the day, I discovered that neat little can. And I discovered that the neat little cap would easily screw off. And I discovered that the stuff inside looked just like water. It smelled a lot different, but it sure looked like water. So I decided to pour some of that "water" on the coal in the coal bucket. "That's funny...it disappeared!"

So, I poured some more on the coal. "Where did it go? I'll just pour the rest of it in there!" Well, the can was empty. It was all in the coal bucket somewhere, but I couldn't see it. Well, this was no fun. On to something else then. Gone and forgotten—until dad came home and decided to stoke up the fire with the coal in the coal bucket. He opened the fire door and tossed the coal in on the hot coals. All hell broke loose! In with the coal went the kerosene I had poured into the bucket. When it, along with the coal, hit the hot coals, it immediately became a roaring inferno! The stove was jumping up and down, the stove pipe was red hot and fire and smoke were coming out every crack and opening in the fire box. I don't think they called the Fire Department, but there was some real jumping around in the kitchen with buckets of water and blankets and whatever else they could get their hands on that they thought would put the fire out. Whew! Well, when all the smoke cleared away, no harm was done and after their hearts had calmed down, things got pretty much back to normal. BUT, they never let me forget my little "adventure".

Aside from my memories as a fire-starter, was the fond memory of my great-grandparents, Jens and Ellen Peterson, who had raised dad. I was their fair-haired great-grandson in whom there was no wrong. Great-grandfather Jens especially spoiled me! Mom and Dad had to be careful about disciplining me. He would chew them out for even being cross with me. They often waited until he was not around before taking me to the wood shed!

I'VE GOT A BROTHER?

Another big deal in my memory was the birth of my brother Gary on October 15, 1939. I was almost two at the time and don't remember a lot about it except that Mom and Dad decided to have the delivery at home instead of the hospital. I don't remember the reason why. All I know is that he was born at home on the living room couch and there was a lot of activity and excitement at our house that day. For some unknown reason Dad could not be there while Mom was giving birth. Somehow he had "roped" Uncle Pete in to staying with Mom during her labor and delivery. Pete and the doctor were very busy tending to a little brother coming into our world! The relatives often kidded dad about that little bit of history! That living room couch must have been a special place, since my Aunt Bonnie had also been birthed there to the Steigs, a few years before. One amusing thing I remember about my brother as we grew up together those early years was that Gary could not pronounce my name. The closest thing to "Gordon" was a sort of growl, like you make when you begin to gargle—ggggah! For a few years that was the source of some family humor.

A major event (a major event for a two or three year old) at our house on Hudson Street, was Mother coming down with something they then called "Lumbago". The main thing was that she was bedfast for several days and Dad had to hire a nurse to come in to care for her, take care of me and the house, and to cook. It was strange having this other "mom" doing things around the house. After a while, Mom was back on her feet, and things were back to normal—and this other mom was gone.

3 years old

Me as a young toddler

Great Grandpa, Jenz Peterson and me

My brother Gary and me (right)

CHAPTER 3

AGE FOUR

STORM LAKE, IOWA 1942, TO
SAN GABRIEL, CALIFORNIA 1946

December 7, 1941, was a major day in the history of the United States. The Japanese bombed Pearl Harbor. It ushered in the beginning of WWII, a huge event in the history of the world, something that did truly engulf the whole world, including the history of my family. The Steig side of the family had already moved to southern California in 1936. We were about to follow.

The suddenly growing war machine needed lots of workers to manufacture the guns, helmets, boots, tanks, jeeps, ships, airplanes, and airplane parts needed to equip our fighting men and women in Europe and the South Pacific. I remember Dad telling Mom and my brother and me that, although he was too old for the military draft, he was not too old to help in the factories building planes or whatever. We were moving to southern California so he could work for Douglas Aircraft in Long Beach. Workers were in extreme demand, the pay was great, and he could do his part as a patriotic American. This was the period in which "Rosie the Riveter" came on the scene. This was a metaphor for all the women who signed on with the defense plants, to help build planes and wings etc. with their rivet guns.

So we crated up what little furniture we had and shipped it to California by rail. In those days you moved that way because there were no moving companies or U-hauls and you often held on to what you had. With war rationing enforced, one might not be able to buy another ringer washer, stove, or refrigerator etc. for some time—maybe several years. I remember dad draining the water system in the house and emptying out the toilet bowl and tank so it wouldn't freeze during the winter months. There would be no heat in the house at that time. We then loaded up the old 1936 Chevy with our clothes, a cooler and lots of food items and headed west on old US-30, called The Lincoln Highway.

FROM A CAR TO THE TRAIN

But I remember something major happening as we neared North Platt, Nebraska. The differential went out of the old Chevy, we had to take her to a garage. After a few hours in the garage, it was determined that it was going to cost more money to fix it than my folks could afford, so other arrangements were made to finish the trip. The mechanic bought the car "as is" and also bought the thermos and ice chest. This gave us enough money to buy tickets on the Union Pacific passenger train to Los Angeles. For a minimal amount, Dad rented a small motel cabin for an hour or two to rest and bathe and put on some clean clothes for the train trip. I am sure all of this gave Mom and Dad temporary ulcers, but when my brother and I heard we were going to be riding the TRAIN, we were in seventh heaven! We started the trip eating sandwiches in the car. We finished the trip eating in the dining car of the train, which was first class all the way, with waiters and servers and all. Wow! What a world! We were the luckiest kids on earth!

SAN GABRIEL, CALIFORNIA

Life in California! We were starting a new chapter in our family life. A different culture, a different neighborhood with different neighbors, and a different climate. I recall the trees being so different! The really different looking ones they called Palm Trees. There were also big gray smooth bark trees with a great aromatic smell that drifted around the neighborhood, these were called Eucalyptus trees. The other thing I noticed about these Eucalyptus trees was that their very smooth bark—it made them nearly impossible to climb—*rats*! However, I did love that smell, even though it reminded me of Vicks-Vapo-Rub!

This was to be a new and different relationship with the Steigs, my other grandparents, and my aunts and uncles. I had not yet met this side of the family. They had left Storm Lake, Iowa before I was born, and I don't ever remember visiting them in California during those early years. But, here we were, and we would be getting to know each other "up close and personal". I say that, because we did live right next door to our grandparents and aunt Bonnie and her husband. When the Steigs moved to California in 1936, they rented their house on San Marcos Street in San Gabriel, California. On this property, along with the main house they lived in, were three small three-room cottages north across the driveway, with a common outdoor bathroom. Bonnie and her husband lived in the front cottage near the street. We lived in the second one, and in the third one, lived an odd, eccentric couple whom I only knew as "Ish" and "Bee"...no last name, just Ish and Bee. Mom coined a last name—she called him *Ish Kerbibble*! Still makes me chuckle as I recall that funny last name! Each cottage had a small kitchenette, a bedroom, and a living room/dining room. Mom and Dad had the one bedroom, Gary and I had a set of bunk beds at the far east end of the living room. I remember each Saturday night as bath night and Gary and I would have our bath together across the drive at Grandma's house, in her big white claw-foot tub.

THE STEIG'S LITTLE FARM

Grandpa and Grandma Steig both worked at Binney-Smith Crayon Factory, which had lots of "fringe benefits" for Gary and me. They were always supplying us with all the "seconds" or rejects. We never ran out of crayons. But they also had a small "farm" at the back of their yard with a tool shed, a large chicken house with lots of chickens, and a large rabbit house with several rabbit hutches and lots of rabbits. I remember collecting eggs in the chicken house. Usually the hens would jump off their nests when they saw me coming, but there were a few hens that could be quite testy when I came for their eggs. Sooner or later, at butchering time "they got theirs"! Butchering the chickens—that was a new experience! Dad and Grandpa would take turns grabbing the chickens by the legs, stretching their necks out, squawking and screaming across an old weathered log round and chopping their heads off with an axe. They would turn them loose, jumping and flapping and running around all over the yard with blood flying everywhere. Then came the smelly dipping in scalding hot water, then the feather plucking, gutting and cleaning. At first, this scene with its sights and smells was just about more than I could handle!

Then about as soon as I got used to the chickens, came the rabbit butchering. Grandpa would hit them in the head with a monkey wrench or pair of heavy pliers. There would be just one squeal, and then he would slit their throat to bleed them out. Next came the skinning. He would anchor the hind legs to a post and then proceed to pull the whole hide right down and off the carcass. Last, he would fit the hide on a wire rack and hang it up to dry in the shed. Wow! What an eye popping, mixed emotional experience this was for a four year old boy! It gave me an early understanding and appreciation of where the food on our table came from. The Steigs also had a large vegetable garden. We saw Granddad spread the chicken and rabbit manure on the garden, hand spade the soil, saw him plant the seeds and seed potatoes. We helped with the weed pulling and then the harvest, digging the fresh potatoes, pulling up the carrots, and picking the fresh peas and beans...memories, still today.

MY SAN MARCOS STREET FRIENDS

I met some of my first childhood friends in this San Gabriel neighborhood. Across the street was Joseph Eddy, with whom I played on numerous occasions. Years later, after moving back to Iowa and then returning California in 1955, I had the joy of reconnecting with Joe. We discovered after being separated by 2,000 miles, during the 3rd grade through high school years, we were both into "Hot Rods" and custom cars. Back in California I had acquired a '54 Chevy pickup which I immediately "customized". Joseph was driving a beautiful custom detailed '56 Chevy 2-door hard-top. We shared some great moments together comparing notes on the past, on cars, on the teen scene etc. amazed at how similar our interests still were.

Another childhood friend was Sonny Grey who lived in the next block north on San Marcos Street. His house was in the middle of a small grove of navel orange trees. I remember climbing into one of those trees with him, sitting on a limb, pealing and eating those huge, sweet, juicy navel oranges. Often, it wasn't just one. One day, after an extended "hob-nob" session in the orange tree, I had so much citrus juice running around in my system, that I broke out in a case of hives. Mom and Dad just couldn't figure out what was causing this rash, until she questioned me as to where I had been, and what I had been doing. As soon as I mentioned the naval orange trees, and revealed how many oranges I had eaten, she knew exactly what was going on. "That will be enough of that young man, there will be no more climbing the orange trees. If you want an orange, you come and ask me!"

FUN WITH OUR COUSINS

Some of my closest friends in California were my own cousins. One block south, and around the corner lived my uncle Milo Steig, his wife Olivia and their four kids, Jerry, Timmy, Beverly and Barbara. Gary and I would either go to their house down around the corner, or they would come to our house. We would ride our tricycles together, or push each other in the coaster wagon, and play all the games kids play; tag, hide-n-seek, annie- anne-over etc.

A near tragedy happened to one of the girls. Her mother, washing clothes in the wringer washer, left it unattended for just a moment. Beverly wanted to "wash clothes too", and began to feed something through the wringer. As she fed it into the wringer, her fingers caught in the rollers and she couldn't remove them. The wringer gradually pulled her fingers further and further into the rollers, then her hand, then her wrist and her arm. Finally, when the rollers could no longer pull in anymore arm, it simply ground her arm down to the bone! Her mother caught the desperate predicament, stopped the ringer, and released her arm. Although her upper arm required surgery and suffered some permanent damage, she did not lose her arm. This was a very traumatic experience for all of us!

MORE TRAINS!

Right across the street from their house were the Southern Pacific railroad tracks. We often (at least the boys) would enjoy just sitting in their yard watching all the trains go by. We saw passenger trains, troop trains, and freight trains go by several times a day. The Southern Pacific RR had some of the most spectacular steam engines in the country. Their passenger trains, especially the Southern Pacific "Daylight", had one of the most beautiful designs and paint jobs I've ever seen. Most engines were just black. The Daylight had side skirting and shrouds that covered the steam pipes and other equipment on the top and sides of the engine. This "streamlining" was painted red and orange with silver trim-stripes. The front of the engine, as well as the side-walls of the big steel drive wheels were silver. Behind the engine was the tender and usually a dozen passenger cars all painted in that same color scheme. What a spectacular sight!

The Southern Pacific also had a series of steam freight locomotives called compound mallets. These engines, like the Union Pacific Big Boys, had four wheeled lead trucks, then two sets of eight drive wheels each, and a trailing two wheeled truck. What was really different about this steam locomotive was the cab. The engine was turned around so the rear of the cab, normally next to the tender, was now in the front. They put a steel "front" on the cab with a double windshield and headlight, and actually ran the engine backward. It was called a "Cab Forward". The reason behind this unusual arrangement was to give the cab crew fresh air when they went through the long railroad tunnels on the Tehachapi grade between Los Angeles and Bakersfield, California. Being young train enthusiasts, we just couldn't help but notice and watch, and marvel!

I SAW GENERAL PATTON!

A very historic event came to our little San Gabriel village The war in Europe had ended or was coming to an end, and General Patton was coming to the San Gabriel Mission to make an appearance and a victory speech. I will never forget the "hoopla", with the motorcade with all the police motorcycles, the big open convertible carrying General Patton. There was Mariachi music with dancing girls in long flowing multicolored gowns, and General Patton with his chrome combat helmet, short military jacket with bars, stripes, and campaign ribbons, and his pearl handled pistols. Dad perched me up on his shoulders, with Gary up on Mom's shoulders so we could see and hear. I don't remember anything of what he said, but it was sure a sight to behold. From up on Dad's shoulders, it looked like the crowd went on forever, over the entire plaza, down the streets and alleys, the sidewalks and even neighboring yards. I didn't realize his importance at that time, but later, as a teen in history class, I realized what a major role he played in WWII. And to think that as a kid, he came to my little town and I saw him in person! How neat is that?!

NO CAR, BUT WE WENT EVERYWHERE

The first year or two at San Marcos Street we did not own a car.

Dad car-pooled-it to Douglas Aircraft in Long Beach. The family often walked to the places we needed to go. We walked to the grocery store on Alhambra Ave, pulling our coaster wagon to haul our groceries home. We often took the trolley or the city bus to places we wanted to go. We would ride the bus to downtown Los Angeles to the Pacific Electric Bus/Streetcar terminal, and then ride the "Electric Car", either to Exposition Park near the University of Southern California campus, or to the Long Beach Rainbow Pier on the Pacific Ocean. My brother and I enjoyed both places and the ride. At Exposition Park, was a wonderful museum displaying hundreds of miniature working factories and mines and mills, with moving miniature cars and trucks and machines and people. Now, it would probably be termed a "Mega Mega Plus" miniature train layout and more! We would walk through the many hallways studying the working models for hours and hours. We didn't want to leave this wonderland of moving toys. Mom would pack a picnic lunch. We would enjoy the lunch and then later board the Pacific Electric car for the trip home. For us two boys, the trip itself was an exciting fascination. No car? We had no car? Who cares! Its more fun on the bus and trolley!

It was sometime later, during our stay in San Gabriel that Dad did buy a car. It was a 1932 Chevy 4-door. Dad had to do an overhaul on the engine, installing new oil rings, bearings and valve job, all of which he did himself. It turned out to be a good running car. I don't remember what happened to it when we moved back to Iowa, but now, as an avid older "Street Rodder", I would love to have it in my garage to restore! But I did miss the trips on the trolley.

The ride to Long Beach and the Rainbow Pier was the same kind of trip—by bus and electric car, except longer and more spectacular. The Rainbow Pier was a large permanently fixed carnival. Actually, it was two piers that curved out over the ocean and met in the middle, forming a large arc. All along this curved pier were carnival sideshows, games of chance and skill, a large merry-go-round and the most (at that time) awesome roll-a-coaster ride in the world—the *Cyclone*! Again, Mom would pack a basket lunch, and we would spend the day there riding the kids-rides, and the giant merry-go-round, watching the street vendors, and the soldiers and sailors on leave trying their skill at all the games of chance. It was also fun to just sit with Gary and my folks, just watching all the interesting and sometimes crazy people that passed by, and feed the pigeons and sea gulls. Then, at the end of the day, we enjoyed the ride home. First, the PE electric car to the LA terminal, and then boarding the bus for the ride back to San Gabriel and the last few blocks walk home from the bus stop to our little three room house on San Marcus street. A little three room house with no bathroom? And no car? Walk? YES! All of that! Those were some of the happiest days of my life!

KINDERGARTEN

It was while we were living in San Gabriel, not long after moving there, that I began my grade school education. I entered kindergarten at Washington School at age four and one half. I had turned four in December of 1941, the year of Pearl Harbor, and entered kindergarten in September of 1942 This was a new experiment for the schools at that time, but there I was, with all the other four year olds, in public school. Things went pretty well, but I do recall a few embarrassing incidents. On one day I got the terrible urge to go to the toilet. I needed to "pee", but was too embarrassed to ask the teacher to visit the restroom. I just quietly slid down out of my desk seat, between the two boards to which all the desks were fastened in that row, and "let-er-go"! Nobody knew anything had happened until the little yellow river made its way to the front of the row. Suddenly, the teacher stopped her lesson and traced the little stream back to me. Caught! I don't remember exactly what happened next. I think they sent me to the principal's office. They phoned Mom to come to the school with a change of pants. Oh brother! Now I've gotta face Mom! I wanna die! Well, I didn't die!

MOVIES, SHOTS, EARTHQUAKES, AND MURDER.

Another embarrassing moment in school was when they announced that there was going to be a "movie" and all the classes would be going to the movie in the auditorium. "What's a movie? I had never been to a movie! I didn't want to do this! I am not going in there!" What shall I do? Act! Act like you're sick! So I told the teacher I had a stomach ache, and was sick to my stomach. That got action, away to the principals office I went. They called Mother and she walked to the school and took me home. After we arrived home, she noticed that suddenly I had miraculously recovered! "What happened at school?" she asked, "You are just fine now. You weren't really sick were you? Were you afraid of something at school?" I marveled at her wisdom at that moment! I explained about the movie we were all supposed to see. I didn't know what a movie was. I didn't know if I should see this "whatever it was". She smiled, gave me a hug and then explained what a movie was. A few months later mom and dad took Gary and me to a movie, the very first movie I would see. It was *Snow White and The Seven Dwarfs*, playing at the San Gabriel Theater. My very first movie—a Walt Disney classic! So this is a movie! Wow! Not so bad after all! Another great treat was going with Mom and Dad for malts and ice cream cones at a classic soda shop in west Alhambra.

MY FIRST SHOTS

I remember my first shots. SHOTS?! What are shots? Dad said that the doctor would use a needle to "shoot" good medicine in my arm so I wouldn't get some real bad diseases. They said I probably wouldn't feel it at all. That just didn't compute with me at all! "Stick a needle in your arm and feel no pain"? Well, to my utter amazement, they stuck the needle in my arm, and I really didn't feel it—much! I didn't even cry. I felt so brave! "BRING IT ON!"

A HAIRCUT?

I remember my first trip to the barber shop for a haircut. "A haircut? What is this haircut?" Again, I was very fearful of having my haircut! "Would it hurt?" Well, I soon found out that hair cuts didn't hurt either! It was actually kind of fun with the clippers "buzzing" on my head, then the powder brush and brushing off the loose hair from my face and ears.

PAIN

I had my first major/minor accident with a trip to the doctor. I was acting up in our little house, spinning around and around. Mom told me to stop. I didn't. I got so dizzy that I fell against the dining table and split my eyelid open right along the line of my eyebrow. The doc said he could stitch it up right then and there in the office, but Mom and Dad decided to spare me the pain and just have it taped up. For several years you could see a faint scar, but now I can hardly find it.

Another painful incident occurred at Washington Grade School. We were playing kickball at recess. The pitcher rolled the ball to me, upon which I was to kick it as hard as I could, allowing me to get around as many bases as possible. Well, I kicked—missed, and when my foot came down it was exactly on top of the ball. As I instinctively shifted my weight to that foot, I found myself balancing on top of the ball like a circus clown. Wham! Down I went, right on my arm. It knocked the wind out me and the pain was so intense it made me sick to my stomach. At first we thought I had broken it. We found later that it was only a severe sprain. Don't want to do that again!

WHAT'S AN EARTHQUAKE?

It was here while living in San Gabriel that we experienced our first earth quake. We were all at home, Mom was in the kitchen; Dad was in his easy chair; Gary and I were playing on the living room floor. Suddenly, things began shaking and swaying and rocking and rolling. It lasted for several minutes, then stopped, but Mom and Dad were frantic. They were racing around the house calling out, "Gordon and Gary!" looking frantically to find us. As it turned out, the rocking and rolling had rolled Gary and me right under our bunk beds and up against the wall. We were fine, but a little stunned with this "strange" event. We crawled out from under the bed to find two shocked but relieved parents. First, there were a few tears, but then laughter, when we all realized what had happened, and that we were still in one piece.

I had my first experience with "motion sickness", emphasis on the "motion". In our back yard on San Marcos Street, north of Grandpa's chicken house was a huge elm or silver maple tree. On one of the highest limbs we could find, we attached a heavy rope which served as a bag swing. Gary and I and the neighbor kids had a great time on that swing. The longer the rope on a swing, the higher and further out it would go. What a blast that swing was! One day Gary and I found we could "wind" that rope swing up higher and higher, and tighter and tighter, knot upon knot. So, I got on and he "let-r-go!" Wow! What a ride! The back yard was a total blur for what seemed like forever! Finally, I came to a stop—but the back yard did not. Totally disoriented, I immediately became violently sick to my stomach and threw up my shoes and socks and everything else! That was the last time I did that. Not until years later upon taking my family to Disneyland and riding with the girls on the "Mad Tea Party" ride—accompanied by a complete stranger whose main intent was to get the cup spinning at warp speed—did I ever experience that terrible sensation again. No more rides on the "Mad Tea Party!"

A WITNESS TO RACIAL VIOLENCE

One dark memory of this period was witnessing a murder! Mom and a friend of hers went on a shopping trip to downtown Los Angeles, taking Gary and me with them. The stores and sidewalks were very crowded. We heard the sound of crashing glass just ahead of us as we walked down the sidewalk. Suddenly the crowd, which seemed to multiply like a stampede of cattle, pressed together and headed toward the sound of the breaking glass. Afraid Gary and I would be trampled, Mom and her friend lifted us up on their shoulders. From that vantage point I could see a black lady lying on the sidewalk with blood running down toward the curb and gutter. The police had a white woman in grasp. The story was that the white woman had kicked out the plate glass display window and used a long sharp piece of that glass to stab the black woman to death. Thankfully, the crowd moved rapidly on down the sidewalk in an orderly way, and we were soon back on the bus, on our way home. A scene like that can quickly put a damper on a shopping trip. It certainly made an indelible impression on Gary and me, and on Mother!

A LECTURE ON RACIAL TOLERANCE

After she and Dad had discussed the happenings of that day, they sat Gary and me down to press home some very important moral lessons. Such as, "although we have a loving and safe home, we also live in a dangerous world where people hate and inflict pain and sometimes even death on others. Don't be naïve. Be aware of what's going on around you! Don't ever let hate rule your life. Especially, do not EVER shun or hate or disrespect people by name calling, etc. particularly because of the color of their skin! We do not see color at our house!" To use the "N" word was treated the same as swearing. You could get your mouth washed out with soap! I don't remember going to church and Bible School very often, but I do know both Mom and Dad did go as children. And I do know from stories told by relatives on the Peterson side of the family, that great-grandmother Peterson was a wonderful, loving and Godly woman and seldom missed church and took her children and grandchildren with her. Many of the Christian values learned there were passed on by her to her children, grand-children and great grandchildren, and are still being passed on to others by them. I thank God that I was the recipient of those moral/spiritual values.

Other recollections of that period were visits to Aunt Fern's and Uncle Earl's on the Steig side of the family, visiting them and their two grown children, Jimmy and Rea. Jimmy was seldom around, but Rea was often there. Visiting with Rea was another new experience for me. She was mentally retarded, and it was difficult to know how, as a young boy, to communicate with her. Yet, she seemed delighted to have my brother and me come for a visit. She seemed delighted, and even excited with the very simple things, so we would just draw pictures together. I had learned to draw at a very early age. Grandfather and Grandmother Steig were both good artists, and some of their genes came my way. As they drew and painted, I watched. I was a natural. It was fun to do cartoons and other pencil drawings for others, especially Rea. I certainly had plenty of crayons to work with! During one period of interest with art, I took to drawing portraits in pencil. Got pretty good at it, but it was not something I wanted to do for a living.

KNOTT'S BERRY FARM, FOREST LAWN, BLACK OUTS AND V.J. DAY

There was no Disneyland in Southern California then, but there were other family attractions. There was Knotts Berry Farm, which at that time was simply a large version of a roadside vegetable and fruit stand. It had grown and expanded into a "chicken dinner restaurant" rumored to be the best in the country, and with it, a gift shop with all kinds of jams and jellies. It was later developed into fun park with kid's rides and games with a big emphasis on the family. It was probably the forerunner of Disneyland.

It may seem strange, but another place we visited was Forest Lawn Cemetery and Mausoleum. Why take a family outing at a place like this? We discovered that it had acres upon acres of beautiful flower gardens with ponds of goldfish, fountains and waterfalls. And all around the gardens and ponds and throughout the hallways of the mausoleum were hundreds of copies of classic marble statues, famous oil paintings, and stained glass windows by all the great ones! In one separate large auditorium was housed a huge oil painting of Da Vinci's "The Last

Supper". The giant reproduction was around 100-feet long by over 25-feet high and was covered by a motorized curtain. It was the only thing in this huge auditorium. Periodically the curtain would be opened for showings and a formal presentation was made about the details of the famous painting. To spend the day at Forest Lawn was a visual, floral, and classic art feast! What an unusual cultural treat for a young, small town Iowa boy. The only art I remember in Storm Lake was a small bronze WWI statue in Chautauqua Park, looking out on the lake from the north shore and the painted mural on the wall in the Storm Lake Post Office. Forest Lawn was my first real exposure to the arts. Others would follow.

There were also visits to our home by uncles and cousins who were serving in the military. On their military leave uncles Glen Peterson, Buddy Sanford, and Gene Steig would stop by "in uniform" to see how the relatives were and get a little glimpse of home. To my brother and me they were heroes, in their sailor suits and caps, and "khakis" with bars and stripes. We were totally captivated by the stories they told of tanks and jeeps and oceans and ships and life in the military—and war.

DAD RETURNS TO IOWA FOR A VISIT

On the subject of getting a little glimpse of home, Dad had mentioned often how much he missed his friends and family back in Iowa, especially his father, and his uncles, Pete and Fred, and his grandparents, the Petersons, who raised him. Finally, he could stand it no longer. Mom encouraged him to take a couple of weeks vacation and make the trip back. So, he bought a round-trip Greyhound Bus ticket and went back to Storm Lake. It seemed he was gone forever. But when he returned he was a different Dad. He was happy; he was renewed; he was re-energized— and he had a million stories about all the folks back home in Iowa and about the trip.

Travel then by Greyhound was a long and rough two to three day trip on two-lane highways. One incident he related on the return to California was coming onto an accident scene. A produce truck had turned over crossways of the highway, completely blocking all traffic. Several of the passengers were military men. They, and my dad, along with others left the bus to clean up the mess and get the truck off the highway. "The mess" happened to be a load of berries, so most of their labor was done, ankle deep in berries. Their juicy work then allowed them to move the truck off the road and get on their way. It was also fun hearing Dad describe the bus driver and the old "Silversides" Greyhound, working their way up and down the grades and curves of Raton Pass south of Denver.

BLACKOUTS

The war with Japan was still raging, and I remember the periodic "black-outs" where all the lights—city lights, car lights, house lights, street lights, and factory lights—were doused, just in case the Japanese were coming to bomb us. With the black-outs came the gigantic search lights panning the dark night skies for enemy planes. On occasion, our own air force would stage a simulated "dog fight", and we would see and hear a flight of P-38s high in the sky, illuminated by the search lights, chasing one another around and around and over and down and up again! This was not real war, thank God, but a timely reminder of the possibility of an enemy invasion. It was also an awesome scene for four and six year old boys to witness.

RATIONING

Other ways we witnessed the war was with the "rationing". Tires and gasoline were rationed, and for a few years cars were not being built, the military needed jeeps and tanks. The main thing my brother and I felt was the rationing of sugar. Two little boys and no sugar?! Need I say more? Even the school children were involved in war materials drives. The schools sponsored contests to see who could collect the most aluminum bottle caps, tin cans, newspapers and cardboard, among other things. My brother and I once got first prize! We used Granddad Steig's big four-wheeled manure wagon to collect newspapers. His wagon was home built and about a half-a-wagon bigger than a regular red "Radio Flyer". I pulled and Gary pushed. By the time we got it to school we had a mountain of newspaper! It may have smelled a little odd, but we did our part, and we got it there!

V.J. DAY

Then, at long last, I remember V.J. Day. Victory over Japan! We had heard something about an A-bomb being dropped but had no concept of what that was, except it being a huge explosion that convinced Emperor Tojo to end the war. The main thing for me was watching the

San Gabriel neighborhoods go absolutely crazy! People were in the streets everywhere, dancing and shouting and singing, all through our little village of San Gabriel. People were packing their cars full with people, even riding the running boards, hanging onto the window posts, sitting on the fenders and even on the roofs. They would be dragging strings of tin cans and waving posters of "Tojo" with holes in his head or a tombstone over his head. It was over! I have never seen such community-wide joy! The "boys" (and girls) were coming home! Big changes, good changes were on the way. Life, people, families, factories, businesses could get back to normal again!

BACK TO STORM LAKE

A big change for Harold, Carol, and the two boys, was on the way! We were moving back to Storm Lake, Iowa. The defense plants were cutting down; soldiers and sailors and air force men and women were being discharged by the thousands. And one day came a call to our home on San Marcos Street. It was a friend of Dad from Storm Lake—Dick Schmitz. He was being discharged from the Navy at the San Pedro Navy base San Pedro, California, and he wanted to talk to Dad. So, the family drove down to San Pedro and spent most of the day at the Navy base and ship yard. As usual, Gary and I became engrossed in the huge ships and ship cranes moving around the docks. Dick Schmitz and Dad disappeared into Dick's office and spent most of the day discussing and planning a partnership in a lumber yard business back in Storm Lake. It was to happen within a few weeks, so we would begin packing and crating our furniture and appliances to be shipped by rail back to Iowa. Dad brought home used crating lumber from the Douglas Aircraft shops, and we crated things up. AND...we were going to get to ride the train again! Yippi! YaHoo! And so we did!

Washington School, San Gabriel, CA
Second Grade Class (top row, sixth student
from the left)

Gary and me with cousins
Tim and Jerry Steig.
San Marcos St, San Gabriel, CA

A Southern Pacific Cab Forward

Mrs. Stout's Third Grade Class (top row, sixth student from the left)

Our '32 Chevy

Me and a neighbor in our
soap box racer

Me at age 7

CHAPTER 4

EIGHT TO SIXTEEN
SAN GABRIEL, CALIFORNIA 1946, TO
STORM LAKE, IOWA 1955

After everything was crated and shipped on its way, we packed our personal things and were driven to the Union Pacific station at East Los Angeles, California. After an exciting train trip back through Nevada, Utah and Wyoming, we arrived in Omaha, Nebraska. From there we traveled by Greyhound bus to Storm Lake, Iowa. Uncle Pete picked us up at the bus station, which was at that time the old Bradford Hotel. We stayed with Pete and Della for a day or two until we could find a rental house. Mom and Dad rented a house from the Koonzs, back in the old neighborhood on the corner of 7th and Hudson Street, just two houses north and across the street from 711 Hudson, where we used to live. But this was to be a bitter, short term rental experience. The Koonzs lived just two doors west and across the street south with their big kitchen window open to everything that went on at our house. It seemed that almost everyday Mrs. Koonz, or as Mom and Dad called her, "Old Lady Koonz", would yell at us or complain to our folks about something we were doing wrong— "Don't climb in the trees", or "Don't play on the dirt piles", or "Don't leave your toys out in the yard!" We soon tired of this constant aggravation, so dad began looking for some other way to house his family. One day soon he announced to us, "I've purchased a lot to build a house on! I paid $500 for it, and we are going to start building right away!"

In the meantime, Dad had to make a living, which meant working long hours at hard manual labor at the Schmitz Lumber Yard. This prompted my first, deep-felt admiration for Dad. Although it was our understanding that the reason for our going back to Iowa was for him to "partnership" and help manage the yard, he would come home late and covered with black coal dust and dead tired. It seemed his "managing" would at times mean hands-on management with a coal shovel. There were no mechanized coal loaders and unloaders in those days. The lumber yards often handled the heating coal needs for private homeowners, and it had to be delivered by truck, shoveled onto the truck and then shoveled off and into the basement or yard of the customer by hand. Sometimes those deliveries had to be made after hours as customers had run out of coal for the furnace. Dad never hesitated to do what was necessary to get the coal delivered. Growing up watching that work ethic inspired me to never flinch at hard word or shirk my responsibilities.

A NEW SCHOOL

Soon after arriving in Storm Lake, I had to start a new school. It would be "North School", just three blocks and across the railroad tacks west of the house. Having just moved to Storm Lake from California, I guess Mom didn't have all the details about the starting date and time, so we got to school a few days late and a few minutes after classes started that morning. Miss Clemons, the principal, wrote down my information and led Mother and me down the hall to Mrs. Stout's third grade class room. She opened the door, introduced me to the class, and "shoved me in". Immediately, a third grader, Gus Pappas, dressed in a little sailor suit, burst out in laughter with the class following his lead. I was mortified! Mom and Miss Clemons had already disappeared down the hallway. Now, what was I to do? I hated this place! I wanted out of there! But, I stayed the day—and the next, and the next. And I made it through third grade—and fourth grade and fifth and sixth! I got over Gus and his sailor suit, shared nine more years of school with him and my other classmates, and now, with both of us in retirement, we find ourselves good friends, visiting by phone about "old times", news about classmates and planning for class reunions. Betty and I recently were invited to stay at their home in Tucson while on our way from California back to Texas. What great hospitality and fellowship! What a great wife he has in Mary! We've never met Gus and Mary's family except indirectly by reading their daughter

Krickett's book about her horrible auto accident and miraculous recovery. What an inspiration!

NORTH SCHOOL

I had many experiences at North School. I got really good on the playground bars. I could hook both legs over the bar and swing back, do a flip and hit the ground on my feet. One day I was showing off for the girls and decided to take it up a notch. I decided to hook both legs over the bar and do a front spin and flip. Not so good! As I swung around face forward, I did not do a front flip, I did not land on my feet. I went directly to the ground and buried my face in the dirt! Wow! That hurt! So did my ego! I got up from the ground in a cloud of dust and found my face and clothes covered with dirt and my nose bleeding! Needless to say, this did not impress the girls! They all just stood there snickering!

The same kind of incident happened at another time on the playground swings. I got pretty good on the swings, too. I discovered I could stand up in the seat and pump the swing and get higher than normal, even to the point it seemed of almost going over the bar. The chains would even go slack, and the swing and I would "dead fall" back to the bottom of the arc. One day I was again, "showing off", pumping as high as I could, and my feet slipped out of the swing seat. Out I flew, straight out and spread-eagled and looking up at the sky! And down I came, flat on my back in a cloud of dust, spread-eagled and looking up at the sky! Boy, did that hurt! It knocked the wind out of me and almost all my brains. It took a little while lying on the ground to get my breath and my senses back, and for the pain to subside. And again, the girls were not impressed! How did we ever live through our childhood years?

SCHOOL SPORTS...A NEW EXPERIENCE

It was also here at North School that I had my first experience at sports and showers. It was Miss Clemons who taught us how to play softball and football. She was a great teacher and principal, very caring, very firm, very feisty and a fun football coach! She explained to us what a "first-and-ten" was. She demonstrated the "forward pass" and how to protect the quarterback. It was amusing to watch her step off a five or ten yard penalty in her "teacher's" dress and heels!

MY PAINFUL SECRET

This was also my first experience with a Physical Education class. Our PE coach was Jake Lafoy, who had us doing all kinds of calisthenics and running exercises and games. Besides doing yard chores and digging ditches with Dad, this was the hardest regular workout I had experienced. This worked up a sweat! This meant SHOWERS! Showers? We had to get undressed and shower together? Another whole new experience! Terror! I just couldn't do that! The reality was that I was a "bed wetter". It exasperated my folks to no end. They had long heated discussions about my "peeing the bed" problem. My problem ruined a mattress or two. Mother was frustrated trying to keep up washing the sheets. I thank God she was patient enough with me to not hang the wet stained sheets out on the clothes line for all the neighbors to see. I felt like a freak and a bad kid. They put a rubber sheet under me; they woke me up in the middle of the night; I was allowed no liquids after supper and, worst of all, Mom sometimes made me wear a diaper—at age eight! They talked to the doctor about it, but he had no answer as to the cause. Was it psychological? Was it physical? Nobody seemed to know for sure. One thing they did know for sure, I slept super soundly at night. I could sleep through anything! One night the Pickett's house, our next door neighbors, caught on fire. There was a Fire Department pumper truck running most of the early morning hours just outside my bedroom window. Mother had also brought Bobby Pickett over to our house and put him in bed with me, and I never realized anything had happened until morning. I woke up wondering "Who is this kid in bed with me?" and "What's that fire truck doing outside my window?" So, eventually they saw the connection. It was no surprise that I didn't wake up when "the urge" came.

But now my bed wetting was creating an embarrassing predicament. We had no shower at our house, so I couldn't always wash up as well as I needed to in the morning. There was not only the odor, but I had also developed a rash in my groin area. How could I shower in front of all the guys!? Coach took me aside and allowed me to tearfully explain my problem. He was very understanding and allowed me to shower separately. I was relieved but didn't realize that doing so would just create another problem. All the guys then wanted to know why I didn't shower with them. "What's wrong with you?" I didn't tell them. Too embarrassing. It just remained my painful little secret! Well, I don't know how I made it through all that pain and emotional trauma, but I did! And I am sure that each of my classmates probably had their own "painful little secrets" or terror they had to live with, some I am sure, far worse than mine.

CHRISTMAS IN THE KOONZ HOUSE

That first winter in the Koonz house was terrible! One subfreezing cold stretch, it got so cold in that un-insulated house, there was frost on the walls behind the dressers and other furniture that stood along the walls. I do have one fond memory of that house and that first and last Christmas there. It was not only cold, but it also snowed a great deal that Christmas Eve. Worried about whether Santa Clause would be able to land his sleigh and reindeer in the deep snow, Gary and I bundled ourselves up, grabbed shovels, and went out to shovel off a large long path on which he could land. We had obviously not yet given up our belief in Santa Clause!

WHAT'S WRONG WITH GORDON?

My brother and I were both very healthy kids. We had the usual head colds, chicken pox, measles, and mumps, but nothing major. I felt good, like a healthy six year old should, but I had one unusual several-week spell where I would feel great one day but the next would suddenly feel sick to my stomach and vomit. Just as sudden, I would feel fine and go on playing. I had no pain, no other symptoms—just this sudden nausea and vomiting. My folks thought it was time to visit the doctor. When Dr. Malliard could find nothing suspicious through a routine check up, he had me swallow a glass of some kind of foul tasting, chalky liquid the consistency of a thick malt. He then stood me in front of a fluoroscope and turned on the switch and shut off the lights. The machine sparked and crackled and flickered and I could see in the flickering light from the machine Dad and the doctor studying the stuff going through my innards. After a while the doc shut the machine off, turned the lights on, and explained to Dad and Mom what he saw. He saw nothing of concern except a little swelling or distention in the bowel region.

After a few more days of this strange and worrisome activity, I happened to get into some delicious navel oranges Mom had recently purchased at the grocery store, and ate a "few". After a few minutes of all that citrus juice working in my digestive track, everything broke loose. I had a "number two" that wouldn't quit! Mom, who happened to be out in the kitchen, let out a whoop, covered her nose with her hand and apron, demanding to know what I had done in the bathroom!!! "You've smelled up the whole house!" All I knew was that suddenly I felt great! No more spells of nausea! Mom and Dad conferred with the doctor about the incident and my sudden recovery, and came to the conclusion that I had simply been constipated! They and the doctor had quite a laugh over that *medical outcome*!

A NEW HOUSE — FROM 7th AND HUDSON TO 604 SUPERIOR ST

It was sometime in 1946, and the conflicts with the landlords did not lessen. It wasn't long before Dad had the solution—the vacant lot at 604 Superior Street. He bought it for $500! They made plans to build immediately. Not having much cash available (not many people did at that time), they determined to build the house themselves, cutting costs wherever possible: choosing good used building materials and taking advantage of the "boy power" available in my brother and me. With Dad involved in the lumber and building business, he not only had the best prices on building materials but also the latest scoop on who was building and what was being built. He knew of a new house being built on the site of an older house which was being moved out to a new location. Someone had bought the house, but did not want the large 2-door garage still sitting on the site. It was a larger-than-normal garage, which Dad began thinking would make a good "start" for our new house. He bought it for $200 and had it moved to our new lot. He hired his cousin, Bob Peterson, to lay the foundation and basement walls. The mover then moved it onto that foundation where it awaited our finishing touches.

It was a very interesting experience, building our own house out of a 2-door garage, paying as you go! We also discovered that we would be moving into it before it was finished. Anything, even a tent, would be better than staying in that rental house another winter. Our first walls were 2 x 4 studs with blankets nailed to them. The blanket walls gave Mom and Dad their private space and Gary and me a room for our bunk beds and stuff. They also provided a make-shift kitchen for mom. There was a toilet in the basement. Later, Dad also improvised a shower in the basement, next to the coal bin—along with the spiders and bugs and coal dust. Until then, we heated water in a tea kettle and bathed in a wash tub in the middle of the kitchen. The house wasn't much to look at, but it was livable, and it would do until we could finish it. So we moved in! What a relief to be out from under the critical eye of the landlords across the street! How wonderful to have a home of our own!

A SISTER ARRIVES

It was during this time in 1946 that our little sister, Margaret Ann, was born. This made our little house with blanket walls even smaller, with a baby bed and all the other stuff that goes with a new baby. I remember also her crying and night feedings etc. with no walls to dampen the sounds. I know it was a very frustrating time for mother with all the extra work, little rest, little personal space, no place for her clothes and nice things, a lot of saw dust and dirt—and two young boys and a husband to take of. I remember one day in particular, when Margaret or "Peggy", as we called her, was sick with an ear infection. She was running a fever and a temperature so high she began to have convulsions. Mother was frantic! She bathed her in cold water, brought the fever down, and stopped the convulsions. But I remember—there she sat with Peggy in her lap, limp as a wet dishrag, and amidst all the mess and emotional trauma of those stressful moments, just cried. I felt so bad for her and wanted to do something to help and to comfort her but, I just didn't know what to do. I just sat there with her quietly, as she cried. But Peggy was fine— her fever broke and her ear infection cleared up.

I remember Peggy being a pretty healthy kid except for a few self-inflicted wounds. On one occasion, when about four, she threw a temper tantrum because she was told she couldn't go to Linda Troidle's to play. She threw herself on the sidewalk and proceeded to bang her head, hoping to change mother's mind. She did not change mother's mind but she did succeed in damaging her two front teeth. I can't remember the outcome but my guess was that she got a paddling on top of a sore mouth.

An accidental wound was inflicted by Gary and me. We were helping Dad break up some old sidewalk in front of the house so we could pour a new concrete walk. Gary and I were lifting one of the large paving squares when it suddenly broke in the middle. Peggy was standing nearby, and as one of the heavy pieces dropped out of our hands, it fell against her and broke her leg. It was an accident, but we both felt bad. For several weeks she had to wear a leg cast. But she was determined to get around to see her neighborhood friends. She would hop along on the good leg, dragging the leg in the plaster cast behind her, leaving a telltale white trail of plaster wherever she went. We never had to wonder where she had gone. We just followed the "white trail".

Another good friend of hers was Linda Illum, a cousin from down the street. She and Linda would often walk to the North School together. On the cold days they would stop in at E.W. Oats Inc., Dad's new employer, to warm up. They would visit with Dad and the guys at the yard and then go on to school a couple of blocks away.

My one regret regarding my sister was the nine year age difference between the two of us. I hardly got to know her. About the time I was graduating from high school, she was entering the third grade. After graduation I left for California. The whole family also moved to California a few months after I did, but by then I was working full time and involved with my new circle of friends. I knew she had entered grade school at Patrero School in El Monte, and later when we lived in La Puente, Newton Junior High. I also knew she attended Los Altos High School, within walking distance of our home but I was very seldom involved in her personal life and activities. Within three years I was gone from California, involved in my college life and studies in Minneapolis, Minnesota. My brother Gary, was the one who was more involved with Peggy on a daily basis. Any questions I have about her during those years of her life, I ask him, and he fills in the blanks. This age difference dilemma is probably very common in families with those "surprise" late arrival siblings. The one thing I always appreciated about my sister is that in spite of my absence in much of her life, she always looked up to me as her "hero big brother". She was always so proud and supportive of me for studying for the ministry. Perhaps someday I can make it up to her.

PLEASE...FINISH THE HOUSE!

Mom began to share her frustrations with Dad about the unfinished house, and he knew he had to proceed in haste. As the money was available, we insulated and sheet-rocked the walls and ceilings of our "starter house" and then added three more bed rooms with closets, a dining room, and a full bath with a shower! At last, our own real rooms! At last, a real bathroom with no more coal dust or spiders! During those months of building, Gary and I learned hands-on skills in roofing, sheet rocking, roughing-in stud walls, installing windows and doors, nailing on sheathing and siding and building chimneys. Not bad for ten to twelve year olds boys. These are skills I still use, making a few bucks here and there, doing carpentry jobs in my retirement and fixing things around the house. We also learned to pour concrete floors, driveways, sidewalks, steps and porches using an old portable cement mixer. We even took a truck out to Kenny Johnson's farm and collected rocks and boulders for reinforcement and fill for the steps and porch. Ready-mix was fairly new and expensive, so Gary and I manned the shovels, throwing the correct proportions of sand and gravel and a bag of Portland cement in the old cement mixer. After mixing, we then carted it by wheelbarrow to where ever Dad needed it.

HUMAN BACKHOES

Since it was before the days of backhoes and ditch diggers, we dug the water and sewer lines to the alley mains by spade and shovel. Dad started the digging, and Gary and I followed up, stepping the ditch down to the level of the main lines. That ditch started at the house at only five or six feet deep. Fifty feet later, at the alley it was ten-plus feet deep! Somehow, for "digging day" we had picked the hottest, most humid and stormiest 4th of July we had seen in a long time. Mom kept watch on the weather while we dug. Now and then she pointed out what looked like the start of a funnel cloud diving down and then back up into the clouds. None ever touched down in our area, but others south of the lake did. We later built a garage by the back southwest corner of the house.

DIRT PILES AND TOY TRUCKS

When we began construction on the house, huge dirt piles were left where the dragline had excavated for the basement. Dirt piles and young boys—what a great place to play! Dad told us a thousand times, "do not play on the dirt piles!" Impossible! We just couldn't resist! Dad finally decided to fight that battle a different way. They needed to be leveled anyway, so why complain anymore. One Christmas during this "dirt pile phase", Gary and I each received large scale model die cast 18 wheeler semi trucks. We crawled all over those dirt piles for hours on end building new roads, mountain roads, towns with a freight terminal, and tunnels, making roaring sounds like truck engines and wearing the knees out of every pair of jeans we owned! The neighbors were not impressed with the dirt piles, but I think they were impressed and even amused at what we could create on those "Mountains" of dirt, even leveling the piles a bit.

Finally, Dad borrowed what was known as a "slip", a primitive tool used for scraping up dirt and moving it elsewhere. It was like an open front wheelbarrow but with no wheel. You hooked a cable to the tongue and yoke on the front of the slip and the other end to a truck or tractor. You then grabbed the two handlebars and hung on! As it was dragged over the dirt to be moved, it would scrape up a bucket load, slide across the yard to low spots and then be dumped and leveled for the new lawn. After a week-end or two of this earth moving, all the dirt piles were gone, and so was our playground. We had to move our trucking business to the backyard and a front corner of the garden. Dad then seeded the yard, and we soon had a beautiful new lawn. And the neighbors were happy.

LIONEL TRAINS

One Christmas Gary and I received a huge Lionel electric train set. It had belonged to Elmer Clark, a relative of our dad, who lived in Linn Grove, Iowa. We had been to his home and had seen him and his train set in action! We were in total awe! It included a Pennsylvania Steam Turbine engine with magna track and a string of freight cars and caboose. Also, a Santa Fe double-E unit Streamliner with passengers cars, and cute little Yard Switcher. It was powered by a big two throttle transformer and what seemed like a mile of track. Elmer had expressed to my folks his desire to sell the whole lay-out—everything, for a fantastic price. They decided the train set would be just the ticket for our Christmas present. And it was! We were so excited! We had long been young train enthusiasts. This was the whipped cream with a cherry on top of that Christmas cake! We snapped all the hundreds of sections of track and switch sections together, running it through the living room, kitchen, dining room and back into the living room again. The rooms were all open to each other, forming a large loop. You could hardly walk through the house but Mom and Dad were delighted, watching the fun we were having hour after hour with that train set. Those fun times with the train set lasted much longer than just Christmas morning. I still have a train set, not that same one, but an HO set that is presently packed away in a box in the attic. What a shame! I must do something about that for my grandsons. And I will!

I HATE BULLIES!

There was another "new experience" to endure at this age, bullies! Yes, every town, no matter how big or small, and every neighborhood, no matter where you live, has to have its bully. They were always older and bigger (very insecure) kids who liked to make themselves look big by pushing other kids around. Kenny Koth was like that. They finally had to kick him out of grade school because he was spending too much time in the restroom shaving! On occasion, just for kicks, he would threaten to beat me up and then chase me home. We were on bikes, which was a tactical error on his part, I could always beat him to the house. I didn't want to fight bullies, I hated bullies, so I found other ways getting around them.

Jerry Johnson was another bully who delighted in pushing me around, and it always would happen at the outdoor roller skating rink in Storm Lake. He would trip me or try to chase me off the floor. On one of those occasions I discovered there was someone that he was afraid of, a neighborhood friend of mine, Paul Fry. Paul just happened into the rink as Johnson was pushing me around and off the floor. Paul saw it and wanted to know what was going on. That was all—end of problem! He was afraid of Paul—Paul was a friend of mine. What's that about line about, "its not what you know but who you know"?

Later, in high school there was "Hick" or Warren Bauers, a senior, the star fullback of our football team. He caught me, a freshman, off guard, walking down the hallway and slammed me into the wall and a cast iron radiator. That hurt! As the months rolled by to football season, I had a sudden "growth" spurt to 6-feet 4-inches tall and 220 pounds and—went out for football. On the very first day of practice on a scrimmage play, with me on the "hamburger squad" defensive team, and "Hick" carrying the ball directly toward me, I remembered the incident in the hallway. Now he would remember! As he came directly into my defensive position, much to his surprise, I nailed him! He remembered! Suddenly, there were no more bullies in my life, ever! But to this day, at age 70, one of the things that angers me most is seeing a bully in action. In later years I've seen it not only in children but mostly in deranged or mentally disturbed men, bullying their wives or children or both, and even their neighbors and coworkers. It is very disturbing!

Ride 'um Cowboy!
KnottsBerry Farm

My sister Peggy and me at age ten.

CHAPTER 5

OUR NEIGHBORHOOD

As the days rolled by at 604 Superior we discovered we were living in a good neighborhood. It was not an affluent neighborhood, but a very good lower middle-class neighborhood. Next door to the north lived Fred and Esther Papp. Mrs. Papp taught classes for the piano accordion. Mom wanted me to give the accordion a try. I did. Didn't work! Couldn't (didn't) learn to read music and lost interest. North of the Papps lived Don and Pearl Troidle and their two children David Lee and Linda, Peggie's friend. Don wanted to start his own business, so he bought an old school bus, overhauled it, painted it and started a city bus service. Their neighbors to the north were the Schaffers. Their son, Jerry, and I played together. We built "soap box derby" cars together and were always looking for a good hill to run them down. North of the Schaffers across the street lived Dick Thomas and his wife Cleta, long time friends of my parents. Dick was a brick layer and contractor and built several houses around town, as well as the new brick house they lived in.

A few houses north of them lived "Stub" and Hazel McConkey and daughter Wilma. Stub had his own trucking business. My brother Gary loved everything about trucks and trucking and he would be at Stub's every free hour of the day. As time went on Stub would take Gary with him on day runs, hauling livestock for the farmers from farm to market and from auctions to farm. He would hire Gary to clean out the truck, wash it and help him service it. He became so attached to Gary that years later, when our family was making plans to move to California, he objected to our taking Gary with us. It was a very bizarre reaction. He came to the house to talk to the folks about it. He felt California would be a bad place to raise Gary with all the bad influences and he was ready and willing to take custody and raise him himself. No way! Needless to say, Gary went with our family to California

Across the street from Jerry Schaffer lived Butch Belding a classmate and his family. Next door to the south lived Joe VeeHoff and family. The VeeHoffs had a strange business. It appeared they did a good business selling keys. Yes, keys. They had two or three cars, each with the trunks loaded with assortments of all the various key blanks used in every possible kind of lock, and a key grinding machine. It appeared that that was their sole business. Dad always suspected that they had some sort of under-the -table, black market scheme going on the side, but no proof. They were good neighbors though, always quiet and peaceful and law abiding.

South of the VeeHoffs and directly across the street from us lived Charlie and Ethel Foote. Charlie was a tinkerer, a stone mason, and wood worker. He had a complete wood shop upstairs in what had been a back bedroom. There, he had a table saw, drill press, wood lathe, jig saw, band saw, and every other kind of tool you could think of. He did lots of intricate lathe and wood carving pieces using various exotic woods. Out in the flower garden south of their house he had fashioned a stone grotto, by mortaring together thousands of stones of various shapes, sizes and types into archways, goldfish ponds, crosses and statues. It was sort of a neighborhood "tourist attraction". South of Charlie Foote's and also across the street from our house was Louis Kolbe's commercial truck garden and plant nursery. Each year he would raise starter plants in his hot beds and then later, fresh vegetables.

Other neighbors next door to our south were the Picketts, and then later in that same house, Henry and Loretta Robotnic. Across the street on the other corner lived the Nixons, Rolly and Doris and their family. Carol was my age and with whom I attended high school; Charlotte, a year younger, and in whom I had an "interest" for a short time; Sharon, my brother's age; and Rolly Jr. who was like everybody's kid brother. Not only were we kids good friends, so also were our parents. Doris Nixon's sister JoAnn Shugar and her husband Art lived in a little house on the alley. They, too, were friends with all the kids and our parents. Art worked with the Illinois Central track maintenance crew and was always a pleasant and "fun" guy, with some funny story or expression. And, of course, he knew everything that was going on with the trains. Across the street, east of Nixon's, lived Wilda Taggs and family. Wilda was another classmate of mine and a wonderfully sweet girl.

Further south on Superior lived the Barnett twins, and more of our relatives, the Illum's, Cardia and Bernice and their kids, LeRoy, Paul, Linda, and later Jimmy. Didn't have much contact with the Barnett twins as they were a year or two ahead of me in school, but the Illum's were relatives of ours through my great uncle, Pete Peterson, Bernice being one of his daughters. We had lots of fellowship and interaction with them through the years at Thanksgiving, Christmas time, and birthdays, etc. This was a great part of growing up. After all these years, Bernice is still like an older sister to me. We still manage to get caught up by phone. She now lives in Pasadena, California with her daughter Linda and family.

On the south end of that block, across from the Illum's, lived the Burmisters. The Burmisters had several boys who were all a few years ahead of me in school. Their dad George was a city cop. He was a very good natured man and well liked in Storm Lake, but was at times excitable, and when he talked, would have a tendency to "spray" bits of saliva on you. Everyone called him *Spittin George*! Next door to the Burmisters were the Lee's. Their daughter, Sharon, three or four years younger than me, had a "crush" on me, and somehow, after weeks of finagling and begging, talked me into taking her to the "Rainbow Girls" banquet and dance. She was a nice kid, and I was a perfect gentleman and treated her with proper respect—but would have rather had a mouth full of root canals. Hmmm... that's the price you pay for being a nice guy!

Across the alley behind us to the west lived Carolyn Schramm and her family and then across Hudson street, west of her lived the Delps, with DeeDee and Eddy. The Delp kids were good kids but at times could be the neighborhood terrors. Dad coined a nick name for Eddy—he called him "Delp the whelp" which, as I write this, makes me chuckle. Then, there was my friend Paul Fry, and Jim Gaze who lived a block east on Hudson Street. The Gazes had a trucking business. Also on Hudson Street lived Shirley Iman. She and Jim Gaze later married. And there were also the Simino's and of course, last but not least, my good and long-time friend Ronnie McManus and his family. His mother "Billie" and my mom were themselves, longtime childhood school friends.

IT TAKES A NEIGHBORHOOD TO RAISE A KID

Why, you ask, and how, do I remember all these families and kids and names after so many years? I remember them all because we really "neighbored" with each other during those times. We shared life together. The parents visited over the back yard fences, and we kids all went to school together and rode our bikes together and shared the latest news and climbed trees together and played softball together in the big dirt field north of Paul Fry's. After dark, under the street light at the corner of 5th and Superior, we would gather and play tag and chase the girls; play Annie-Annie-Over and Kick-the-Can and sometimes Hide and Seek. There were no TV's or video games then. There were no computers with "my space", no remote controlled race cars and Nintendo. "Ken and Barbie" weren't around yet, either! We spent our time outside being active and interactive.

On the subject of toys, the latest things out were Lincoln Logs and a neat new boy's toy called an "Erector Set" with miniature metal girders and angles and thousands of little nuts and bolts with which to assemble whatever your mind could conceive of—PLUS...PLUS—an electric motor which turned a winch or transmission to power up a crane or windmill or merry-go-round or whatever thing you had made. Other than these newfangled things, we made up our own games to play and toys to play with. As I think back now on the great life I've experienced, and the values I have lived by, much of that is because I was raised by a whole neighborhood. Oh, it was not all perfect, but there was a camaraderie that gave us all a sense of accountability to everyone to do what was right. Any news of any bad behavior on our part always arrived home before we did. It seemed that all the parents had this conspiracy where they all knew what we were up to and reported to one another anything shady.

THE IMPROVISOR

In our play, we had great imaginations and often improvised with whatever was at hand, sometimes causing our parents great frustration because we had "improvised" with their good stuff! Like when some of the neighborhood boys and I, after seeing a western at the local theater, wanted to create a stagecoach "just like in the movie". So five or six of us found some rope and some sticks and I borrowed my sister Peggy's baby buggy sitting on the front porch. The buggy had a brake on it, and springs, and it even looked like a stage coach except without a roof. This was great! So we took turns being the driver and his "shot-gun" guard, while the rest were the horses, each tethered to a rope tied to the buggy. We would tear up and down the alley kicking up dust and dirt and whinnying just like the horses in the movie—until Mom came out of the house to see what all the ruckus was about. We all got a tongue lashing, had to untie all the ropes and put the buggy back on the porch. And that was the end of stagecoach!

At other creative times, we would rummage around for wheels and axles and build "soap-box" race cars. We would take turns, one would drive, and the other would push, or we would get really ambitious and push it to a neighborhood with a long hill and run it down the hill. What a ride! The long walk pulling the car back up the hill was the pits, but the ride down the hill was a blast!

THE BUDDING INVENTOR

Gary and I created the first "walkie-talkie" in the neighborhood. We heard you could do it with two cans and a string. So we found a couple of 20 oz. cans in the trash and a half mile of string and tried it out. I punched small holes in the bottom of the cans with a hammer and nail, then threaded the end of the string through the holes and tied knots on the ends so they wouldn't slip out. He took one can, and I took the other. Whoops! A half mile of string was way too long. We shortened it up to a half a block. We pulled the string tight, talked into the can, and "voila" we could actually hear each other talking—as long as the string was kept tight. It didn't work well at all around corners and in the woods around trees etc. Ah, well, every new invention has its problems. But, it did work on the sidewalk in front of our house. We thought we were geniuses!

GORDIE'S MANUFACTURING

At one time I even started a small, short-lived business. Mom asked me if I could take some peach crates and make a little table with two chairs for my sister Peggy. With dad's hammer and hand saw, I went to work. I stood the peach create up on end, left the bottom half in tact but sawed the bottom and two sides off the top half, leaving the remaining side as the chair back. I made a second chair and used the left over for a table. When my folks' friends and relatives came to visit and saw the table and chair set, they wanted to know where they got it, and, finding that I had made the set out of peach crates, they all wanted some made for their kids. I had orders waiting! I had to start making the rounds of the grocery stores in town to get all the used peach crates I could find. With simply a hammer and saw and coping saw, I started cranking out sets of tables and chairs. I discovered I could really get fancy with my designs. With my art talent I began painting copies of some of the Walt Disney characters on the tables and chairs. I have no recollection of how many sets I sold, but I was a busy boy for several weeks and made some good money. Not bad for a kid in seventh grade. I do remember Mother and Dad being very proud! So was I!

A THREE WHEELED BICYCLE BUILT FOR TWO

I improvised a lot, creating new things with junk already available in the house and garage. I discovered I could build a bicycle-built-for-two by taking the front wheel off my brother's bike, loosen the wheel nuts on the rear wheel of my bike, and fit his front fork onto the rear axle of mine. Of course, I had to remove the fenders off our bikes to make them "fit". But I tightened the rear nuts down on my bike and there you have it...a (three wheeled) bicycle built for two! Turning corners was a little tricky with that "third" wheel in the middle, but we rode that contraption all over town and turned a lot of heads. I am so smart!

A FIGHTER PLANE SWING

Another invention of mine was a substitute wood "wing" in place of the gunny sack bag swing hanging in the big old box elder tree in the front yard. The new wood wing was one of Dad's old grain boards he laid down in the yard to serve as side walks. Since he had a few extra ones lying around the yard he wouldn't miss just one. I appropriated it for a new concept of flight! Grain boards were approximately six feet long by 16 inches wide. I took dad's hand drill and a one inch bit and bored a hole in the exact middle of it. I then cut the bag off the rope, threaded the end of the rope through this hole, slid the board up the rope as high as I could reach by standing on a ladder, and tied a big knot in the rope. This left a six foot to eight foot length of rope dangling below the wing, just perfect for propelling this fighter plane in its erratic dog fights! We would boost the "pilot" up on the board or find a stepladder from somebody's house. As he held on for dear life, two or three of us on the ground would man the rope "tail" by yanking it as hard as we could back and forth and around and around as hard as we could. Wow! What a ride! I don't know for sure how long we played with this new fighter plane or why we eventually stopped. It could be that the rope broke or Mom and Dad thought it was a little too dangerous. But it was fun while it lasted!

THE BUDDING CARPENTER

During those years growing up at 604 Superior I became pretty good at building all kinds of things. From 4th grade, 5th grade, through jr. high and high school, I crafted a lot of neat things, from stick-built model planes, to simple furniture built in shop class in high school, to helping Dad build the house and garage. I could be pretty creative with simple hand tools, like a hammer and saw, coping saw, and hand drill. Hunks of 2 x 4s became the bodies of toy cars and trucks and airplanes and boats! The round plugs cut by hole saws in sheathing for blow-in insulation, became great wheels. Just drill a small hole in the center of the "plug", and screw four of them to the sides of the 2 x 4 truck or car, and there you go—good solid toys! I could make good use of a pile of scrap wood.

I also made rubber-band-powered stern wheel boats by taking the end-cut pieces of 1 x 4's and 1 x 6's and cutting a pointed bow on one end, and a large square notch at the other end for the paddle wheel to fit. I then stretched a large rubber band across the two arms of the notch, fit a thin piece of wood between the rubber band and wound it up. I would wind it up as tight as I dare and set the boat in a puddle or pond or the tub, and let her go motoring around until the rubber band was unwound. Later, I upgraded the two blade paddle to a four blade one which turned out to be much smoother.

Another building project was a two story frontier "fort tower" which I located out behind the house. Where did I get the lumber you ask? From Dad's pile of lumber for the new garage that had been stacked out back for months and months—getting gray—that I figured he wasn't going to use anymore! To me, it was just lying there getting rotten, just waiting to be used for this fort project! I was already pretty well along with the fort when Dad came home from work and was shocked with what he saw! He demanded an explanation, trying to be tough and stern, but it also seemed to me he was trying to conceal his amusement and amazement at my ambitious undertaking. So, I had to take it all apart, pull all the nails, and re-stack all the boards. The boards had a lot of nail holes in them but were still good for building a garage—which Dad decided to do very soon, before I decided on another use for the lumber!

THE CIRCUS PERFORMER

As a normal healthy boy, I just had to try all sorts of things. We went through one episode where we tried "circus" type tricks we had seen. After days and days of practice and several tries, I mastered the art of riding my bicycle backwards by sitting backwards on the handlebars and cranking the peddles backwards. It was a little tricky AND nobody else in our end of town could do it. I don't recall ever taking a spill doing this trick. I thought this was pretty great! I was famous!

At another time, while the city was installing new storm sewer lines down our street, I became an expert juggler, balancing on the large 16-inch. clay tiles they had laid out along the street. I would balance on the tiles and would then roll them up and down the street like "log rolling". This was great fun—until I smacked into another tile and broke a piece off the "bell". I must have been doing this on a week-end when the crew was not around. When Monday came and the crew saw many of the tiles scattered all over the street and one broken, they put two and two together and "read me the Riot Act", along with some of the other circus performers in the neighborhood! Well, that ended the circus act! I don't think Dad ever found out about that trick. I am still alive!

There were also the times we went against our parents expressed wishes, like no climbing trees. I'm not talking about an apple or cherry tree, I'm talking about the biggest elm, or oak or silver maple in the neighborhood. I just couldn't help myself; I just had to see how high I could go. Usually, that meant climbing high enough to get up into the small limbs, limbs that were getting almost too small to hold my weight. I would get high enough to see over all the two story houses and about a half mile or more to the downtown area, where I could read the name "Storm Lake" on the water tower. I knew I would get yelled at, but what a high!

Sometimes it was amusing. Mom would come out of the house looking for me, calling my name, but couldn't see or find me anywhere. I just sat up on my limb with my mouth shut while my brother, down in the yard with Mom, was laughing his head off, trying to look ignorant and innocent, not giving away my perch. I guess you would call it "hiding in plain sight". I could hardly hold my laughter. Then when she found out where I was and the trick I was pulling on her, she could hardly hold back from giving me the thrashing of my life. "Young man, you get your butt down here right now. Just wait 'til I tell your dad! Do you want to live long and die happy?" But, she would cool down and I guess she figured "boys will be boys". But, she would tell Dad and I would hear about it again—big time! The lecture always had to do with falling out of the tree and breaking an arm or leg, or worse yet, breaking my neck or knocking my brains out.

THE LONG ARM OF THE LAW

Then there was my "tangle with the law". Some of the guys in the neighborhood stopped by to tell me they were going up to look around the old Bellow's place. The Bellows were a father, mother and son who had been living in recluse-type conditions in what seemed like an old haunted house, a block and a half north of our house. The father had passed away and the house at that time seemed vacant. It seemed like a great way to kill some time and maybe see something rare and unusual, so I went along. When we arrived at the house I could hear laughter and breaking glass. Some of the guys were already there and were trashing the house. I didn't like the way things were going, so after taking a quick look around on the first floor, I left and went back home. I wanted no part of trashing someone's home and personal stuff.

But, after I had been home for a while I saw a Storm Lake City Police car pull up to our house and two officers talking with Dad. Dad wanted to know if I had been up to the Bellow's place earlier that day. After affirming that I had been, he informed me that I would have to go with him down to the police station and answer some questions. Oh boy! What's this about? I had no part in trashing that house—Oh, I know—I just happened to be there. Guilt by association! Bad decision! Important lesson learned!

The police chief singled out each of the boys and questioned us as to our part in the vandalism. I could honestly say that I was there for only a short time but left when I heard the glass breaking upstairs; that I had nothing to do with the vandalizing. Then an amazing thing happened.

My dad spoke up and vouched for my whereabouts, that yes, I did go there for a few moments but then came back right away, wanting no part in whatever was going on. Whew! He believed me! I figured I would get the axe just for being there and for "dragging" him into it by having to come to the police station. But, I was honest, and he had a handle on what I had been doing! He had also seen me return soon after leaving. That was a great moment for me! I really appreciated my dad and his wisdom and insight! And I wasn't going to die after all! The only words from him I remember about that incident was, "you've got to be careful about who you hang out with and what's going on around you!" Nothing more was ever said by him or the police. End of police story!

PYROTECHNICS EXPERT

One Summer, on the 4th of July, while Peggy was still an infant, Dad introduced us to FIREWORKS! I had no idea what this was. He had purchased from somewhere, what looked to me like miniature sticks of dynamite all tied together by the "strings" that came out of each one. He also had a bunch of what looked like cherries with strings coming out of them. These were, as I later found out, "Lady Fingers" and "Cherry Bomb" fire crackers. Dad demonstrated by first telling us to stand back, and then lighting one of those strings (fuses) with a match. Ka Pow!!! Wow! Neato! "Let's do it again dad! This time he lit a cherry bomb. BIG TIME Ka Pow! Next, he told us to get some of Peggy's Gerber Food cans out of the trash. We promptly did so and then he stuck one of those lady fingers under the open end of one of the cans. Ker Bam! The thing took off like a rocket a couple hundred feet in the air and hit the ground with the end all bulged out! "Wow, what a blast that was"—literally! This new stuff was really neat! As Gary and I went on to bigger things, bigger cans, dirt clods, (which really maximized the effects of explosion) and then pieces of cement blocks and rocks, things got a little dangerous. The pieces of "shrapnel" began hitting the house and windows. Immediately Dad stepped in..."That'll be enough of that boys, just stick to the tin cans!" Again, I reflect, how did we ever escape killing ourselves while growing up?

MY SECOND MOVIE, "GREAT EXPECTATIONS"

Other experiences I had while still in grade school include another school trip to the movies. This would be only my second movie after *Snow White and Seven Dwarfs*. It wouldn't work again to fake a stomach ache, besides, I was getting too old to be afraid of something like a movie. This movie was based on what was considered to be a Dickens classic, *Great Expectations*. Snow White was great, after which, I had "great expectations" for this movie as well. My "expectations" were dashed. It was in black and white with a dark story line contrasting the privileged lives of the rich of England against the grinding poverty of the poor and several brutal scenes scared us all out of our wits! I had nightmares for days after seeing that "classic".

A DAY AS A "CAT SKINNER"

Big machines totally fascinated me! A rare experience was spending the day riding with a "cat skinner" on a big D-9 Caterpillar dozer. Buena Vista county was re-grading a mile section of gravel road at the northeast edge of our neighborhood. We lived right at the edge of town where the farm road began, so it wasn't far from our house. As the earth movers, graders, and dozers made their way from the county sheds to their work location, they moved slowly right past our house, shaking the earth as they went. The dozer operator saw me standing in the front yard in total awe, as all these huge machines rumbled by, shaking the ground. Suddenly he stopped, wanted to know if I would like to ride along? If I did, I was to get permission from my mother or dad, and he would wait, I could spend the day with him on the dozer! Did I?! I was away like a flash! "YES", was the answer from Mom, and at mach speed I was out of the house and up on that huge dozer. This was really unbelievable. This could never happen today. The liability risks for the county would never allow it. But then, I don't recall anybody ever suing anybody back then over taking a risk like this. Allowing a kid to have an experience like this, in the awesome world of machines and construction, was just something you did, and the men enjoyed it as much as the kids!

So, I spent the day watching, feeling, hearing that dozer push and dig enormous amounts of dirt, belching black smoke and thunder out the exhaust stack, creating newer and deeper ditches and a higher, wider road bed. In the process, we unearthed a huge boulder the size of a car. We pushed it to the center of the road and then moved about a quarter of a mile down the road and stopped. He told me to get off and get down behind the dozer; they were going to dynamite that boulder. The two of us watched as an expert set the charge. But what he did surprised me. He set the sticks of dynamite on top of the boulder and covered it with a bucket of thick mud. I asked the driver why he was doing that; how would putting it on top of the rock even scratch it? His response was only, "Watch this!" Suddenly there was an ear splitting, ground shaking BOOM! It seemed like it was raining gravel for the next five minutes. When stuff stopped dropping from the sky, the guy said, "Come on out, take a look". To my astonishment, that car sized boulder was gone, except for a few pieces lying by the shoulder of the road! The cat driver explained that the blast wouldn't do much to the pile of mud; it was too pliable and plastic, but it would deflect the blast down into the rock and turn it to bits and pieces. Wow! They also dropped a big cottonwood tree that day, using dynamite. This time they dug a hole down under some of the big roots and set a charge. Chunks of wood rained all over the place, and down came the cottonwood! The driver dropped me off at my house later that afternoon as he made his way back to the county shed. What a story I had to tell Dad and Mom and Gary!

HANGING OUT WITH FRIENDS

Some of the other things we did were just "typical friends getting together" kinds of things. Dewy Harr, who lived on a farm close by town on that very road that had been re-graded, would occasionally invite several of us guys out to his farm to play in the hay mow. This was a great thing for Dewy. He couldn't play sports, and I am sure, felt very self-conscious. Dewy suffered from cerebral palsy. It didn't seem as severe as some cases I've seen. It mostly affected one leg. But Dewy felt very comfortable with his friends, friends who really didn't even "see" his affliction. He, and the rest of us buddies totally enjoyed playing all day up in his huge hay-mow. The thing I remember about it was that it was unusually long. It went on forever and was always full of hay bales. His dad didn't seem to mind our being up there and re-arranging many of the bales. We worked our tails off creating forts and tunnels and mountains of hay bales, and waging war either between the Cowboys and Indians or between the Good guys and Bad guys. We would come home at the end of the day with hay in our shirts and pants, hay in our hair and ears and wheezing, our lungs being full of hay dust and pollen. Ah, but what a day! We always seemed to sleep good at night!

TAKE A HIKE

Occasionally my good friend Ron McManus and I would plan a hike up the Milwaukee tracks a mile and a half north of town, to a wooden road-overpass and a railroad trestle, with a creek flowing beneath it. It was a favorite hike destination. Our moms would pack us some hot dogs and buns, some pork-n-beans, a jug of cool-aid and some matches to build a fire. We were always careful with the matches and as well, about hiking the tracks. The old "try-weekly" freight train, as Dad called it, (leave town one week and try to get back the next) was pretty predictable and pretty slow. It seemed that if it went faster than a walk, it would jump the tracks. But, never-the-less, we paid attention to any train whistles and sounds we might hear. As many times as we hiked those tracks I don't remember seeing any trains go by. We would hike out, make a fire, cook the beans in the open can, roast our hot dogs on willow sticks we would find along the creek and then dine! We would then spend the hours checking out gopher holes, snakes, frogs, ant hills, minnows and just stuff along the creek. We would hike back and get home around four o'clock.

On another occasion, when a year or two older, we planned a bigger adventure, an all-day hike around the lake, about a fifteen mile trek. This was a major adventure! We hiked along the lake shore to avoid fences and private property and saw parts of the lake that we had never seen before. We saw red tailed hawks, turtles, beaver dams and dens, fox, ducks, snakes and just about every other thing of nature you can imagine. After a ten hour day on our feet, we finally trudged back into downtown, and to the Lumber Yard, where Dad worked. He knew about our planned hike and congratulated us for successfully completing our trek. We wearily finished the few blocks to our homes, and put our feet up for the rest of the evening—and ate our moms out of house and home.

It was amazing, as I look back on those times! If our parents were worried about us, they never seemed to show it. They seemed to trust that we were always pretty safe. And I guess maybe, except for an occasional careless moment and resulting scrapes and scabs, we were. I don't ever remember hearing of kids being shot and killed, or molested, or raped. There would be an occasional broken arm or leg from falling out of a tree but not major violence. It seems now, that my world then, in Storm Lake, was a pretty safe world. I am so very thankful for that! And it makes me sad that the world doesn't seem that safe for many kids today. One of my hopes is that it could be safe for every kid in every neighborhood, especially for my grandchildren.

JUNIOR HIGH

At North Grade School, my world consisted of one teacher and fifteen fellow students with whom I interacted during the hours of each school day. But Junior High was a big, new, and different world of multiple teachers and multiple classrooms. Each subject had a different teacher and a different classroom, and when the bell rang we moved on to the next classroom and teacher on our schedule. It meant men teachers and a male jr. high principal, Ed Nielson, who was the quintessential, strict, by-the-book, black-suit-and-tie, part-your-hair-down-the-middle disciplinarian. It meant confusion and getting lost a few times until we learned the ropes. It meant lots more kids. Those of us from the North School were combined together with kids from West and South grade schools (East School had not been built yet), making a much larger student body.

Next door to the junior high building and a few steps away was the high school building, the very building where Mom and Dad had attended high school. I would soon attend classes in that same building and be taught by some of the same teachers they had. All those really big high school kids looked really adult and like giants to us junior high "munchkins". Junior High meant study-halls where you were now on your own to get your research and homework done. It meant homework! It meant no more recess but instead, P.E. classes, with running and calisthenics and conditioning. Football was now pads and helmets and shoes with cleats. It was more running and push-ups and jumping jacks etc. Track was still more running and strength training, and high jumping, and shot putting. Junior high was male coaches teaching us the fundamentals and pushing us higher, further, faster. Basketball was not in the picture for me. I was tall enough but knew nothing about the game and didn't have the ball handling finesse and abilities some of the other guys had. Baseball didn't interest me much either. There were never any baseball enthusiasts around our family. Consequently, whenever they picked teams, I was usually chosen last and felt like a total drawback to the team.

Junior High meant being age 12 and 13 and puberty and noticing new things around us—like girls! And for me, it meant being shy and afraid of girls but—wanting one! I thought having a girl for a friend would be a wonderful thing but felt there was no way in a million years a girl would want to have me for a friend. I felt self-conscious of how I looked (although I was handsome enough), and how I dressed (although I dressed like everyone else) and how "dumb" I felt (although I was as smart as the average junior high student). As the years rolled by and life played itself out, as is so often the case, many of those we thought were smarter, and more good looking and more talented, turned out to be fizzles at life. And those of us we thought were "Ugly Betty's" and class nobodies turned out to be the successes at life!

CHAPTER 6

CHURCH AND FAITH

As big a change as junior high and high school was, something else came into my life that was much bigger. It was Faith in God. Through my elementary years I don't remember ever attending church and Bible school but a few times. I remember one Sunday morning my folks, taking Gary and me to the Church of Christ Bible school at 6th and Cayuga while living at 711 Hudson in Storm Lake. The only other time I remember our attending Bible school was when we lived in San Gabriel, California during the war. There, we attended the Alhambra Christian Church. It seemed strange to me that we were not more involved with faith and church. I had often heard Dad's aunts, uncles and cousins speak of "the good old days", when they were all kids and Grandma Peterson (Dad's grandmother) would take Dad and all the kids every Sunday to the Elk Baptist Church in rural Linn Grove, Iowa. Several years ago I had the opportunity to ask Dad why, with such an up-bringing, did our family so seldom talk about Faith or attend worship. His response was that when he got into his high school years, "he thought he didn't need it anymore!" That attitude persisted through the early years of their marriage and even as we kids arrived on the scene. Consequently, I knew nothing about God or Jesus or Faith or Church or the Bible. I was biblically illiterate. By the Grace of God, that was about to change!

FAITH AWAKENS

It was during my junior high years that Faith was awakened in me.

Several of the youth in the Storm Lake Church of Christ youth fellowship, who were school classmates, began inviting me and urging me to come to their church youth events. Finally, I decided to accept their invitation. It was fun! I had never been part of a "group" or fellowship of kids, but now I was! It felt good to be included, to do good fun things together. I began attending Bible school and church on my own, as well as the Sunday evening youth meetings. The junior high boys class met in the bell tower classroom (what better place for a bunch of junior high boys to meet for class)! The teacher was Royal Dean Fortune. I don't remember a lot of what he taught about the Bible, but I do remember him taking us fishing at the lake on Saturday mornings. Later, in the high school class, my teacher was Mark VanVoorhis, and we met in the church kitchen. Again, while I don't remember specific things he taught, I do remember his taking several of us boys who had never hunted with a real gun, pheasant hunting—with real loaded shotguns! I think back now with amazement at such an undertaking and risk. This was my first experience firing a shotgun. What a powerful experience that was! What a great witness to a bunch of boys! What a powerful witness to me that he cared enough to take the time and risk to take us hunting with real guns and live ammo!

MENTORS

Others in the Storm Lake church who influenced me greatly were several adult youth sponsors, such as the Earnie Wises', who entertained us at their farm home with wiener roasts and swimming parties at their gravel pit. Earnie would, later in the evening, take us upstairs to his Ham Radio Shack, and we would short wave radio other "hams" around the world. I even remember Earnie's "ham" ID. Mark Van Voorhis' parents, would treat us all to a waffle supper and an evening of board games at their home. It was such a good feeling for me to feel included in such activities. It made a lasting impression. The same was true also with the Platts, the Kramers, and the Meffords, as we would be invited to their homes for various kinds of food and fellowship and parlor games. Their involvement as youth sponsors included trips to neighboring churches for youth rallies, summer church camp, and even trips to Minnesota Bible College in Minneapolis, Minnesota for special conferences. We would be housed in the student dormitories. We were impressed with the hospitality of the Bible college students. Our acquaintance with many of them has lasted long into our adult years. Their mentoring, personal interest in and acceptance of me as a young man has had an everlasting impact and outcome on my life.

A PERSONAL TESTIMONY LEADS TO A PERSONAL FAITH

My closest personal friend during those years was Ronnie McManus who lived a few blocks from my house. He too, had been positively influenced by the ministry of this congregation. One Monday on my way to school, I stopped by his house to walk with him. As we walked I asked him how his weekend went. He answered that "he had gotten baptized on Sunday evening". I as yet knew little about the Bible or church doctrine, so I asked him what "getting baptized" was all about. He said that he had gone forward at the alter call at the close of the church service and had made "the good confession", which I also had to have explained to me. Then he said he went to church again later that evening with a towel and change of clothes for the baptism. He said he needed the towel and change of clothes because he was to get into a tank of water with the preacher and then be "dunked" under, as a symbol of salvation, that is, "washing away the sin and burying the old person and rising to walk in a new life". This discussion really got my attention!

"They really dunk you under the water?" I asked.

"Yes." he responded, "and if you've never been baptized, you'll go to hell!" That really got my attention!

That theological discussion was the stimulus to get me really involved in the Bible and listening to the morning messages by Alvin Geise the minister. I would attend Sunday a.m. Bible class and then sit with my friend Ron for worship in the auditorium, on the right side, third pew from the back, usually close to the end, or the easy-gittin'-out seats. There, we would sit together Sunday after Sunday, taking in the excellent Bible preaching and stories by the minister, until a picture of truth and reality, about God and me began to be painted in my mind and heart. Then suddenly the pieces of the puzzle of life began to fall into place. I had not become a theologian, but I knew basically what God had done, and where history was going and how I could fit into that big picture. On Sunday, March 2, 1952, without any previous warning or discussion with my parents or anyone, not even my friend Ron—at the invitation, I left my seat and made my way forward to the front of the auditorium. To everyone's surprise I had come to make my confession of faith—publicly, and be baptized into Christ. This was an enormous decision and action on my part. I was a very shy kid, terrified of speaking before a crowd, of even being seen before a crowd. But I was focused on one thing and one thing only, starting my walk with Jesus Christ and living for God! I think that my purpose driven life really began in those hours and minutes of that Sunday in 1952.

A CHILD SHALL LEAD THEM

That decision really was MY decision. I hadn't even told my parents what I had planned to do. I really hadn't planned it in advance at all. I had thought about it at different times, but on this occasion everything clicked! "GO!" God seemed to be saying. I did. I stood before that 300 member congregation and made my confession of faith—that "I believed that Jesus was the Christ, the only begotten Son of God, and take Him as my personal savior". As I made that confession I could overhear sniffing and noses being blown. As I turned to face the congregation I could see many of the ladies dabbing their eyes. I could not imagine how I could ever have that effect on anyone. What normally would have been a terrifying act for me became one of the most pleasant events in my young life. I couldn't believe the affirmation and support from what seemed like everyone, young and old! Well, just like my friend Ron, I was to bring my towel and a change of clothes to the evening church service, and after youth meeting and the church service, I would be immersed into Christ.

CONFRONTATION

Dad stopped by to pick me up at church after making his weekly run downtown to the local drug store to pick up the Sunday paper and a cigar. The rest of the family was not attending church at that time. When I got in the car Dad wanted to know how church went and I informed him that, "I had gone forward" this morning.

"Gone forward, what do you mean, gone forward?" he asked.

When I told him that I went to the front of the church to make my confession of faith and I was to be baptized that evening, he hit the ceiling!

"Why didn't you consult with your mother and me before you went and did this! Why do you always go and do these wild things without telling us? You have always been two blocks ahead of us on everything!" Which was true. I've always been un-accepting of the status-quo, the "same-old-same-old". I wanted to see what was over the hill or beyond the mountain. I wanted to see new things; I wanted to explore. And if I see something important that I could do to make things or me better, I am not afraid to do it. This was about God and me, this was right, this was absolutely necessary for me.

When we arrived home Dad was still mumbling about it. Mom suspected we had been having a major discussion about something. When Dad informed her of what I had done she responded with a classic question for Dad. "Well, would you rather have him down shootin' pool at the pool hall?" End of discussion!

The day of my Baptism

MY BAPTISM

That evening I took my change of clothes and a towel with me to youth meeting and church. At the close of the service I made my way downstairs to the change room and then up the narrow back stairs to the baptistery. There, I met the minister in the water. I was surprised, the water was warm! He then opened the curtains to the baptistery and announced "I was being baptized in the name of the Father, and the Son and the Holy Spirit". He then lowered me under the water... "united with Christ in His death, burial and resurrection, arising to walk in newness of life." What a wonderful feeling as my face broke the water! Fourteen years old and I am starting a new life with God! I wonder where He'll take me?

To my pleasant surprise Mom and Dad, Gary and Peggy were there to witness my baptism. There was a fellowship coffee in the fellowship hall following the service. I dried myself off, changed and made my way back upstairs to join my folks and the fellowship and was greeted by the minister and many of the congregation and especially by my family who openly expressed how proud they were of me and my decision. I was blessed by all the kind words and affirmation. It made me see, even then, what a positive, character building experience a person's conversion /baptism experience can be. You feel God and peers and parents putting their stamp of approval on your commitment and on you as a person. Christ is there, with you in the water! To this present day, that event had the most positive effect on my life, over any other. It was the beginning of a very special Moses-like personal calling of God on my life that involved my life's work, my life mate, and my family. It is as though from that time on God has "never let me alone"! At every stage of my life He would show up to call me in a new direction to do some new and often, to me, a scary mission. What an odyssey!

DAD, MOM, AND GARY, TOO

One act of faith inspires another! Dad took me aside one day not long after my baptism to inform me that what I had done had gotten him and Mom to thinking, that they had never made a public decision for Jesus Christ nor had they been baptized. They decided that the two of them and Gary were going to do the same. On Sunday morning April 20, 1952, the three of them responded to the alter call at the close of the church service, to make that same confession and then be baptized that same evening! What a great thing that was! Although I had seldom seen them attend church before, after their act of faith and baptism I don't remember them ever missing. And not only did they attend regularly, they became involved in the work of the church. Dad even learned to pray in public and at one time was a deacon in the church they attended in California. Their church activities became a major part of their daily life. What a marvel, the way God works! Little did I know the effect my life would have on others. That is the major plan of God for His people. It starts with just one life and then like a lump of yeast, begins to effect the whole lump of dough, overflowing into the whole neighborhood. Where does this story go next?

CHAPTER 7

HIGH SCHOOL

My high school years happened to be the early 50's. These were very good years, much like those depicted in *Happy Days*. For that reason the *Happy Days* series was very special to me. I could identify with many of the characters. I saw myself in "Richie Cunningham" and attended school with guys like "The Fonz" and "Ralph" and "Potsie". Those were the days of the soda shop/malt shop, the jute box, the drive-in burger stand, sock hops and hot rods. The 50's were Buddy Holly, Ritchie Valens, and Rock and Roll. It was *American Band Stand* and *Rock Around The Clock* with Bill Haley and The Comets. It was Rickey Nelson, The Everly Brothers and Fats Domino singing *On Blue Berry Hill*—and Bobby Darin. It was the crooners like Nat "King" Cole, Frank Sinatra, Perry Como and Dinah Shore. Teens were sporting the latest fashions—blue jeans, poodle skirts, saddle shoes, white bucks and girls wearing their hair in "pony tails" and the guys with "flat tops and "duck tails". James Dean had just hit the screen in *Rebel Without A Cause*. On TV were *The Honeymooners, Father Knows Best, I Love Lucy, Ozzie and Harriet* and *The Ed Sullivan Show*. The FM radios carried *"Jack Benny", "Fibber McGee and Molly", "Amos and Andy", "Henry Aldrich"* and *"The Life of Riley"*. Hula Hoops were the rage! Harry Truman was president until 1952, after which Dwight D. Eisenhower became president until 1961. Our high school staged its own political debates and elections, giving us teens a hands-on experience at the political process.

Ah yes, high school—more new experiences, another different

69

building with different teachers, new classes with new and harder challenges. Subjects like History and English and Health were similar, but simple math turned into Algebra I, then Algebra II, and then Geometry (what's this?) and Science with complicated math calculations, and Speech Class (oh terror!). There was advanced woodshop and metals shop and advanced art and drafting. Now, those last classes, the shops and art and drafting, were a snap for me. I've always been gifted in these areas—straight A's. But the math just never clicked. Science really grabbed me, but the math involved was always a problem. Being one year younger than most in the class, having started school in California at age four and a half, my brain just hadn't developed to where I could fully understand the algebra and geometry. What is ironic is that a few years later, when I did decide to attend college and study for the ministry, I was required to take two years of Biblical Greek. My comprehension, vocabulary, and reading/translation skills and grades were excellent! I often thought, if only my English and Composition teacher could see me now! She would faint from the shock!

One of the results of being gifted in art and shop was usually being called on by my classmates to design and lead the construction of homecoming floats and similar projects. In my senior year our float committee came up with the slogan "Our Boys Can" for our float. I suggested we borrow someone's outhouse, as there were many of them still around in 1955. So we did, as well as a hay rack, some large potted trees, and some astro turf. We painted some signs to hang on the chicken wire and tissue skirting, and presto, we had our float proclaiming to the folks along the main street parade route— OUR BOYS CAN! We had our best football season in years. Our boys not only *could* but *did*!

Another part of high school I enjoyed was choir. I sang in the boy's choir, mixed choir, and a small mixed vocal ensemble. The most fun was singing with a male quartet, both acapella and accompanied. We even worked up some good Barber Shop. At different times of the year we sang at festivals, school events, and traveled to and performed at multi-school festivals and music competitions. This was just some of the great fun of my high school experience. Much of my vocal music experience carried over into my church life and Bible college experience a few years later. I enjoyed a new experience singing in the church choir, having been urged by Cecil Miller, a church member, who mentored me in reading the music and singing the bass line. Later, at Minnesota Bible College I sang in the "King's Choristers" college choir and sang bass in a male gospel quartet named the "Gospel Foremen", traveling with Professor Jerry Gibson on spring tour. Later, I sang bass in a mixed acapella quartet. It was all a great life building experience—and fun!

THE HIGH SCHOOL ATHLETE

The absolute best high school experience was competing in sports, from intramural wrestling, to track and football. In intramural wrestling, I won all my matches but one, in which I tied my opponent. Probably my best sport was track. I competed in the running events; the two- mile relay my freshman year; the mile my sophomore year; the half-mile my junior year and the quarter-mile my senior year. I never won any firsts in any of those running events, but I excelled at the shot put and discus throw. My freshman year Coach Spatcher sent me over to the discus practice area to look up "Hick" Bauer, a senior, and a star fullback on the football team. He had a reputation as a weight lifter, a fast, powerful running back, and a premier discus thrower. He grudgingly took a few moments to "show me the ropes" of discus throwing and then turned it over to me to give it a try. It seemed quite easy to me as I wound up a few times. So, when I felt comfortable, I let her fly. Even without a spin, my first throw landed out about 120 feet. Bauer took one look and then, in disgust, walked off to do other things. As it turned out, I had thrown it further than he ever had! The coach later called me aside and told me that the discus throw would be my main event. It turned out to be my main event all through my high school years. As I practiced and perfected and gradually developed the spin, I was able to throw a consistent 120 to 130 feet at our track meets. My senior year, at Estherville Iowa, at a regional meet, I threw the discus 142 feet, setting a meet record. I loved it! At every track meet the field events were held first in the afternoon. Usually, being able to place first in the discus throw and sometimes in the shot put, I was able to score the first major points of the day, giving our team early leads. I can't tell you how good that felt to make a major contribution to the team.

Football was a major event for me as well. I had grown to 6'4" and 220 pounds by fall my senior year. My assignment was left tackle on offence and middle guard on defense. Our front line from end to end averaged 220 pounds, allowing us to use a seven and five man defensive line much of the time and sometimes allowing us to manhandle some teams. The fall of 1954 was our best season in several years. We won some games many felt we would lose; we tied two teams that were supposed to trounce us; and we upset two powerhouse teams that should have beat us! We started the season as usual, in the Lakes Conference basement. From 8th place we climbed up the ladder to 3rd place. Third place doesn't seem like much, but it was a major accomplishment for a high school team. We were good! We had a great coaching staff, great team spirit and effort, and now, for me—great memories!

At the close of the season I received scholarship offers from Buena Vista University in Storm Lake and later from the University of Minnesota. Surprising everyone, I turned those offers down! I was not ready for more academics. But I wanted to get out of Storm Lake, to find something new do and to experience—and to find instead something I didn't know at the time—would turn out to be "providential". For someone who often struggled with self image and the feeling that I would probably never excel at much of anything, those sports accomplishments were huge confidence builders. I thank God for those experiences. The discipline and physical conditioning were great character and body builders and instilled character assets that have lasted a lifetime.

JACK BARBER

Sports also contributed to a camaraderie with fellow athletes that has lasted a lifetime. Although Jack Barber was a year ahead of me in high school, there was, nevertheless, a bond cemented between us through the church youth program, our participation together in track and football and later, as fellow students at Minnesota Bible College. I first became aware of Jack through football, and our football coach Cecil Spatcher. The coach had scheduled a preseason, non conference scrimmage with the Laurens, Iowa high school team. Coach warned us about their red headed, lightening fast halfback, Jack Barber. We won that scrimmage, but we were all in awe of Jack's speed. Then came an amazing blessing to Storm Lake's football program. Jack Barber was moving to Storm Lake! Jack and I would be playing together as teammates! How great is that?! Jack became a left halfback on our football team, running behind my blocking as a left tackle. Jack was faster than greased lightening, the fastest running back in the conference. If I could open a path in the line for Jack, he was gone! That bond of friendship has continued due to our college experiences and ministries, and has lasted for over fifty years. He and his wife Lucille have been close friends of ours even though at times many miles have kept us geographically apart.

After Jack graduated from high school, I lost track of him. What I did not know at that time was that he had enlisted in the paratroopers and was stationed mostly in Germany. I did not see him again until I was in Minneapolis, Minnesota in the fall of 1957, enrolling as a freshman at Minnesota Bible College. I was standing in the large main foyer of Old Main waiting in line for my turn to sign on the dotted line when suddenly, I could not believe my eyes, there he was, old "carrot top" coming through the front doors to the foyer. I hadn't seen him in five years, nor did I know where he had been or what he was doing.

"Jack" I said, "What in the world are you doing here at Minnesota Bible College?"

He responded with, "What do you think I am doing!!?? I am enrolling here! What in the world are you doing here?!"

"So am I, Jack!" Fantastic! In a few minutes we were comparing notes and getting caught up on each other's chain of events. Jack explained to me that while he served in the military he felt called to work with the base chaplain and became a chaplain's assistant. He enjoyed it so much that he began to feel "the call" more and more and decided to make it his life's work. Thus, through the years we've enjoyed getting together with Jack and Lucille, whether they were in Iowa, Illinois, or Palisades, Colorado. We always enjoyed reminiscing about our experiences playing football together at good old Storm Lake High or studying theology together at MBC or sharing stories about churches and ministries, and families. Jack and Lucille have retired now from their last ministry which happened to be at our home church, the Storm Lake Church of Christ. We spent some time helping them pack and move, giving them encouragement and moral support. (Moving is hard and stressful work.) We know, we've done it more than fifteen times! We continue to stay in touch not only by cell phone from anywhere in the country, but by the 21st century phenomenon of "e-mail".

CARS, CARS, CARS

Planes, Trains and Automobiles! Up until this point in my life my odyssey did not include planes or flying or cars but lots of trains. However, in high school, a romance budded with cars. As I have alluded to several experiences in the past with automobiles, my memory continues to focus on the "cars" in my life.

First, while still a kid, there was the big 1929 or 30's 4-door Buick with huge wooden spoke wheels. I remember taking a long trip from Storm Lake, Iowa, to Hammond, Wisconsin to see relatives Clyde and Annabelle Hanson and family in that car. What stands out about that trip was Mom taking along a "pee can" for Gary and me to go in while traveling. There were no rest stops then and gas stations it seemed, were few and far between. So, when Gary or I would need to relieve ourselves we would use the pee can while on the move! Then, out the window it went! If it was after dark, we would just stop along the road. If no cars were coming we would just pee in the ditch. Or, as would often happen, we would have a "contest" with Dad to see who could pee the furthest across the ditch! We had a great visit with the Hansons. The Great Northern Railroad tracks ran practically through their back farm yard. Naturally, Gary and I did not miss a train. What is interesting, is that's about all I remember about that visit—the trains and the pee contest. Isn't it funny, the things kids remember!

Next, there was the old Chevy that broke down in North Platte, NE, on our move to California in 1942, and then the 1932 Chevy that Dad overhauled when we lived in San Gabriel. When we first returned to Iowa in 1946, our "car" was the Schmitz Lumber Company business car and/or pickup. The pickup was the best! It was a 1941 one ton Chevy flat bed with stake-racks. If we took a ride when the weather was favorable, Gary and I would ride in the back end, standing behind the cab and hanging on to the front stake rack. What a blast that was, with the wind in our hair and bugs in our eyes and mouth! People did not think of this then as being a dangerous thing to do. Life was slower then, cars were slower and people were not in such a hurry. You didn't go for a ride around town or in the country at 65 and 75 miles per hour. People were more careful then of others and themselves. In all the months we used this as our means of transportation, I don't ever remember even a close call! It was unlike nowadays when most of the time I don't feel safe even if I were in an armored truck!

DRIVERS ED AND THE 1948 OLDSMOBILE

Eventually we owned a car again. I believe it was a 1939 Chevy. And then came *the* car—a new or "newer" low mileage, used, comfortable 4-door family car—a 1948 Oldsmobile straight six with an automatic transmission! Wow! We were coming up in the world! *This* was the car I learned to drive in! Unbelievably, this was the car Mom and Dad allowed me to drive after getting my learners permit! And...*AND*...when I received my drivers license, allowed me to use it *ON MY OWN!* Miraculously, during those first months of driving I never had a ticket or an accident. This was probably due to the new Drivers Education programs being adopted in all the Iowa schools at that time. It was new; it was extensive; it was serious! It was considered as part of the curriculum of every high school student. If you missed it, you didn't drive! It started out in the classroom with all the books and paperwork of Drivers Ed—even the drivers' exams.

Later, after the classroom work, you were in the car, learning all the "ropes" of safely and efficiently handling an automobile. At the close of this extensive program the local Police, and State Highway Patrol put together an all-day driving Rodeo, utilizing several of the city blocks of downtown main street. There were traffic cones set up everywhere depicting turns, curved roads, parking spaces, cross walks, etc. The trick was to negotiate the whole stopping, turning, parking, backing, course without touching or knocking over any cones or flags. An added excitement and challenge came from it being a "competition" with other high schools. I did well— second place! This education experience served me well through the years. I have driven everything from a motorcycle, to a hot rod, to a sports car, to a family car, to a log truck, and several years driving a school bus. I've done it all with a nearly-perfect driving record. I thank God for that!

OWNING MY FIRST CAR—MY 1941 FORD

One of my most pleasant memories of cars and driving was getting my very own first car. Dad and Mom were usually very slow in allowing us kids to try our wings with things. It came as a very big shock when one day Dad took me aside "man to man", and suggested that maybe it was time for me shop around for my own car! What? Me?

"You think I should own my own car???!!!"

"And, what's more," he added, "I am ready to go shopping with you right now!"

"Now?" I asked.

"Yes, now! I know you have been saving your money, I know a good car you may like out at Hansen Motors. Let's go now and take it for a drive." he said.

I couldn't believe it! This really is my dad? Now? A car of my own? I must have died and gone to heaven! "OK Dad. Let's go!" And we did. We took it for a drive. We kicked the tires. We checked the oil. After asking the price, I paid my money—$150, which I had in savings and more. I had my first car! A 1941 Ford 2-door sedan with a V-8 engine and "stick" transmission. Dad made a perfect call! I loved that car! I couldn't have picked a better one myself!

But the trouble came later as I wanted to make some improvements on what Henry Ford had manufactured in 1941. I wanted to lower it a couple of inches. It was easy to do when you listen to tips from the hot rodders and race car guys. Take off the nuts from the eight spring shackle bolts on the suspension and replace the factory shackles with longer ones—however many inches lower you want it to go. I did it easy in one afternoon. I lowered the car two inches in the front and back. It looked great! Dad hit the ceiling! I could also very easily add a duel muffler and tail pipe to the exhaust system using "glass pack" mufflers. This gave it a powerful, deep-throated rumble as you took off from a stop sign and as you slowed to a stop. Wow! What a great sound! It also ran better and got better fuel mileage! Dad wasn't convinced. He hit the ceiling again! Later I decided that maybe it needed an overhaul so I borrowed a block and tackle and pulled the engine. I asked Uncle Pete (actually Dad's uncle), who was a seasoned mechanic and owned his own garage, if he would come over and check it out for me. He was glad to do so. He checked the engine out and determined that it was really in excellent shape and wondered why I went to all the work to pull it out before checking it while in the car. Gee! Why didn't I think of that! And—yes, Dad hit the ceiling again! "What are you trying to do, ruin a good car?" Pete said, "Just put her back in the way it came out, and it should run just fine!" I got some engine cleaner and cleaned the old greasy thing spic and span then bolted it back in. I learned that I had gone to a lot of work just to have a clean engine. She did run just fine for several years, my last two years of high school and then a trip to Southern California after graduation.

She was a good car! She was a pretty car! She was a great sounding car! She was an eye catcher! On a beautiful Spring day in 1955, the area high schools had a senior "Skip Day" where senior teens came to special festivities planned in Storm Lake. High school teens were there from all around the area, enjoying the lake, the fellowship of new found friends, and all the new "Boys" and the new "Girls" in town. They were everywhere, walking along main street and strolling along the lake shore sidewalks and parks. My bud Ron and I found we could meet all kinds of girls by offering taxi service either to downtown or to the lake whichever way we or they happened to be going. On one shag-of-the-drag through the downtown area, we had three or four girls with us and stopped at the light at 5th and Lake Avenue, right in the middle of where "things" were happening. When the light turned green I decided to peel some rubber. I revved the engine, popped the clutch and snap, no rubber, no smoke, no glory—just a broken axle—right there in front of God and the girls and the students and the parents, watching and listening at 5th and Lake! Oh, mortification! Oh, embarrassment! The girls piled out immediately and Ron and I were left pushing my dead Ford down the street and around the corner out of the way. And as if the embarrassment wasn't enough, I had to get the car home, tear it down, find a new axle, and install it. In those early Fords that was not an easy, quick task. You had to take the whole rear end apart to install the axle. With the help of Uncle Pete and a local junk yard, I got the job done—but way too late for the activities of Skip Day. And, oh yeah...Dad hit the ceiling! After a while he learned to stop "fussin" about me and my car. I paid for everything with my own hard earned money and bought all my own gas and oil and did all my own tune ups and oil changes—and repair jobs. It was good for me to learn to take care of my car and sometimes pay the price for my poor judgment. The one thing he did have to admit though, that after all my tweaking and tuning, the car looked good, sounded good and ran good!

Graduation 1955

Storm Lake Church of Christ Youth Group, 1955

1948 Oldsmobile

Discus thrower, 1955

CHAPTER 8

IN THE WORK FORCE

More about cars later. There was much more about my high school experience than automobiles. There was another brand new experience— the experience of WORK! My early jobs consisted of mowing lawns in the summer, shoveling sidewalks in the winter, and managing a Des Moines Register paper route. The mowing and shoveling jobs paid pretty well, but the paper route was kind of a pain in the neck for what little money I earned. There were always the dead beats who would not pay their paper bills, and I would have to carry the cost until they did pay.

I also acquired a Saturday job working in a "blacksmith" shop, or metal fabrication shop a few blocks south of my home. My job was mainly washing parts and operating the power metal band saw, sawing tubing, flat steel stock and sawing the ends off early Ford axle housings. They were manufacturing post hole augers for the three point hitch/power take-off system on farm tractors, utilizing and recycling thousands of old Ford drive shafts and rear ends. It was fascinating to see what these guys could invent and fabricate from some junk and a few pieces of steel

Later, I had jobs sacking groceries and stocking shelves at Trobridge's Grocery and later for Marx's Market on the north side of town. These jobs provided me an income but were kind of boring. I wanted to do something outside, something where I was part of creating things. Since I was getting bigger and stronger and Dad was in the know with what was going on in the home construction business, some contractors began calling. I had some jobs doing carpenter work, concrete work, and roofing. These jobs usually paid $1.50 per hour. This was good pay and very valuable experience! We built new homes, remodeled older homes, poured sidewalks and drive ways, and installed new roofs. I found my early home building experiences with Dad very valuable. I knew what to do with a hammer and saw and a level and square. And I was strong enough to handle the concrete work and loading shingles on a roof. I could also lay down a good row of shingles and could scramble around on toe holds and scaffolds. It was all hard work but fun and rewarding.

Dad also put me to work. By the time I was in high school he was working as the yard manager for E.W. Oats & Co. He was always very "sly" about these jobs. He would call home, ask to talk to me and would ask "if I wanted a good job today". He would never tell me what I would be doing, but just "come on down to the yard and I'll get you going". So I would show up at the yard and he would take me for a walk. One time it would be to the cement shed. We would walk through the shed to a large sliding door. He would push the door open and there before my eyes was a railroad boxcar full of bagged Portland cement.

"Just take that two-wheeled cart over there and fork up six or eight bags at a time and stack them in the warehouse. Empty the railcar. Take your time. Don't kill yourself. See me when you are done," he'd say.

Other times he would call, I would go to the yard, and he would lead me out into the rail yard to a long gondola railcar. We would climb up the climbing irons on the end of the car, and there before my eyes was a full carload of stoker coal.

"There's the truck. You know how to drive the truck. There's the coal shovel, just start at this end of the car and work your way to the other end. Take your time. Don't kill your self. See me when you are done".

Needless to say, the coal took more than a day to unload. Nevertheless, I got it done! The nice thing was, I not only stayed in good shape, but Dad saw to it that I was paid very well. This was not the kind of work that just anybody would do.

On yet another occasion he called me to the yard to "deliver brick". I was to load the brick on the flat bed truck and then deliver it to the location of the new Church of Christ parsonage across from the church and unload it there wherever the brick layers wanted it. This I considered to be a very special job. This was my own church and I knew all these brick layers—Dick Thomas and his crew. It was a good job and good environment and again, good pay.

Being Storm Lake was very much a farm community, I also got called to farm jobs. One summer I worked for DeKalb Seed Corn Co. as a "detasseler". The job consisted of riding in the back end of a large truck with a large crew of other detasselers, to the corn fields of local farmers. We would hit the ground, then spend the day walking the corn rows, each taking two rows of corn and pulling the tassels out of the eight "female" rows of corn. This allowed the two "male" rows of corn of another variety to cross-pollinate with a standard variety, thus creating the various "hybrids". We did lots of walking and got lots of corn cuts from the leaves and spent most of the mornings soaked from the dew on the leaves. But again, the pay was very good. Usually, the money we earned from this summer work would last well into the school year if we were frugal in our spending.

Still other farm jobs consisted of baling hay. Usually it meant either taking the bales off the baler and stacking them on the hay-rack or working in the hay-loft, taking bales off the elevator and stacking them as high as possible in the loft. I always spoke for the wagon. It was cooler, and there was less dirt and dust. Besides, being tall and strong, I could pile lots of bales on the wagons. I've gotten as many as one hundred bales on one wagon. A few times I was asked to not stack so many bales on a wagon. They didn't want to risk blowing a tire. Again, the farmers paid well, $1.25 to $1.50 per hour.

Probably the most unusual job was working for a hog farmer, rounding up hundreds of feeder pigs for tagging, vaccinating and castration. That was a crazy day! First, just try rounding up hundreds of little pigs squealing and scattering in a million directions, then catching them, cutting out a notch in their ear, sticking them with a needle, and snipping off their private parts. We earned our pay that day! What a valuable asset these work experiences have been through the years. They not only instilled in me a good work ethic, and provided an outstanding resume, but they also enabled me to learn to use the tools and develop the skills I would need and use for many years, to do many different things. I never saw something broken that I couldn't fix, and never saw a needed project I couldn't build—from remodeling my own home, to building a home and school for Native American children at American Indian Christian Mission in Show Low, Arizona; or a real log church building for Peninsula Christian Church in Hancock, Michigan, or building a "Godzilla" dog house for a giant English Mastiff for my wife's niece. I've also built kitchen cabinets, a Murphy Bed, and a portable fireplace. These skills have also allowed me to help friends and neighbors with their "fix-it problems" and to help in major disaster rebuilding. I often joke that I work for a great guy—He was a Jewish carpenter. As the years rolled by, I was involved in other types of jobs and work experience. But more about that later.

MY OTHER FRIEND, EDDIE

There were many other experiences during my high school years. Another good friend from school was Eddy Barrels, a year ahead of me, and whose family, along with Eddy, were members of my church. Eddy and I were on the football and track team and spent a lot of time working out together. One Saturday before the fall practice workouts, we decided to get ahead of the conditioning game. We donned our football cleats, shorts, and tee shirts and ran the railroad tracks the fifteen miles from Storm Lake to Newell, Iowa. Between running the track ties, the ditches, hills, railroad bridges, and culverts, we discovered we had picked a real obstacle course! We had bitten off a big chunk of physical conditioning. We were two really beat football players! Eddy's mom gave us a ride back to Storm Lake, which had been the original plan. We were sure glad we had made that arrangement! But that workout had put us ahead of the game! The fall "two-a -day" workouts and conditioning drills were much easier. We noticed a big difference in our endurance. That same camaraderie carried over into the track season.

Eddy also introduced me to some very new sports—sailing and water skiing in the summer and ice boating in the winter. What super fun they were! There was no way I would have ever experienced these things without Eddy's friendship. His family owned a boat marina and bait shop on the north shore of the lake. His family had the speed boat, and the sail boat and in the winter, the ice boat. They were already seasoned veterans of water sports. Sailing was fantastic! I developed a hunger for it and later in life, owned my own sailboat.

Ice boating was really different. We took the big sail off the sailboat, rigged it on a cross beam rig with steel runners and a rudder, and on the cold winter days with a foot and a half of smooth ice, trimmed the sail and screamed across the ice at eighty miles per hour! Other kids who lived along the lake would bring out their rigs, and there would be races—high speed races, where the upwind runners would come up off the ice! What a rush! On one run we were milking as much out of the wind and sail as we possibly could, pushing the limits and suddenly, at full speed, it spun out. It threw me off, landing me on my back on the ice and catapulted me for what seemed like a quarter of a mile, spinning around and around. I didn't get a scratch or even a bruise. There is nothing out on that huge expanse of ice to hit or stop you. You just slide and slide until you stop. What a trip! One summer Eddy talked his dad into letting us take out the speedboat and water skis. After a few attempts and trial runs I had my first experience on water skis! What a great way to spend the summer days!

Eddy and I also attended church camp together at a rented, state owned 4H camp facility at Dolliver State Park. I had been urged to go in previous years but declined due to my bed wetting. I had been afraid to take that big risk. But in high school that problem had improved, so I decided take the gamble. Camp just looked like too much fun to miss. So, I went! I had no "accidents", and had a terrific time, doing Bible classes, hiking, playing softball, volleyball, and getting acquainted with lots of new kids—girls! Not only did I not have an accident at camp, I never had a problem with it again. That week of camp seemed to heal me of an excruciating problem that had plagued me all through grade school. Suddenly, gone! That was God's greatest blessing to me that week of camp—and girls!

That week Eddy and I met some great Christian girls from the Clarion and Hampton, Iowa churches and later in the year, upon hearing of youth rallies in those churches, decided to make the trip there and "renew our acquaintances". Those were great times and we made many great friends. Many of those church camper kids later turned up on some of our bible college campuses and in missions and ministries.

Prior to Eddy's senior year, his family moved to Newell. He then changed high schools, and we saw less and less of each other. Upon graduation, he entered Minnesota Bible College in Minneapolis. I did not see him again until four or five years later when I enrolled there. It was good to see him again and know he was committed to the same calling I had received. But upon graduation he became involved in ministry somewhere else in the country, as did Betty and I and we never saw each other again. I understand he has retired in Montgomery, Alabama and I hope we will, on some future occasion, be able to see each other again before we leave this earth.

OTHER WINTER SPORTS

We found other winter sports to do, like driving our cars out on the ice of Storm Lake. One "sport" was to get up some speed then deliberately spin out, cutting huge "doughnies" across the ice. One afternoon Ron McManus and I were on the ice in his 1947 Plymouth coupe cutting all sorts of "dydos" when the two wheels on the right side slid off into a deep crack in the ice. The crack ran for hundreds of yards. The car's frame and axles were hung up on the ice, and there we were, miles across the lake from home with no tools or—cell phone! "Work, brains, work! How do we get ourselves out of this jam?" We decided to walk the shore line to see what we could find in timber, or planks or logs. With what few things we could find and with one lonely bumper jack, we jacked and blocked, and jacked and blocked until we extracted the right side of the car from the crack before the ice froze. Finally, we could crank up the engine and make our way back home, thanking God we didn't end up on the bottom of the lake. How did we ever live to adulthood?

JUNIOR/SENIOR PROMS

High school was also about the Junior-Senior Prom and the Senior Follies and Skip Day. As a junior, the prom meant that the juniors were in charge of carrying out the theme, arranging for the music, food and decorations. It was not a lot of fun but a lot of work. Of course my responsibility was to help with the decorations. That year, the surprise blessing for me was being asked by Joyce Blake to be her escort to the prom. I was delighted she asked me and excited to be her escort, but once there, seated at the table with her, I had absolutely no idea what to do or what to say. Suddenly I was a "shy dork" and at a total loss for words and how to socialize with a girl!

Of course my senior year we were the "honored guests" with the juniors doing the work. I had done no dating during the year since the last prom and felt no more comfortable with the opposite sex by Prom, '55. Being afraid to even try to invite a girl to be my date, I decided to attend alone as did some other class members. Having looked back at times on high school and Prom Night, I wish I hadn't been so uptight about girls. High school would have been a lot more fun. But, all is well that ends well—and it has all ended well!

The Senior Follies featured the senior class before the student body doing jokes, skits, parodies and musical "spoofs". The class members put me in a head lock/hammer lock and talked Jane Sorenson, my cousin, and me into doing a duet, lip sync to "Whatever Lola Wants, Lola Gets". It brought down the house then and during our class's 50th reunion, summer of 2005, they "goaded" us into doing that number again—without accompaniment—and no lip sync. Jane and I were sure they had forgotten that whole thing, but all these old "geezers" hadn't forgotten a thing! We did it again. It was fun!

The Sorensons
Gary, Carol, Harold, Gordon & Peggy

CHAPTER 9

A WHOLE NEW WORLD

Finally, came the Spring of 1955 and graduation! Down the isle we marched to Pomp and Circumstance. On Thursday evening May 26, 1955, at 8:00 p.m. our long awaited "graduation" was under way. I don't remember anything the speaker said. I do know that I participated with seven other classmates in a mixed quartet presentation of the song *The Halls of Ivy*. Then came that one all-important moment—hearing my name called to cross the stage and receive my high school diploma. Sixty-four of us crossed the stage that evening and received our coveted "sheep skin". The next event facing us was life! What do we do now?

My buddy Ron McManus and I had itchy feet. We wanted to see what was beyond Storm Lake, beyond Alta, Truesdale, and Sulfer Springs. We wanted to see what was beyond Iowa, and beyond the Rockies all the way to California! My family, as well as Ron's, had relatives in southern California. After I pretty much insisted I was heading to California, Mom and Dad helped me cash my $50 savings bond and arranged for me to stay with Grandmother Steig in El Monte. She had a guest room where I could stay and she looked forward to having a grandson for company. Besides whatever job I found, I could also earn my keep by doing her numerous household and yard chores. Ron's family arranged for him to stay with an aunt and uncle who lived in the Eagle Rock area of Los Angeles.

GO WEST YOUNG MAN, GO WEST!

So, it was all set! A few days after graduation we checked out my old '41 Ford, gassed her up, tossed all our earthly belongings in the trunk and back seat, and with all our savings money in our pockets, headed for Omaha, Nebraska and US 30,then west to Los Angeles. The weather was already hot, the old Ford was running warm, and I had to watch the temperature gage pretty close. By the time we arrived in Rock Springs, Wyoming, it was very hot and the temperature needle pegged out on the hot side of the gage. We stopped in a gas station and an old "veteran" mechanic there advised us to dump a can of lye in the radiator, drive to the next town, drain it out, put in fresh water and a box of baking soda and drive to the next town. There, we were to drain out the baking soda and put in fresh water. I followed his instructions and all that messing around did help a little. It still ran on the warm side but at least not boiling over. Later, after we finished the trip, I found the real problem. Someone had taken both thermostats out of the main hoses to the radiator, letting the water circulate so fast that it didn't have a chance to cool down. Nevertheless, we arrived at our destinations having had very little sleep or relief from the heat. We were in Los Angeles, and it was wonderful to get out of the heat of the desert! What a relief to sleep horizontally in a real bed! We had been taking turns driving and sleeping in the passenger seat. What a delight to be with family and to taste a good home-cooked meal!

OUR FIRST JOBS IN CALIFORNIA

After a day or two of rest, the next thing was to find a job. Somehow, through the "grapevine" I heard of a job with a small roofing outfit in Baldwin Park, California. I went to work immediately for D.A. Burt Roofing Co. as a "grunt" laborer , loading shingles and colored roof rock and granules onto new roofs in the many new housing developments. When the boss, D.A. Burt learned I was from Iowa, he immediately gave me a nick name—I was known as *Corn pone*! Corn pone is a southern cornbread baked in small oval loaves called "pones". I didn't get the connection with being a kid from Iowa except that they grew CORN in Iowa but since he and the crew got a charge out of it, I didn't mind. The money was good, and the work I was doing kept me in great shape. I was riding high! Ron found a job working in the large Van Camps Bakery in Burbank. Both of us were doing well, enjoying southern California, the big city, and lots of things to do. Neither of us were party-goers or hell raisers, it was just fun meeting new people, going new places and doing new things—like surfing at the beach. We had a wonderful time discovering the many surfing beaches along the Pacific, many of them famous from popular movie scenes of that era; Malibu, Venice, Santa Monica and of course, Muscle Beach. Actually, for consistently good surfing, Huntington Beach was as good as any.

MY FIRST CRUISE

One of those "new things" I experienced was a weekend boat trip to Catalina Island with my Aunt Bonnie Davis and her husband Gail. We had a great day going over, but during the evening the wind came up. We also discovered the two engines on his boat were stalling out and the harbor at Avalon was full. We had no choice but to try to anchor in a nearby bay. But we discovered that we had the wrong type anchor for the strong winds and high seas. We kept dragging anchor and drifting into the rocks, so spent all night manning the engines when we could get one or the other to run. We were constantly resetting the anchor, and navigating away from the rocks and cliffs. In the middle of that awful night I became sea sick and spent one of the worst twenty-four hours of my life. We finally made it back to the port of Long Beach late afternoon the next day and then back to Grandmother Steig's house to collapse! Actually, by the time we drove in the driveway my stomach was feeling back to normal. My brain had adjusted to the motion of the boat and car. But now my brain would have to readjust to land again and no motion. Not good! I was *land sick*! More ugh! and double ugh! Through all of this boat trip my Aunt Bonnie slept like a log and ate everything in sight. On the boat that morning after that terrible night of seasickness, she awoke to fix me a breakfast of orange soda and a pimento loaf sandwich—on six foot swells! Over the rail it went! Even the thought of that food combination brought retching. So much for my first big Ocean Cruise! It was back to work, pitching 125-pound bags of rock up onto roofs and carrying bundles of shingles up ladders.

THE REST OF THE FAMILY COMES TO CALIFORNIA

As that summer ended , I was in for an unexpected surprise! Mom and Dad phoned me from Iowa and announced that they too had decided to move to California! Dad was looking ahead a few years to retirement and was concerned that he would have no retirement income other than Social Security, as the lumber business in Iowa offered him no retirement pension at all. The lumber industry in California was unionized and the Lumberman's Union offered a good pension. They already had the house in Storm Lake sold to some friends in their church. All that was left was to have an auction sale for all their household goods and then drive to Los Angeles. They arrived in California just before school started. Grandma Steig had a nice small rental house right next door where they could live. Mom , Dad , Gary, and Peggy lived there, and I continued living in Grandmother's guest bedroom.

One of the great things I enjoyed while staying with grandmother was her patio. Adjacent to the back of her house was a thick grapevine covered patio with a large aviary of canaries and parakeets singing and talking nonstop and of course a couple of wonderful porch swings and some easy chairs. After a hard days work and a shower it was heavenly to sit in one of the porch swings and rock and listen to the birds. And on a hot day, under the vines, it was especially cool. A little bit of heaven for a seventeen year old young man! Dad did find a job in a lumberyard nearby, and with union benefits. Gary enrolled at El Monte high school for his junior year. Peggy enrolled at Puttrero School, in the third grade. Mom was having the time of her life making our new quarters home and enjoying being near her mother, siblings and other relatives. Life was good!

CHURCH

One of the rock solid institutions in my life was my sense of God's presence and my relationship with Christ and His church. It may sound odd for a healthy, active, seventeen year old to say that, but it was true. I couldn't help myself! My worship, sense of connection with Christ and camaraderie with, and acceptance by other Christian college age kids had built a solid world in which I could really grow. I wasn't about to set that aside as nothing. For me, it was everything. No one had to tell me to go to church, it was as natural as eating and breathing. Immediately upon arriving in California, I began looking for a place to worship. I began attending the El Monte Christian Church. It was okay, but not much going on with the college age kids. When my folks arrived, they too sought a place to worship and set out "visiting". They happened to visit the Rosemead Church of Christ where Richard Miller and wife Mary and family ministered. It was a hit with them from the very first visit. Richard and Mary were graduates of Minnesota Bible College, a school very familiar to all of us. The people were very friendly, and they had a great high school and college-age fellowship group and—a beautiful college-age woman by the name of Betty Smith! More about her later! Needless to say, this church family was a hit with me as well!

So, I attended the Bible classes and worship each Sunday and the college fellowship meetings and social functions. Later I even agreed to sing in the choir! They had a great college group! We went to the beach together for surfing and cookouts; we went to the mountains together to hike, ski or toboggan; we went to each other's homes for eating and games; we went to huge youth rallies together and met hundreds of other great kids and, or course, we dated each other, enjoying many great times together! And then...there she was. Betty Smith—singing in the choir— the voice of an angel and the looks of a movie star! But, surprisingly for me, I found no opportunity to get acquainted with her. We saw each other in church, but our day to day lives went in different directions!

LIFE IN SOUTHERN CALIFORNIA

I soon learned one of the realities of life living in a large city like Los Angeles—union labor and power movements and labor strikes. What could that possibly have to do with me, a grunt laborer? The concrete workers went on strike, which gradually shut down the carpenter/framers, which in turn, finally shut down the roofers. D.A. Burt called the roofing crews into the office and announced that we could all "go fishing"—there would be no more work until the strike was over! No one knew how long that would be, so I started looking for another job.

There were plenty of other jobs available, and I was able to find new work immediately. I hired on with the Bank of America as a bank courier, beginning work at 3:00 a.m. in their mail room and then delivering that mail from the home office at 7th and Olive in downtown Los Angeles to all the suburb branch banks by their 9:00 a.m. opening. This must have been the first version of overnight delivery—*When it absolutely, positively has to be there overnight.* We never knew if we had just some papers to be signed or a billion dollars in big bills. Each driver had his own unmarked company car and a set of keys to every branch Bank of America on whatever route he was assigned. My first route was to Pasadena, Monrovia, Arcadia, Temple City, San Gabriel, Alhambra and all points in between. Later, I was given the Hollywood/San Fernando Valley route. This was truly exciting for a kid named "Cornpone" from Storm Lake, Iowa. As with all the bank deliveries, I actually locked myself in and out of the Hollywood branch at Hollywood and Vine! How great is that?! I would then go on to the San Fernando, Burbank, and Glendale branches etc. and do the same, leaving the "incoming" mail bags in a locked compartment and bringing the "out going" bags back to the car. There were not many movie stars around at four, five, six o'clock in the morning, but it was fascinating to see Hollywood and the movie lots, etc. at that hour of the day.

Finally, I was given the route from Los Angeles to Garden Grove, Santa Ana—"Anaheim, Azusa and Cucamonga"—to use a famous line from the Jack Benny show. Actually, it was Anaheim, Corona, Riverside, San Bernardino, Redlands, Fontana and *then* Cucamonga! (Yes, ladies and gentlemen, there really is a place called Cucamonga!) Near there, I would often eat an early lunch in the car at a freeway pull off near the Ontario International Airport, and watch the fighter jets come and go on training runs. Then it was time to head west on I-10, back to downtown Los Angeles and the home office. I then had to fight the traffic on the return trip back home to La Puente (yes, it is hard to believe, but as early as 1956 Los Angeles was suffering "gridlock" on its freeways!)

There were a few times I had errands to run in downtown Los Angeles or I would decide to go for lunch at "Clifton's" a famous classy cafeteria, or some "burger joint" before going home. It was on one of these rare occasions that I saw her. THERE SHE WAS, right there on the corner of 6th and Olive—that beautiful Betty Smith! And she saw me! She recognized me! She actually stopped on the corner to visit with me and exchange a few pleasantries! Wow! You don't suppose?—Naaaa! More on her later!

HE'S COMING OUT OF HIS SHELL!

There was a major change taking place in me at that time, as it pertained to GIRLS! I actually began to feel brave enough to ask a girl for a date—so I did. I met some girls at the bank's home office whom I asked out—each just once. One, I took to a UCLA/Iowa football game at the Coliseum. She hated every minute of it. She was more of a party person. Not me! The end! I dated a couple of El Monte girls, Carmen and Carla. Nice girls, but we just didn't "click". Carmen moved away to Silver City, New Mexico. I had two weeks vacation coming, so I decided to pay her a visit there and meet her family. Nothing she had told me added up. Never got to meet her mother or father. She fabricated stories about them that never added up. Two days of that was enough! I was out of there in a flash! That was one of the dumbest wastes of time of my life! Carla, the other El Monte girl's former boyfriend became jealous, got drunk and with his "goon" buddies surrounded me in the dark one evening at the end of her hedge-lined driveway and threatened to kill me if I kept dating her. The next day I went straight to the police, filed a report and called for his arrest. I also arranged for temporary permission to carry a gun with me in my pickup. But God's providence intervened. I just happened to meet him face-to-face in one of the back aisles of an auto parts store in El Monte where he worked. Before I could get a word out of my mouth, he backed up and practically pled with me on hands and knees to forgive him for his stupidity. I did. But no more dates with "Carla". Ah yes! The realities of living in the big city! On to better things!

Rosemead Church of Christ

CHAPTER 10

THE NEXT BIG STEP OF FAITH

There was also a major change taking place in my faith. I began to sense there was more to life for me than the simple job of delivering mail for the Bank of America. I knew very little of the Bible, but I knew that faith meant more than just attending services. It meant sensing some sort of call from God to do something different than the usual, safe, expected, well mapped-out secular pursuits. For me, it meant doing something I had never done before—something big! I would quit my job and trust God to take me in a really new direction. Faith meant doing something God would want me to do—whatever that might be. I had no preconditions, only that God would take me into His new purpose and destiny. WOW! Did He ever!

I turned in my resignation of the bank courier job to my supervisor, Mr. Wilcox. My first "sign" from God that I was doing the right thing came in a surprising discussion with Mr. Wilcox as to why I was leaving the job. I told him honestly about my decision to take a step of faith with my life and let God lead me into some purpose He had for me. I couldn't believe his reaction! A smile came over his face. He stood up and reached out to shake my hand, congratulating me on living out my faith in such a real way! He hated to lose me, but he wished me God's blessing and God speed and told me God would have something special for me! WOW! This, coming from a "secular" bank mail-room boss? I left his office in awe at what I had just witnessed. It was a secular job, but how wonderful to find one of God's people there lifting me up!

I can't help but reflect on Abram, in the Old Testament and what he felt when he listened to God's call to leave what he had in Ur of Sumer, and "go to a land I will show you, and I will bless you"—no road-map, no address, no detailed plan—just that He would bless him! The Hebrew's writer says simply, "He obeyed and went, even though he didn't know where he was going!" Faith means being willing to leave our *comfort zones*! I had certainly left mine!

CONFIRMATION

My next sign from God that I was doing the right thing came the day after my visit with Mr. Wilcox. The very next day was a Saturday and I attended a huge college-age youth rally at the South Gate Church of Christ, a sister congregation. There was a program with a speaker with the usual time of fellowship and refreshment following. As I stood visiting with some Christian friends, someone approached to tell me that my minister, Dick Miller, was looking for me. Hmmm—I wonder what he wants? So I wandered through the crowd to locate him. As I approached him he immediately turned to me and said, "I've been looking for you— DO YOU NEED A JOB?"

Again, I couldn't believe my ears! This was getting eerie! I began to find that when you decide to get serious about doing things by simply trusting God, you had better be ready! He appears on the scene sooner than you might think! "Do I need a job??!!"

I responded, "Yes, yes, I do need a job! How did you know?"

"What do you mean how did I know? Know what?" he asked. He had no idea I had just resigned my job as a step of faith. When I told him what I had done just the day before the rally, and why, he was shocked at how fast God had moved and that he had unknowingly become a part of God's action in my life. "What's the job", I asked.

"Angeles Crest Christian Camp is badly in need of a qualified lifeguard for their swimming pool", he responded.

Wow! Was I interested? "YES! I love the water! I love swimming! I would love the job! When do I start?" I was to start as soon as I could be certified as a fully qualified lifeguard. At first that looked like a problem because I had never been qualified as a lifeguard. Dick assured me that getting qualified would be no problem. He knew a qualified swimming instructor at the Alhambra YMCA, who would be willing to work with me during her lunch hour to get me certified. "Great! Where do I sign up?!"

GETTING IN SHAPE

So, I signed on and began one of the most rigorous daily water workouts I had ever experienced! I swam laps upon laps for endurance; laps upon laps carrying weights (as if carrying a drowning victim); laps with a real live person (the instructor); laps upon laps under water. At the end of two weeks, she had me doing hyper breathing techniques, allowing me to do two full laps of the pool under water! But all-in-all it was great! I always loved a physical challenge and staying in shape. And—I passed the test with flying colors! I was now a certified lifeguard, able to work at any pool or at the beach.

ON THE JOB

This job would not be like life-guarding at the beach, watching for sharks, and swimmers caught in rip tides and swept out to sea. My main job here would be keeping order. But even more important, I would be serving others in the great Christian enterprise of church camping. I would be watching over and working with kids, young adults, and adults from every walk of life, while they enjoyed Bible camp and the beautiful new swimming pool. The job included; taking care of all the pool equipment; the upkeep and maintenance of the pool; the testing and treating the water; the cutting and maintaining of fire breaks around the entire camp complex (the camp was 40 miles into the Angeles National Forest) and cabin clean-up and maintenance. From time to time, it also included my help with leading hikes in the surrounding mountains and taking care of an occasional rattlesnake! I couldn't have found a more suitable and terrific job! Correction. GOD couldn't have found me a more suitable and terrific job!

CAROL

Just previous to and during this change of jobs another girl came into my life. She was a great gal from our youth fellowship at the Rosemead Church of Christ (I had placed my membership there by this time). I knew her very well and saw her every Sunday—but didn't see her—she was hiding right in plain sight! Gradually, Carol Sickinger, a student at Occidental College, and I became good friends and as that friendship grew, began dating. We spent a few Saturdays at Huntington Beach surfing, went to the movies together, and was her "escort" to Rush Week at Occidental College. And of course, we had become a "couple" at college church functions. She was comfortable to be around and truly a good friend. But about the time I started lifeguard duty at the camp, we took a trip there together so she could see where I would be working and what I would be doing. It was then she explained to me that she had to move north to the University of California Berkley campus for the summer to complete her studies. But I would be life-guarding and living up at the camp for the summer, except for weekends. There would be no way I could ever drive clear to Berkley and back in 24 hours! Bummer! I wouldn't be seeing her for the entire summer! But God had many other major things planned for me that Summer of '57!

THE LIFEGUARD—"THERE'S A NEW SHERIFF IN TOWN!"

Carol moved to Berkley, I moved to my new job at Angeles Crest Christian Camp and the camp kids started making their way up the mountain for their weekly stays at church camp. Actually, I had started two weeks before the camps began to help get things cleaned and painted and to make sure the pool was in ship-shape before the "invasion" of nearly 200 to 250 kids and/or adults each week of the summer. The first two weeks were extremely trying. We had nearly 250 high school students each week who were not use to having a lifeguard telling them what to do and enforcing the rules at the swimming pool. The camp had tried to operate previously without a lifeguard, but things became so rowdy and there were so many accidents occurring, that their insurance carrier insisted they get a lifeguard to keep order or they would have to close the pool. So, I discovered, I was the *new sheriff in town*, which, of course meant "let's test him to see if he can take it" tactics. They deliberately broke the rules, threw each other in the pool, threw the pool equipment in the pool when I wasn't looking, and then—big mistake—they tried to throw me into the pool as well! Finally, my patience had run out! Then— shock and surprise—faster than you could wink I threw them all out of the pool area (some bodily) and locked the gate! After three days of this deliberate ill behavior, I went to the caretakers cabin (office) and threw my whistle on the table and resigned! "These are church kids?—these are Bible college student staff—and they carry on like this?" Harold Stanwood, the camp manager, calmed me down and urge me to stay with the job. "Things would change the next week", he promised! I stayed, and things did change—they got much better. Manager Stanwood had informed the President of Pacific Christian College about the conduct of the PCC students and the next week he, and the Dean of Students drove up to the camp to personally set them straight and apologize to me. I was impressed! I had drawn the "line in the sand" they knew that we meant business! We had turned the corner at the Angeles Crest swimming pool. I guarded there the rest of that Summer and for three succeeding summers and never had but a minor problem or two.

Angeles Crest Christian Camp pool

Marcy and me...the lifeguard showing off

98

CHAPTER 11

GOD BRINGS "THE" GIRL INTO MY LIFE...
BETTY

On the weekends, I would drive down the mountain to La Puente, to be with my family and attend church. I washed my dirty clothes, spent some time with them from Saturday afternoon to Sunday afternoon, then drove back up the mountain with my swim-trunks, whistle and clean clothes. Church was still the main thing on my schedule those weekends. On one of those Sundays, as I drove my pickup out of the church parking lot, there was "that Smith girl" standing at the edge of the driveway, flagging me down! Who is this? I couldn't believe it—it was Betty Smith wanting me to stop so she could talk to me. Me? Me?—she wants to talk to me? I say that, because we had accidentally gotten together earlier that year at a New Years Eve youth fellowship. We had visited, played games, shared scripture, prayed, ate and were getting our coats on to go home when someone in the crowd asked Betty if she needed a ride home. I heard her say yes—but then heard no offers. So—(good guy that I am) I offered her a ride with Mike Williams and his girl friend and me in my customized '54 Chevy pickup. She accepted, and there we were, bouncing along, four in the seat, on our way home. Suddenly Mike said, "Hey, its New Years Eve, and we don't have to go home. How about us riding around Hollywood and see all the activities and crazy people?" Everyone agreed—and Betty agreed!—awesome!

A NIGHT ON THE TOWN

We had a good time—drove all over Hollywood; then to the Griffiths Park Observatory; then to Pasadena to see all the "crazies" gather for the Rose Parade the next day. We decided to park the pickup and just walk down Colorado Boulevard, the parade route, and watch all the activity. As we walked along, suddenly something amazing happened—Betty slipped her hand in mine! What's this? Could it be? I was thrilled! Later, as dawn began to break, we all decided to head to our homes. I took Mike and his girlfriend home and then asked Betty if she would like to go to my house for breakfast. I knew mom would be fixing French toast or pancakes, and it would be great for Betty to enjoy it with us and meet the family.

AND BREAKFAST TOGETHER TOO!

She said, "YES!" Yes, do you hear that! Yes! I was pumped! The prettiest girl in California, the Crawford's Market "Miss Sweet Sixteen", a Rose Parade Queen runner-up wants to hold my hand and eat breakfast at my house with my family? I must have died and gone to heaven! After breakfast we went back to Pasadena to watch the Rose Parade. We experienced the amazing sights and aromas of this floral parade with some other friends from church, and then took her home. We both needed some sleep. At the Wednesday p.m. church service, I saw Betty again. After the service, I took her, along with her younger brother Chuck, to a drive-in for ice cream, sodas etc. As I dropped her and her brother off at her house, I lingered a few minutes for a parting visit. She would be leaving to go back to Minneapolis, to Minnesota Bible College where she was a freshman. I would not be seeing her for a while, but urged her to promise me her first date when she returned home in the Spring. She did promise, but little did we know the circumstances that would bring her home early from college.

A HEARTBREAKING LOSS

Betty's mother, Pearl, entered the hospital early that Spring. One of the deacons called to ask if I would consider going with him to the Ontario hospital to call on Pearl. This would be a different experience for me. I had never made hospital calls on church members in general. I did not know her mother. I didn't know what to say, but not for long.

She was a delight to visit! It was a very pleasant experience! She was a very pleasant woman! Now, I see it as a providential meeting. Little did I know at that time I would be marrying her daughter and that this would be the last time I would see her alive. A few weeks later she passed away.

Betty came home for the funeral along with the rest of her family. I attended the funeral as well. I am so glad I did. Betty was home for about a month before returning to M.B.C. The famous movie *The Ten Commandments* premier was taking place at the Pantagis Theater in Hollywood, and I thought it might be good to take her to it and spend some time with her before she left again for Minnesota. I called her to make the date and was shocked to get a flat NO! End of conversation! Well, that's the end of that! "I knew it was all too good to be true!" On to other things!

AN UNEXPECTED MEETING IN THE PARKING LOT

Now, here she is. "That girl"—Betty Smith, the one who promised me a date but then turned me down flat—is flagging me down in the church parking lot for something. What does SHE want? To tell me I forgot my Bible or to apologize for the cold shoulder earlier? What now? Knowing how much I loved to swim, she figured I might like to go to a swimming-pool party at her friends house. I kind of figured she just wanted a ride, and after all, I did want something to do before going back to camp that weekend! Postmen take walks on their days off. Lifeguards go for a swim. So, I halfheartedly said yes and taxied her to her friend's pool party. I spent that afternoon with her, cavorting at the pool and being mischievous. Upon returning her to her cousin's home where she was staying for the summer, I decided to ask her directly the big question... "Do you want to go out, i.e. date me or not?"(make up your mind)! And, I got a yes! I GOT AN AFFIRMATIVE! She actually does want to date me! OK, now that's better! Lets get on with it! We did date the rest of that summer on the weekends after I returned home from camp. On one of those dates I gave her our first kiss. This began a relationship that has gone on for 49 years of marriage, three children, and eight grandchildren. How did that happen?

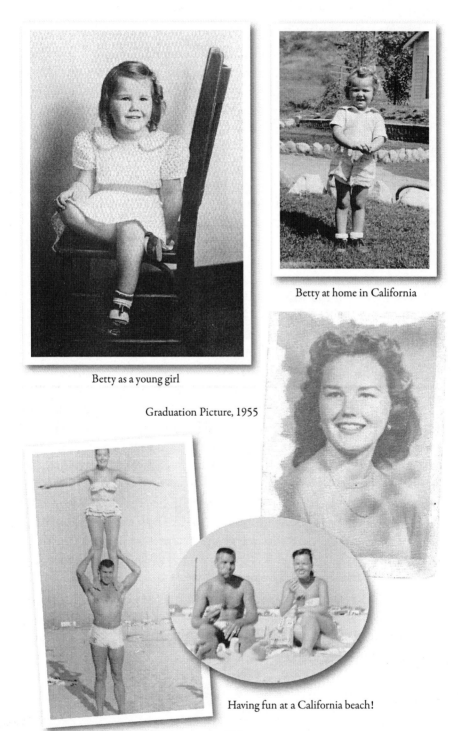

Betty as a young girl

Betty at home in California

Graduation Picture, 1955

Having fun at a California beach!

CHAPTER 12

GOD'S PURPOSE UNFOLDS

The rest of that summer of camp was wonderful. I met many great Christian leaders and teachers. I met hundreds of campers of all ages, many whose lives touched mine, as they would spend time visiting with me by the pool both during pool hours and even during off hours while I cleaned and maintained the pool. Many of the campers just wanted someone to talk to. I began to recognize a great need to simply be their friend—to be their sounding board, as they shared the deep concerns of their life. A light began to turn on in my head. On a few occasions I had church teachers and leaders tell me that they thought I should prepare to be a minister. I always immediately rejected those comments, explaining that they didn't realize how ill suited I was for public speaking and being up in front before the people. It just wasn't ever going to happen! Ministry was just way beyond my abilities! Except—except here at camp with so many of these kids needing someone to shepherd them. I began asking myself, "Is that something I could do—could I be a minister to youth?" I thought about that question every week of that summer, as the kids would come and go from each week of camp. All summer that question remained in the back of my mind.

The last week of camp that first summer was college week. There was a great turn-out of college students from several different campuses in southern California that week. The speaker was tops in connecting with that age group—of which I was a part. Harold Gallegher was the featured speaker, at both the morning service and at the evening fireside program at the open amphitheater. Although I was hired staff, I completed my chores early so I could get in on his fireside chats. I can't speak for the others, but I can truthfully say that he really challenged my thoughts big time! On the last evening, his message was based on the story in John, of Jesus and the woman at the well. Jesus spoke to her about the "living water" He could give her and about her personal life, that she had been with several men, and the one she was presently with was a "live in". She was so impacted by Christ and his compassion for her that she "left her water pot to run into town to tell everyone she could find, that she had found the Christ and to come see!" It was then, as I sat there listening to that story unfold that the "lights" for me totally came on! If that simple messed up woman could do what she did, then I could certainly do something. Having not planned ahead at all to do so, I suddenly got up out of my seat at the invitation and went forward to declare my intentions to give my life to "full time Christian service". The lifeguard?!! He's not even a camper! But "God works in mysterious ways, His wonders to perform!" And for me to do *that* was a wonder. After the close of the fireside service I took a walk on a mountain path in the moon light and had a little talk with God. I needed to make a deal with God—that although I had committed myself to Christian service, it didn't mean I would be doing any preaching or *up front* kinds of stuff. I was committing myself to working with youth—only that! Well, God didn't listen! God didn't argue with me about it then, but HIS plan for me unfolded subtly as the months and years rolled on.

A BIG CHANGE COMING

That week of camp meant the end of that summer of camping and the end of that year of employment as a lifeguard. The campers left on Saturday and I stayed for a few hours to help clean up, pack up, straighten up the camp facilities and then made my way down the mountain for the last time that summer of '57. I arrived home to then surprise my family with the news that I had committed my life to college studies and full-time Christian work. I would be packing my bags for Bible College! They were again in shock! "When? Where? Where are you going to Bible College—Pacific Christian College in Long Beach—right?" No, my plans were to leave immediately for Minneapolis, Minnesota, to attend Minnesota Bible College! "What? All the way back to the cold mid-west—Minnesota? Are you sure you want to do this? Are you sure you can go back to being a student—you know, books, homework, etc. and at a college level? We just moved out here to sunny California where we can all be together and enjoy the warmth! And now you are moving way back there? Why?" And so I did.

COLLEGE LIFE—MINNESOTA BIBLE COLLEGE 1957

Many thought it was that Betty Smith girl that turned my head to Minnesota and bible college. But it was not! I had developed a great appreciation for MBC years ago on their youth campus visitation programs. I determined then, that if I ever decided to attend college, it would be Minnesota Bible College...Betty had little to do with that decision even though presently she was a student there and would be starting her sophomore year. So we packed what few earthly possessions we owned, hitched a ride with another couple headed for Minnesota, and hit the road for the long trip east.

Before we left for Minnesota, I had to make the ultimate sacrifice for a 17 year old hot rod enthusiast—I had to sell my beautiful '54 Chevy street rod pickup! Those funds provided the money for the first year's tuition and college expenses, which worked out wonderfully, but—I was walking! Culture shock! I went from being a carefree, tanned, hot-rodding teenager to a car-less, academically overloaded, sleep deprived pedestrian! We arrived in Minneapolis in the middle of the night (like 3:00 am) and dropped Betty and her things off at Leverton Hall, the girls dorm. I bunked on a couch in Hayden Hall, one of the men's residence houses. Six a.m. the next morning it was "up-n-at-um", signing up for classes; getting class schedules, and getting moved into my room (which turned out to be a third floor attic, two room with bath, $85 per month, apartment shared with four other guys). Living off campus was never suppose to happen to freshman students, but the college had no choice due its exceptionally large incoming freshman class. And as we all know, murphy's law was immediately in affect. The attic apartment ceiling sloped down on each side just like the steep roof of the house. The only place the bunk-beds would fit was in the middle of the room. All four of us were 6'3" or taller! Head ache! This quartet of freshman giants consisted of Art

Collier, John Luther, and Larry Howell from Council Bluffs, Iowa, and me, from Storm Lake, Iowa by way of La Puente, California.

SECOND THOUGHTS

So, there I was, after three years of being free from classes and studies and term papers, back up to my ears in academia! I had some of the best professors you could ever study under, but I was overwhelmed. Some would compare a Bible college education to a "Sunday school" level education. It is not! We met students who were transfers from secular colleges, and they were shocked at how difficult this so-called "Sunday school" education turned out to be The college felt that any Minnesota Bible College student ought to be able to compete with any other student from any other college—even the University of Minnesota, which was right across the street. Many of our MBC students took classes and did graduate work at the U of M and did very well. But for me, this new college work was tough. I was studying harder than I had ever studied while in high school and could hardly make average grades. I got so discouraged that I began to consider quitting and returning home to California. But little did I know how much the professors and staff cared for each and every student on their campus. Someone "tattled" that I was considering quitting and immediately I received a message from Professor Jerry Gibson, that he wanted to see me in his office. Appearing at his office, He expressed his concerned for me and that the school might be losing me as a student and that the Lord would be losing a good servant! Wow! They all cared that much? He then continued to visit with me about my struggles with the work load and suggested ways the school could help me with it. Then he asked me what had brought me to MBC. I responded that, "I guess I had felt the call of God to do so". His response came in the form of a question.— "had God taken back the call?" Suddenly, we looked directly at each other, and I began to grin—I knew exactly what he was driving at! No, God hadn't taken back the call—and He still wanted me in school, and in ministry of some kind! No further conversation needed. I knew what I needed to do—just keep on with my program, keep working, keep studying, and God would take care of the rest. That is exactly what I did after leaving his office that afternoon. To this day, I have no idea what happened to turn things around. All I know is that the load seemed easier, my grades came up, and I stayed with it for six more years, when in 1963, I graduated with my Bachelor of Theology degree. Since that day Betty and I have served 45 years in church ministry and in mission service around the country.

A MARRIAGE PROPOSAL

Other than my birth and my baptism, the other most significant event of my life began to unfold those first months in college. As the beautiful fall days and colors arrived, Betty and I took walks together near the campus. A favorite spot was Van Cleve Park, a few blocks from the campus. One beautiful Saturday, while we could hear the fans cheering the U of M football team at Memorial Stadium a few blocks away, we sat down on one of the benches to just relax and enjoy the beautiful Fall colors. As we sat there, I began talking about "us getting married" and about when and where. At which time she responded with, "Wait a minute. Aren't you forgetting something here?"

I thought for a minute. Hmmm, what am I forgetting?

"You don't know?" she asked! "YOU HAVEN'T ASKED ME YET!"

Duh. She was absolutely right! How could I be so dense and make such a huge assumption? So, immediately I took her hand, got down on one knee and "popped" the all important question "Betty Smith WILL YOU MARRY ME ?" To which she responded—YES! Yes!—and it seemed that the providence of God was at work again. Two years later on June 6, 1959 we were united in marriage, or as our dear MBC friend Robert Eckman would say, "...united in the solemn vows of woolly headlock!" The wedding was at the Rosemead Church of Christ in Rosemead, California, performed by our minister Richard Miller. This began a 49-year "TEAM extreme adventure", in raising three beautiful daughters, and serving God together in ministries and mission work. Looking back on our lives and work and sacrifices and hard times and victories, it seems we really did have a marriage made in heaven—in spite of a few times of woolly headlock! Most marriages would not have survived those pressures.

FIRST A BRAKEMAN, AND THEN A BUSBOY?

During those wonderful, busy, pressure packed years there was more than just classes, studies, outside reading, and a half a dozen research papers each week. There was outside employment and student activities and a great camaraderie within the whole student body. My first paying job was, I thought at the time, really pretty neat. Somehow, I had landed a job with the big railroad yards in Minneapolis as a railroad brakeman. It was entirely switch yard work in the middle of the night with what seemed like a million different switches and switch tracks. I had to learn the layout of the switch yard, throw the proper switches and be able to assemble trains and group car orders, all in the dark of night. I started work at 10:00 pm and worked until 6:00 am. But, I had to have breakfast eaten and be in class by 7:30 a.m. What was I thinking? I couldn't keep that up for more than a week or two! I was dead! I knew I had to quit and look for something with better hours and that would bring sanity to my schedule. I found a part time job as a bus-boy at Sigma Kappa sorority house. I helped serve meals, buss dishes, wash dishes, and tidy things up after meals. I was paid by the hour for my time, PLUS—meals! "Meals" is a big fringe benefit deal for an 18 year old at 6'3" and 220 pounds—thats good pay! Plus—the beautiful scenery of a whole house full of college girls! Pay and meals plus, *fringe benefits*! But what a paradox—from being a railroad brakeman, to a sorority house busboy! I truly loved railroading, but that was an idea I had to give up for the sorority house job. Isn't God truly good!

Minnesota Bible College, Minneapolis, MN

Betty and me as
Freshmen

Dressed for the
M.B.C. Banquet

Earning my
bread & butter
(far right)

CHAPTER 13

STUDENT LIFE AT
MINNESOTA BIBLE COLLEGE

At the college campus we enjoyed the fun of student activities, such as "Skip Day", where the students "kidnapped" the dean, and they, and the professors took off for a day at the park. There was a big picnic, games, and great fellowship between students and faculty. The professors also invited the students into their homes at different times of the year for a family sit-down dinner. One of the first of these dinners I had the privilege of attending was at the home of M /M Russell Boatman. Russell Boatman was actually "President" Boatman, also "Professor" Boatman, who taught the freshman class, *The Church In The Scriptures*. I couldn't believe that he would invite me, a lowly freshman student, to his home for a wonderful dinner of northern pike, which he had caught himself on a lake in Canada. There was no stuffy academic or theological "table talk" that evening. Instead there were great fish stories and lots of great jokes and stories about his hobby—restoring and driving around his 1910 Model T Ford. What a great evening! It sure put me and the other students who had been invited, at ease with the president of MBC! There were similar occasions with other faculty as well. I could see very soon that this was not just any college campus—*this was a family!* That personal care and attention helped just an average kid like me to succeed at college academics—far beyond what I had ever imagined! As I look back now, I again see it all as a "God thing"!

Besides Professor Jerry Gibson, whom I mentioned earlier, who taught Old Testament and Hebrew classes, and President Boatman, there was Professor Don Riggin, my Greek professor, who not only got me through 1st year Greek with flying colors (miracle of miracles) , but also taught me more English than I had ever learned in high school. If my high school English teacher could have seen my ability with Greek, she would have fainted from shock! Then there was the beloved Dean, the professor of the four Gospels and second year Greek, G.H. Cachiaras. Under his tutelage I learned not only the life of Christ from the four Gospels, but in addition, could translate, read and speak the Gospel of John from the Greek text to English—quite a miracle for an "average" Iowa boy! There were also Professors Ronald Keeler and Harold Haskell, teachers of English/Composition and Speech/Homiletics. Another of my professors was Howard Hayes, who taught Church History. Professor Hayes was a task master, demanding excellence, yet had a great dry sense of humor and a dedication to and compassion for the students. You couldn't help but admire this dedicated servant.

But of all the faculty, the one who touched my life the most with his biblical and theological insight, wisdom, and sweet reasonableness, was professor Earl Grice! Professor Grice taught various New Testament books as well as studies in Theology. During the second or third year, Betty and I began Sunday worship at the 48th Street Christian Church where Earl, his wife Betty and family also ministered. As the weeks rolled by we became involved there, singing in the choir and leading the high school students. Through that involvement, we became closely involved with the Grice family, which meant knowing their three boys and being in their home for occasional dinners and social events.

Later in our college years there was more involvement with Professor Grice, as he and I participated together in an a cappella quartet Gospel Team at Spring Tour time. We traveled the central and northeast states, presenting gospel concerts each evening at different churches in different towns, over a two week period. Our friendship has remained close to this day—over 45 years later! Tragically, Betty, Earl's first wife died of cancer several years ago. In 1993 Earl retired from teaching but is still closely involved with the college alumni activities in a major way. Earl Grice will always be a servant of God—to his family, to the college, to the church and to his neighbors and friends. He and his present wife Irene will always remain our close friends.

M.B.C.—THE FRINGE BENEFITS

With the University of Minnesota across the street from MBC, and located in the twin cities of Minneapolis-St Paul, students had available many great opportunities for culture and entertainment, and access to some of the greatest minds around. The U of M offered free concerts at the Northrup Auditorium. We attended the annual Bach week, with free pipe organ concerts by organist Heinrich Fletcher, as well as string ensembles. We attended lectures in archeology by the renown archeologist, W.F. Albright, who presented his travels and finds in Egypt, and the Sinai, and insights on Moses and the Exodus. We heard the great Montovanni and his orchestra at another Northrup concert.

MY STINT WITH THE ROYAL BALLET OF LONDON

And then there was the time two or three fellow students and I, as a dare, answered an ad in the University campus newspaper, to hire on as "extras", to perform with the London Ballet in the "Firebird" performance at the U of M's Northrup Auditorium. We were to be Russian Cossack soldiers, performing in the last act. They hired us!! We were shocked! There we were, with the Minneapolis Symphony at full crescendo, and us, in full Russian Cossack battle dress with battle axes, and dancers flying all over the stage! What an experience! The grandchildren will hardly believe that story—"Grandpa was in ballet??!!" We did five weekend performances getting $8.00 per performance. Not bad for a weekend! All of these experiences—plus special concerts at MBC by our own King's Choristers; and outside guest speakers such as Dr. Carl F.Henry and Dr. James Sire—right on our own campus!

I also remember an afternoon with Bill Miller, a student at MBC and a consummate pianist and organist, who invited Betty and me to go with him to St. Marks Cathedral in downtown Minneapolis for his "pipe organ lesson". After riding the city bus to St. Mark's, we found ourselves alone, sitting in this huge cathedral, listening to some of the most majestic Bach organ music we have ever heard—*Toccata and Fugue in G Minor*, etc—for free! What an experience! Our own private concert! What a country!

MUSIC TOUR GROUPS

Many MBC students became involved in music and drama. Each year the students would form drama teams or quartets and trios, then during spring break, would travel the length and breadth of this country presenting gospel music concerts and drama programs for churches large and small. Faculty members would team up with a quartet, trio or drama team. Then, using their own automobiles, would drive the teams (five to six members plus equipment) from city to city for evening concerts and programs. Each team plus luggage and gear would rush to make it to the next church, sometimes driving through the night and sometimes through snow storms or even blizzards to make a scheduled performance .

THE "GOSPEL FOREMAN"

Since I had loved singing in the ensembles and choir in high school, I was immediately recruited to a men's gospel quartet that was forming, as the bass. We called ourselves "The Gospel Foreman". We collected some Blackwood Brothers quartet music, and with hours and hours of practice, worked up an impressive repertoire of reasonable quality gospel music. We sounded kind of like a "not-quite-ready-for-Nashville" version of The Oakridge Boys. Our first two week Spring Tour was with Professor Jerry Gibson in his 4-door Studebaker. We squeezed—rather jammed—our suit cases, MBC display board, boxes of pamphlets and pictures, into the trunk of his car and together (I mean TOGETHER—all six of us were over 6 feet tall) headed down the road through a blizzard to our first destination and presentation—the Church of Christ in Hammond, Indiana! That tour took us on through Indiana, Ohio, a corner of Pennsylvania, and Bethany West Virginia. We then made our way back through southern Ohio, Indiana, Illinois and home, to Minneapolis. What a great adventure! We presented not only church concerts, but programs at high schools and other Bible colleges. Our quartet even put together a collection of Barbershop favorites which we presented on "lighter" occasions, such as social events at Sigma Kappa Sorority house where I worked as a busboy! None of us had ever been performers, but we all enjoyed the experience so much, that most of us (members of twelve different teams) signed on for tour every year of college.

The Gospel Foreman went on tour again the next year. The two following years I sang with the Kings Choristers choir tour. My senior year, I sang with a mixed acappella quartet consisting of Professor Earl Grice, tenor; Maurice Butler, soprano; Arlene Frick Eckman, alto; and me singing bass. We toured some of those same states, singing at churches, high schools and even a chapel service at Lincoln Christian College. I remember the Lincoln Christian College presentation as a wonderful but scary experience. Their chapel service was held in the huge college gym. The acoustics were terrible. The only musical assistance an acappella quartet has is a pitch pipe! On that occasion I don't remember anyone having even a pitch pipe. We simply had to depend on our musical ears and perfect pitch to get each musical number started and then stay on pitch. God was with us as we presented our acappella selections to this large impressive group of peers and were well received! The members of our quartet stay connected to this day in 2008. Whenever we are in Rochester, Minnesota we look up Maurice "Squeek" Butler and Earl and Irene Grice. And whenever we are in Montrose, Colorado we fellowship with the Eckmans. I performed their daughter Heather's wedding this summer—as I did for Bob and Arlene many years ago 1963 at Ladysmith, Wisconsin. MBC folks stay close.

MBC Quartet: Mr. Grice, Arlene Frick Eckman, Squeek Butler and Me

CHAPTER 14

SPRING 1958
BACK TO CALIFORNIA
AN AMAZING EXTREME ADVENTURE!

As the '58 school year ended Betty Smith informed me that she would not be coming home to California that summer. She was required to do an internship toward her Christian Education degree by spending the summer doing Vacation Bible Schools, first at a church in Sciota, Illinois, and then other churches in the upper mid-west. I wouldn't be seeing her again until the start of the Fall term of 1958. Since I had sold my pickup to attend college, I had no transportation of my own to return to California. Phil Davis—a friend and fellow student also from California—and I were discussing the fact that we were both headed in the same direction and that we both needed a ride. We decided we ought to work something out to travel together. Yes, we could travel together, but how? Neither of us had the money for a train or bus ticket—what other alternatives did we have to get home—2000 miles away? "Lets hitch-hike!" Travel was still pretty safe at that time, and not much danger for two big college guys hitch-hiking together. We decided we would leave Minneapolis Wednesday p.m. following the graduation service, at which we both sang in the King's Choristers. That night we would thumb our way south out of Minnesota through Iowa, and then west to California and home.

RAY BOCK—AND A NIGHTMARE UNFOLDS!
Somehow, news of our plan made its way to the ears of other students

and before long fellow student Ray Bock met with Phil and me to suggest yet another idea. He had just purchased a car—a 1947 Buick "Woody" station wagon and was planning to transfer to Platt Valley Bible College in Scottsbluff, Nebraska. He would be packing all his stuff in the station wagon and heading out that same evening following the graduation service— "would Phil and I want to ride with him as far as Scottsbluff, sharing the driving and gasoline expenses?" he asked. Sounded like a great deal to us, since it would get us at least a third of the way home!

Graduation night came, and after the service Phil and I said our good-byes, threw our gear in the station wagon along with Ray's, and began making our way out of Minneapolis. I knew the way south out of Minneapolis quite well, and was elected to take the first shift of driving. But as I drove up University avenue to connect up with one of the major thoroughfares south to Lake Street and out of town, Ray informed us that, "first we had to pick up his wife!" What? Pick up his wife?

"Ray, we didn't even know you were married—you have a wife? What street does she live on? Give me directions."

Ray responded, "She doesn't live here—in Minneapolis"

"Then where does she live, Ray?"

"She lives in Staples."

"STAPLES! That's over 200 miles northwest of here, Ray! That's the exact opposite direction we should be going—it will take us the rest of the night just to get there and get her stuff. Then we will have to chart a completely new course down through South Dakota and Nebraska to get you to Scottsbluff! Ray—why didn't you tell us?"

Many have advised us that we should have stopped the car right on the spot and got out. Well, we didn't. Bible College brothers don't do those kinds of things—even though I know we would have been justified. But had we bailed out, we would never have experienced the amazing adventure that unfolded. So, on we drove into the night—to Staples, Minnesota. We stopped after a couple hours to fuel up. Phil and I purchased the first tank of gas. Phil then got behind the wheel and took us the rest of the way to Staples where she was living with her parents. We arrived there at about 2:00 am and immediately began loading her stuff into the Buick wagon with Ray's—mainly a big old steamer trunk full of newspaper clippings, memorabilia and junk, which we tied to the roof of the wagon. The rest of her junk, along with Ray's, filled up the back end of the old '47 Buick. With Phil's and my bags in the back seat, there was only one cramped place left back there to sit. Ray and his wife and whoever was driving (either Phil or me) sat in the front seat, and which ever of the two of us was not driving sat in that cramped cubical in the back seat—trying to get some sleep before our next shift of driving.

Off we went again into the night, with me and Phil doing all the driving and me and Phil buying all the gasoline. It was sometime during this segment of the trip that we asked Ray when he was planning to buy some gas and take his turn driving that more of this nightmare unfolded. Ray informed us that he didn't have any money for gas—AND, he did not have a drivers license—he could not take his turn driving! Phil and I looked at each other—we were stunned! We would be doing all the driving—we would be financing their whole trip to Scottsbluff, Nebraska! We had not slept in 24 hours, we had not eaten in over 12 hours—and now we couldn't afford to. We wouldn't have enough money to rent a motel room or hardly enough for food—barely enough for gas! We just pushed on, hungry and exhausted!

THE '47 BUICK—JUNK!

We traveled south-southwest through Sauk Center, Morris, Ortonville Minnesota, and Milbank, South Dakota. Thursday morning around 6:00 a.m. found us crossing the border of Minnesota into South Dakota and nearing Milbank. Suddenly, the worst racket you could ever imagine broke loose under the hood. The connecting rods were hammering like mad, and I knew we had a major problem. We found an auto repair garage open on main street in Milbank next to the railroad depot and limped in to see about the damage. I knew this would mean an engine overhaul. I had been enough of a shade tree mechanic to know what a major engine blow up was about. We would have to replace all the main and rod bearing inserts in the old "straight eight". It didn't take long for the mechanic to tell us the bad news—she did indeed need a complete engine overhaul BUT—there were no parts available for an old '47 Buick straight eight and we couldn't afford them even if there were. Now what do we do? Since I supposedly had the practical automotive expertise, the group looked to me for answers. My suggestion was to begin looking around town for another car (cheap car) to buy. I then asked Ray if he had serviced the car during the days before leaving. He said he had—that "He had even drained all the old oil out of the crankcase and filled it with kerosene and drove it around town to flush the gunk out of her!" "You did WHAT?" I asked in disbelief! He explained again his stupid idea to clean out the old engine and then I knew why all the bearings had gone out!

I could hardly stand being around Ray and his wife, so I suggested they just sit tight on a park bench somewhere, and Phil and I would see what we could find. The next question I had to answer was money—where would we get the money for another car? In the meantime, while walking past a Dodge/Plymouth dealership we saw a nice 2-door Plymouth on the car lot with a private For Sale sign in the window. We talked to the dealer and discovered it was his son's car, and not a dealership used car. He then asked questions about the two of us and upon finding we were Bible college students and the details of our travels and problems, offered something to us that was very amazing. He offered to sell us the car "on paper" with a small down payment and co-sign with us himself, trusting us to send the rest of the money later. The problem was the down payment. It wasn't much, but we just didn't have it. I decided to phone my dad—surely he would go along with this deal and send some money. I would pay him back at the end of the summer. "NO WAY!" was his reaction. "Where in the world are you? What in the world are you doing in Milbank, South Dakota? I'll wire you $85 for a bus ticket. Forget that bunch and get your butt home!"

STUCK IN MILBANK SOUTH DAKOTA

So, that was it—$85! What could I do for $85? The money wire was to come by Western Union at the train station next door to the garage sometime that day—Thursday. So I hung around the train station to check and then check again and again and again—nothing. The time was 4:30 p.m. Milbank would be rolling up the sidewalks and locking all the doors at 5:00 p.m. At about 4:30 p.m. we struck a bananza! The owner of the garage said he had a '47 Chevy 4-door in good mechanical condition and would sell it to us for $75. That seemed "do-able". It wouldn't leave us much for gas but it seemed to be the only answer. Finally, at 4:30 p.m. the $85-dollar money order came through at the train depot next door. But at 5:00 p.m. we were going to be faced with another problem—everything would be closing up, not just for the day, but for the long Memorial Day weekend—Friday, Saturday and Sunday. We discovered that in order to buy the '47 Chevy and get it on the road, we would have to have it inspected at an inspection station; get it registered at the courthouse; get the new plates on it and rent a U-haul trailer for all of Ray's junk—all by 5:00 p.m. Literally sprinting up and down the streets of Milbank, and up and down the steps of the courthouse, and in and out of garages and inspection stations, we were able to get it all accomplished by 5:00 p.m.! Whew! Talk about a miracle! It had to be a miracle!

The last thing to be done was to dispose of the old Buick at a local wrecking yard on the edge of town. We figured she would run that far and possibly get us a few needed bucks for the rest of the trip. I didn't want to let the Buick go without draining as much of the precious gasoline out of the tank as possible, so I borrowed a hammer and a punch from the mechanic and slid underneath and punched a hole in the gas tank. Phil found me a short stick that would fit the hole and as the last of the gas was draining out into the gas can, I jammed the stick in the hole. After getting directions to the wrecking yard, I started her up and sped off to the Buick's final resting place. Phil followed me in the Chevy and together we pulled into the yard just as the owner was locking the gate for the long weekend. We asked him if he would buy the Buick for salvage price and a good spare tire for the Chevy. He agreed and gave us $25 for the car plus a good spare wheel and tire. At last—we could be on our way and end this nightmare!

ON THE ROAD AGAIN!

Phil and I were both exhausted and suffering from hypoglycemia, having not slept nor eaten anything for all those hours. We decided we had better get something to eat. We picked a local Mom and Pop café on main street. Ray and his wife found themselves a booth, and Phil and I found a booth to ourselves and ate some soup and a sandwich. At 7:00 p.m. we gassed up the Chevy and were on the road again, with Ray and his wife and the U-haul trailer and their "junk". On we drove into the night through places like Watertown, Huron, and Winner, South Dakota, and then Valentine, Gordon and Alliance, Nebraska—finally arriving in Scottsbluff at about 9:00 a.m. Friday (Memorial Day). We left Ray and his wife with the '47 Chevy and their "stuff", trusting them to pay me for the car when they got settled. There was no way we could afford to keep the car and put fuel in it for the rest of the trip home. We asked the Dean of Students at Platt Valley Bible College, who just happened to be on campus, if we could use one of the men's dorm rooms to clean up and take a nap. He was very gracious and allowed us to do so. We showered and shaved and tried to sleep for a few minutes. We found we were too "wired" and the temperature too hot to sleep. We decided to start thumbing a ride from Scottsbluff. The college dean gave us a ride to the south edge of Gering, Nebraska, just three miles south of Scottsbluff, where the main highway headed south to Kimball. This would be a more advantageous place to catch a ride.

About that '47 Chevy. Ray called me 20 years later and said he wanted to pay me for the car—would I accept payments at $20 per month? I would, and Ray paid his bill. God bless him!

THE WILDEST RIDE OF MY LIFE

It was 98 degrees in the shade on the south edge of Scottsbluff-Gering that day and there was no shade! And, there was very little traffic on that Memorial Day that was headed south. Finally, after an hour had passed, a truck driver in his car, deadheading back to Denver to pick up his semi, stopped to pick us up. It was 50 miles south to Kimball and US-30, the main east/west route to California. As we rode along with this truck driver, we visited about our travels and "happenings". When he heard about our meager meals, he immediately stopped to rifle around in the trunk of his car for some canned goods and food stuffs that had spilled from their cartons as he made deliveries in his semi. Much to his disappointment, he could find only one can of Spam and a quart jar of dill pickles. He said he was sorry— "it ain't much, but ye'r welcome to um". So we ate some of the pickles and saved the can of Spam for what might be "our final hour" if we were starving to death beside some cactus out in the desert of Nevada. We arrived in Kimball, and US-30 somewhere around 2:00 p.m. The truck driver dropped us off and headed on to Denver. And there we stood on the side of US-30, in our cleanest and best college dress, with our cardboard "Ride To Los Angeles Please" signs—waiting on the mercy of some California bound motorist.

RIDE NUMBER ONE...

We stood there for some time watching an enormous amount of

westward bound traffic whizzing right on by us. We also noticed that most of the cars with California plates had only one person—the driver. How often we said to one another during those moments, "why couldn't or wouldn't they stop?" Then, suddenly from the stop sign of an intersecting north/south highway, came a 1956, 4-door Plymouth, with what looked like a full load of passengers. They pulled up, opened the back right side door and yelled, "come on—get in—we'll all scrunch over!" A girl, whom I took to be a teenage daughter was at the wheel, with grandma and grandpa beside her in the passenger's seat. In the back seat was her mom, with her little brother and sister. Phil and I sat "scrunched up" in what was left of the back seat with our luggage on our laps. Zoom! Down the two lane highway we went, bouncing along on the overload stops! Being next to the window I could look out and view the light poles going by—faster than one per second! How fast is she going, I wondered? I stretched my neck around my suit case to get a look at the speedometer. I couldn't believe what I saw—*90 miles per hour!* I began praying..."I sure hope we don't blow a tire—God, please keep this thing on the highway!" And, of course we passed car after car. She was not reckless in passing and in handling the car—speed yes— but reckless no. We sped on, passing everything and—every California car we had seen pass through Kimball.

Finally, arriving in Laramie,Wyoming, all in one piece, she dropped us off at a Dairy Queen along the highway and sped off to the left, to who-knows-where! Phil and I decided that an ice cream cone would sure taste good and that we could spare a few pennies for a "sugar lift". Then, as we stepped back to the edge of the road with our thumbs out, along came all the California cars we had seen go by us in Kimball and had then passed on the highway. Suddenly, all these drivers were noticing us! We could imagine them saying, "Hey, those two hitch hikers...didn't we see them back in Kimball? HEY—they're making better time than we are!" We began laughing as, one by one, they would pass us by again—but craning their necks to look at us and wonder how they could be seeing us again!

RIDE NUMBER TWO...

Another car pulled up—this time in a cloud of dust and oil smoke. The door flew open and a voice hollered "get in"! We did—and away we went. This time it was a single young military boy in uniform and "hell bent for leather" as Dad used to say. Oh no, here we go again! The guy confessed that he had been partying all night and was late FOR HIS OWN WEDDING! At that very moment he said he was suppose to be in Jackson Hole, Wyoming, over three hours away, saying his vows. "Keep me awake and hang on" he said, and we did! Again, I peeked at the speedometer and wished I hadn't—95-plus miles per hour! Unlike the last ride, this was a real nail bitter—passing cars by the "skin of our teeth"—all those California cars! At last—relief from this maniac ride! He dropped us off in downtown Rock Springs and dashed off to the north on US-191 to Jackson Hole—and whatever fate lay ahead! And there we were again, walking with our suitcases and signs, west through Rock Springs, to the west edge of town where we would start "thumbing" again. AND HERE THEY CAME AGAIN! All those California drivers were passing us by again and really giving us the stares. I am sure they couldn't believe their eyes! We imagined them saying to themselves, "There are those guys again! They're everywhere—they were in Kimball, they were in Laramie, they were in Rawlins, now here they are in Rock Springs! How are they doing that?" And again, we were rolling with laughter! It brightened our trip and lightened our load!

GUARDIAN ANGELS

As we neared the west end of Rock Springs, the highway widened briefly to four lanes to accommodate the roadside cafes, shops and gas stations at the edge of town. We also noticed to the west a very threatening black storm cloud on the horizon, with brilliant, straight-to-the-ground bolts of lightening and earth shaking crashes of thunder. We walked west past a restaurant when we heard, just over a sand hill to the south, a Union Pacific freight train barely moving westward, but opening its throttle to pick up speed as it headed west to Salt Lake City, Utah.

"Hey, Phil" I yelled, "let's run over there and see if we can catch that freight! It will get us to Salt Lake City and get us out of the storm". I immediately sprinted across the highway to the south, toward the train about 100 yards ahead. Then I noticed that Phil was not with me. As I looked back to see where he was, I could see he was visiting with some people in a new white 1958 Oldsmobile with Iowa plates. "Come on" I yelled, "we've got to go before we miss it!"

"No" he yelled back, "these people know you. Get back over here!"

As I crossed back over the highway, I could see familiar faces. I couldn't believe my eyes! It was my dad's cousin (my second cousin and a favorite) Bernice Illum and her daughter Linda in the back seat and at the wheel, Mavis Mefford, the wife of a church elder, all from Storm Lake, Iowa, and my home church. Mrs. Medford was taking her mother-in-law home to Santa Cruz, California! Bernice and Linda were riding along for the "company" and—bless her heart, it was little Linda who saw me run across the highway and recognized me."That's Gordie Sorenson!" she shouted! They argued with her that it couldn't possibly be Gordie! But she kept insisting, "that's Gordie, that's Gordie!" And as I approached the car they could see she had been right! As I came to the car, they all looked at me in disbelief and exclaimed, "Gordie Sorenson, what on earth are you doing out here in the middle of this God forsaken desert?" I replied that "We were trying to get home to California from MBC in Minneapolis! "Well get in, you're both going to get wet!" When I explained that we were running to try to catch the freight train, they responded with "Oh, no you're not! You're riding with us! End of discussion."

FOOD AND REST

And so we did—driving through pouring rain and wind and lightening to a tourist oasis called "Little America" west of Green River, Wyoming. There, they bought us a meal and a motel room for the night—the first good meal and sleep we had had in days. I don't remember ever sleeping that hard again in my life. It was early, 8:00 or 9:00 p.m. thank God, for they wanted to get going again at 4:00 a.m. the next morning—which we did. They bought us breakfast and then informed me that since they knew I was an excellent driver and knew the way, I would be doing the driving all the way to Los Angeles. Isn't it amazing how God works? I start out rattling along in a worn out 1947 Buick "antique", with every possible thing going wrong that could go wrong, and end up finishing the trip rested, with a full stomach and driving a brand new 1958 Super 98 Oldsmobile—with power steering and power brakes! That had to be another "GOD THING" in my life! Phil was utterly amazed. Fifty years later we are still talking about it and telling the story to our kids and grandkids!

HOMEWARD BOUND

We left Little America around 5:00 that morning after breakfast and headed west to Salt Lake City, then south through Provo Canyon, and St George, Utah, then on to Las Vegas, Nevada and Barstow, California. At Barstow I wanted to get my family ready for a surprise and allow them time to get the house ready for guests. I didn't tell them who it was—just that some wonderful fellow travelers had picked us up in Wyoming and were bringing us all the way home to Los Angeles and the least we could do is give them beds for the night and some good down home cooking. I also told them to get the coffee pot on because these were "coffee drinking Danes".

Later, as we pulled into the driveway at about 10:00 p.m., the family all came running out of the house to greet me—only to pull up short because I was behind the wheel of this new car, and out of the other doors were exiting all these wonderful cousins and dear friends from back home! They didn't know which way to go—didn't know who to hug! Confused, we heard, "How?...Where?...How could this be?...What are you all doing here together?" Then, after hugs and the initial shock wore off, we all sat down in the living room and Phil and I explained the misfortunes of the past days and then this "God thing" that happened out in the middle of Wyoming! They all sat in open mouth wonder at this amazing, providential chain of events. I then drove Phil to his home and family in West Hollywood and closed that chapter on the "Amazing Extreme Adventure"!

Ray Bock (Left) and friend Roger with the infamous '47 Buick wagon

Jack & Lucy Barber with their family

CHAPTER 15

SUMMER AND FALL 1958

With hardly a moment to unpack, my schedule was full. I was needed immediately at Angeles Crest Christian Camp to help get the camp and swimming pool ready for another summer of church campers. Things went very smooth that summer. I had established the pool rules and limits the summer before. The kids knew me and they knew the routine and that summer was a piece of cake! I missed Betty very much and wrote to her often at whatever church location she was working. I did things with the college fellowship gang at the Rosemead Church, but the summer was boring without her.

MY "NEW" '46 FORD

The main event for me that summer was accidentally finding another car. I was tired of walking or borrowing or thumbing a ride. One weekend while driving through an El Monte neighborhood in my dad's spare car, I happened to see some "vintage tin" out of the corner of my eye, sitting behind a resident's garage. When it came to recognizing hot rod potential, my eye/brain coordination was like the sharpest radar! I stopped, backed up for a closer look and sure enough—it was a primered 1946 Ford 2-door sedan—just waiting for a home! The owner came out to meet me, and I inquired as to the status of the '46. He assured me that it ran and the tires would hold air (although flat at that moment), and it was for sale. I must have also had some kind of X-ray vision to be able to see any potential in that car. It had been sitting in the man's chicken yard. There were chickens inside, chickens on the roof and hood, and chickens underneath. You might say it was a 1946 Ford "rolling chicken coupe"! When he had prepped the body for the primer job, he had stripped the chrome off and stored it in the back seat. I found it all there, and in good condition! But I also noticed all the upholstery was shot. The headliner was gone and most of the stuffing in the seats was either gone, or hanging out, leaving the bare springs exposed.

Looking beyond those flaws, I asked the man what he wanted for the car, to which he responded, "$50 bucks!"

Hmmmm...$50 bucks! I could easily afford $50 bucks! I gave him $10 to hold it, while I ran to get the rest of the money, a good 6 volt battery and a can of gas. I returned with the money and some hand tools, battery, portable air tank and gas. In no time the gas was in the tank; the air was in the tires (I couldn't believe the tires actually held air); the battery was in place. I was ready to go—except for one problem—no keys! The man had lost the keys! So, I simply hot wired it directly from the battery to the coil. After pouring a small amount of gas directly down the carburetor to prime things, I pushed the starter button. Expecting nothing to happen, since it had been sitting so long as a chicken coupe, it suddenly scared me to death—it actually started up with a roar! As the radiator fan pulled fresh air through the engine compartment, it sent spiders, cob webs and chicken feathers flying everywhere! I made one last check of the water level in the radiator, which was okay and after paying the man, headed my new wheels down Valley Boulevard for home in La Puente, sitting on a pop crate seat—with spiders, chicken manure, feathers and dust all flying out the open windows! What a ride!

As I pulled my "ramblin wreck" into the driveway, Dad and Gary came out to see what the commotion was about and to try to figure out how suddenly this piece of junk wound up in our driveway. When they saw me get out from behind the wheel they were amazed again! "Big brother, what in the world have you gone and done now?" I explained that it only cost me $50 bucks and that I would be cleaning her up, putting her in a paint shop for a brand new coat of paint, and then into an upholstery shop for new seat covers and headliner. In a few weeks they would never know it was the same car. So, on my weekends from the life-guarding, I was busy talking to paint shops, upholstery shops, picking out colors and material and getting prices. The paint job was stunning! In a week, she was back in the driveway with a new coat of GM Olds Cutlass Bronze paint and all the chrome pieces back in place. It was flawless—it was impressive! I then lowered it two inches front and back and installed dual exhausts. It was even more flawless! Then, the insides. I sent it to a shop in El Monte where they installed a new headliner and seat and door upholstery. What a machine! I began driving my "new" 1946 Ford back and forth to the camp. It was a head turner!

As summer was drawing to a close, I began making plans for the return trip to Minneapolis and MBC. Dad and Gary thought the engine in the Ford although running well, was using oil and needed an overhaul before making that long trip. I suggested making a quick change by installing a new "short block". They agreed it was a great idea and volunteered to do it for me while I was away working at camp. And they did. They located a new short block at a good price, pulled the old one out, and with much work and several hours time, bolted the new engine in place. I will be forever grateful for their wonderful help. I have often felt guilty that I wasn't there to help with it. My lifeguard duties kept me busy at the pool earning tuition and travel money for the next college year. They did an excellent job for being backyard, shade tree mechanics!

ROUTE "66"

Finally, the time had arrived. I loaded my gear into the Ford, along with a new Christian friend who was transferring from Pacific Christian College to Ozark Bible College in Joplin, Missouri. Bill McClure, a member of the Rosemead Church, had heard I was making the long trip back to the mid-west and asked if he could hitch a ride and share the expense and driving. I agreed. After some emotional goodbyes, we headed east on the famous "Route 66". We left California in the late afternoon to avoid the heat of crossing the desert at mid day. We drove through the night, passing through Barstow, and Needles California and then Kingman and Flagstaff, Arizona. Of course at that time there were no freeways, and Route 66 really was "Route 66", the main east/west two lane highway between Los Angeles and Chicago, IL.

After many long hours of switching off driving/sleeping duties, we finally arrived in Joplin at the old Ozark Bible College campus. I dropped

Bill off and made my way north on US -71 through Kansas City, Missouri, and then on through Clarinda and Carrol, Iowa to Storm Lake, where I grew up. This would be my first time back in Storm Lake since I had left after graduating in '55. Arriving in mid afternoon, I drove to Bernice and Cardia Illum's home, my second cousin, and "bummed" a bunk for the night. It was Bernice and her daughter Linda who had rescued me in the desert of Wyoming earlier that spring. They were delighted to see me, especially after the hitching hiking episode in Wyoming and offered me a bed, meals, and whatever else I would need. We had a great visit, recalling the details of meeting Phil and me out in the middle of nowhere. I got caught up on some much needed sleep and after breakfast the next morning, made my way on the final leg of the trip to Minneapolis.

My first priority upon arriving on campus in Minneapolis was to locate Betty. She was no longer living in Leverton Hall, the girl's dorm, but in a second floor efficiency apartment a few blocks northeast of the college with a college friend, Mary Etta Dorrough, from Fort Smith, Arkansas. After a joyous reunion, Betty fixed supper, and we got caught up on all the past summer's activities. Then, it was back to the books and part time work and research papers and outside reading! My outside job for this year would be cashiering at a Snyder Drug store in the St. Anthony shopping center a few miles north of the campus. I worked there with fellow students John Luther and Carol Fulford, stocking shelves, waiting on customers and checking out at the cash register. Back then, there were no price codes to swipe, no credit cards to swipe, no "beeping" scanners—just price tags and stickers with numbers to be punched on the keys of the cash register and a drawer lever to be pulled for the total to be posted and the cash drawer opened. We would then accept the customer's cash and return their change by counting out the cents and dollars, starting from the total cost and ending with the amount tendered—unlike today where the cashier puts a handful of change and bills in your hand and just says, "Your change sir".

THE SPRING OF 1959

I don't remember a lot of details about that school year except the adventure of another MBC Spring Tour with the quartet, traveling through America. But as it began to come to an end my thoughts were on getting back home to La Puente and our rapidly approaching wedding.

For this return trip home Betty would be with me. We also acquired some other fellow travelers from MBC. Tim Coop and his girlfriend Sandy Gray, "hitched" a ride with us. They were needing a ride to Tim's home in Bridgeport, Nebraska, at about the same time we would be traveling west near there, so invited them to share the ride with us. Betty and I got some needed sleep at the Coop's and then finished the trip to California—a straight through dash for home.

As usual, there was no money for a motel and very little for gas and restaurant meals, and since Betty did not drive, I just put the hammer down and ate up as many miles as I could as the hours rolled by. Early the next morning around 6:00 am, after driving all night and with little to eat, we decided to stop in Cedar City, Utah—I was tired and hungry. We entered a café across the street and sat down to order. As we were waiting for the food to arrive, I began to feel sick to my stomach and very light headed. We asked the waitress to wrap up the food to go. We made our way back to the car. I sat in the drivers seat and rested my head on the steering wheel. The beautiful morning and fresh mountain air helped to clear my head. My appetite began to come back. We sat in the car and ate our eggs and toast, drank some coffee, and by then my strength had returned. I was ready to go! "Lets git-er done!" I know now, what I experienced was an attack of low blood sugar—hypoglycemia. It was a long haul from Cedar City, Utah to Los Angeles, California, but the trip went well—my beautiful '46 Ford carrying me and my beautiful-bride-to-be—HOME!

CHAPTER 16

A NEW CHAPTER
MR. AND MRS. GORDON SORENSON

Upon arriving home, there wasn't much time to relax. We had a wedding to plan. We had tuxes to rent; we had singers and players and people to line up; we needed to spend some time counseling with our minister and help Betty's family in whatever way we could. Her cousins, aunt and uncles had taken on the responsibility for the flowers, the cake and reception and the picture taking. Betty borrowed a wedding dress from Alys Haugen, an MBC friend. It fit perfectly! She was beautiful! God bless them all. We are indebted to them forever. They put the entire wedding together for $150—and it was beautiful! It was wonderful—and we've been married for 49 years—as of June 6th 2008! Everybody "done good work", as they say down on the farm.

In a very few days it was time—June 6th had arrived! The Rosemead Church of Christ was decked out with flowers and candles. Everyone was in their places. Mrs. Ruth Dart sang "Oh Promise Me" with Mary Miller accompanying her at the organ. Pastor Richard Miller, my best man and brother, Gary Sorenson and groomsman Chuck Smith, Betty's brother, and I were all in our places. The wedding march began, everyone stood, the female attendants marched in, her sister Jill the maid of honor and Jackie Kersey, bridesmaid. And then, there she was—at the side of her father Louis Smith! What a picture of beauty and grace she was coming down the aisle. As the wedding march ended, we joined hands and faced each other. After the invocation, her father gave her away, "to be married to this man". We exchanged vows and rings, kissed each other, and headed out to participate in this great adventure of life together!

THE HONEYMOON

Actually, after the service we didn't go very far. After exiting the chapel with all the rice throwing and congratulations etc, we went a few blocks west and around the corner to "Boots" and Mickey's, her cousin's and husband, where things were ready for our reception. They had set everything up on their backyard lawn next to a small pavilion/gazebo. After the opening of gifts, great fellowship, and refreshments, we were off! Dad gave me the keys to his nice '58 Oldsmobile, and we headed for Bakersfield, California and the Red Woods. We had hoped to get further north into the Kings Canyon/Sequoia National Park resort area, but we had started too late in the day, and we were both exhausted! As we approached Bakersfield, we saw a Holiday Inn, considered the best at that time. They had a nice room available for us and that became our "Honeymoon" suite. Some couples honeymoon at Niagara Falls, Hawaii, or Las Vegas—we honeymooned in Bakersfield, California—near "Pumpkin Center", "Weedpatch", and "Oildale", with "Buttonwillow" and "Greenacres" just up the road! We did enjoy the tour of the Red Woods in Kings Canyon the next day, but then decided we had seen enough big trees.

THE REAL HONEYMOON

Although the trip through the Red Woods was scenic and interesting, we were still exhausted. We decided that what we really wanted to do was head back to our respective homes, pick up our summer necessities and work clothes, and make our way up to Angeles Crest Camp to the little camper trailer (and I do emphasize LITTLE camper trailer) we would be living in for the summer. My folks owned the trailer but wanted us to use it while working at the camp. They had towed it up and set it up for us earlier, before the wedding. It was great! It was restful! It was scenic! It was truly a honeymoon! The camp crew was quite surprised that we had cut our original honeymoon plans short to come to the camp to work. They insisted that we forget about working—"you guys just relax, get up when you want to, eat when you want to and go to bed when you want". We did just lay-back for a day or two, but we just couldn't help ourselves—

we wanted to get busy helping prepare for the coming weeks of camp. Betty worked the summer in the kitchen, which happens to be her cup of tea, and I resumed my duties as the lifeguard, with pool maintenance, lifeguard duty, cutting firebreak and general campground upkeep.

As usual that summer, we met and worked with several great people, one of whom was quite notable, Fredi Liu, a happy-go-lucky Hawaiian kid who served as a terrific kitchen helper. Everyone loved him! Also a talented musician, he often entertained the campers with his guitar, singing Hawaiian songs. He would have everyone on their feet doing the "hoola" to the "Hooki Lau". Fredie's pride and joy; and his main transportation to camp was his 1931 Model A Ford coupe! Yes! With a trunk! When he found out I was also a shade tree mechanic, he begged me to turn his trunk into a "rumble seat". I did just that! He and Betty and I had a blast on a few weekends, driving down to the San Fernando Valley with Fredi as the chauffeur and Betty and me riding in the rumble seat. The three of us would attend church, with Betty and I sometimes providing special music in the form of duets, with Fredi accompanying us on his guitar. What a great summer for a pair of newlyweds!

MR. AND MRS. SORENSON RETURN TO COLLEGE

Naturally, the idyllic summer of 1959 came to an end, and it was time again for reality. We shut down the pool and kitchen at the camp. We pulled the little honeymoon camper back to La Puente and prepared for the long trip back to Minneapolis. We decided to "extend" our honeymoon by taking a new and scenic route back east. There were new places we wanted to see and since there were no freeways and the two-lanes ran everywhere, why not see some new country en route?

Leaving Los Angeles we took a new route north and east instead of the usual trek across the desert through Las Vegas. We traveled north through Lancaster, Lone Pine, and Bishop, California, and then through Carson City, and Reno, Nevada before crossing the desolate wasteland of northern Nevada. We then traveled east through Winnemucca, Battle Mountain, Elko, and Wells, Nevada, turning north on US-93 to Twin Falls, Idaho. We then proceeded east/northeast through Pocatello and Idaho Falls to the northwest corner of Wyoming and the Jackson Hole/Grand Teton/Yellowstone National Park area. We had heard so much about these scenic places but we were now there in person, seeing them all for the first time, with our own eyes! Southern Idaho was beautiful, but the Grand Tetons—Wow! What a visual feast! And Yellowstone— we could have stayed there for a month! We still have old Kodak "Box Camera" color pictures we took of these places tucked away in picture albums. What a wonderful way to cap off our honeymoon!

BEARTOOTH PASS!

But, we weren't finished yet! After Old Faithful and the Mud Pots, there was that "cute little cub bear" as Betty described him, who stood up to his six feet height and tried to crawl through the open window on Betty's side! We enjoyed the breathtaking Yellowstone Falls and Mammoth Hot Springs. Toward the close of a marvelous day in Yellowstone we found ourselves at the northeast gate or "Silver Gate" of Yellowstone. The road map showed what seemed like a short distance from Silver Gate through Cooke City to Red Lodge, Montana. Although it was late in the day and dusk was upon us, we figured the 64 miles to Red Lodge would be an easy drive. Little did we know that this section of highway was soon to be closed (open only in late May through mid-October). They close it for the winter season due to its extreme altitude, narrow, difficult curves, and impossible weather conditions on the "top". What we also failed to notice was that on this section of highway 212 there was a place called "Beartooth Pass", where the elevation was a lofty 11,000 feet. Young and adventurous, we headed off for Red Lodge, Montana. Up we went, like a roller-coaster—up and up and up. It got cold, we had to roll the windows up. Still, up and up we went! Then we saw a moose in the fading light, standing in a pond near the highway! Then—what is this?! SNOW? Snow! This early, in August—snow! Snow on the rocks, snow on the highway and along the highway! Then we saw the sign— "Summit, Bear Tooth Pass 10,947 feet."

Then, as they say, "what goes up, must come down", and did it ever! Down and down and around and around the highway went, doubling back over and then under. Then up again and down again, with hair pin turns so sharp we had to stop the car, back up and take an even sharper swing to negotiate the turn. It was like meeting yourself coming back! In places, I was in low gear to make the grade up or down. Then, as we neared Red Lodge—three hours after leaving Silver Gate in Yellowstone—the bottom really dropped out of this roller-coaster highway. Down and down and down we went with the transmission in second gear to help brake. The temperature gage pegged clear down on the cold side. We finally leveled out just as we came into the edge of Red Lodge. It was like doing a hammerhead stall in an aerial stunt plane with a 10,000-foot tailspin right down to the landing strip! WHAT A COUNTRY! WHAT A RIDE! Never before, nor since, have I ever had such a ride on a two lane highway in an automobile!

We stayed the night in a motel in Red Lodge, thankful to be alive! The next morning, after breakfast, we continued our long trip east through places like Billings, Miles City, and Glendive, Montana. From Glendive, we crossed over into North Dakota and passed through places like Dickinson, Bismarck, and Jamestown. I must say, this latter part of the trip was truly boring compared to Beartooth Pass. As nice as North Dakota is, it is truly the flattest geography I have ever seen. For the 350 miles from the Montana border to Fargo, I don't remember seeing one hill or even a tree! You could see forever—not a curve, not grove of trees, not even a bump in the road! Just enormous fields of waving grain that went as far as the eye could see. As the breezes blew over the fields, it looked like an ocean of golden waves!

In Minnesota, we made our way through Fargo, Morris, Wilmar, Litchfield, Dassel, and Howard Lake, names of towns that sounded much more familiar to us and indicated we were nearing our destination. Not only were the city names familiar to us, the roads looked familiar as well. As Bible college students, we traveled these roads around central Minnesota often, as we served weekend ministries and held gospel music concerts in the churches in many of these little towns. Some of our professors also ministered to congregations in these places. Howard Hayes ministered at Dassel, and our beloved Dean G.H. Cachiaras ministered for years with the congregation at Howard Lake. Before we ever reached the campus, we were feeling "good to be home!"

Betty, me and the '46

Camp Cooke: Summer of '59

Graduation Day
with Betty and Cynthia

Our first honeymoon home at Angeles Crest

Beartooth Mountains

CHAPTER 17

FALL 1959
BACK TO CLASSES
INCREDIBLE PRESSURE AND STRESS,
INCREDIBLE BLESSING

It was now back to the grind! Betty and I both carried full schedules of college classes. Plus, she worked 20 hours per week making sodas, malts and Sundays at Bridgeman's Ice Cream Parlor in "Dinky Town" (campus village), and I worked nearly 30 hours per week delivering furniture for B and C Furniture a mile north in the East Hennepin shopping center. We lived on little sleep and lots of coffee, keeping up with work and studies that year. We worked the hours we did to pay the bills, the rent, the tuition and book costs for school. We had no scholarships and now married and on our own, no money from home—although there had been little from home before we married. Now, as a married couple, we did whatever we had to, to pay our own way, which we did. It was a back breaking schedule, juggling work and school and time for each other. I, in particular, felt the stress of it. First, was the responsibility of providing for my wife, then the responsibility of staying on top of the academic work, which was enormous with the number of research papers due each week. The easiest part was my furniture delivery job. As I look back on those days, I wonder how I ever made it! There were moments of what I now know to be panic attacks, where I feared my mind would explode, where actually I may have been on the edge of a nervous breakdown. I am sure that what I was also feeling was isolation from my new bride. As we both buried ourselves in our schedules and work loads, we found very little time for each other. It was one of the loneliest and saddest times of my life. I was overwhelmed!

Added to these feelings of desperation, came another jolt to our lives. We were renting an upstairs two room apartment in Dinky Town, above a knitting shop. We had to share the one miserable bathroom with all the other residents on that floor. There were lots of people sharing this space with very little privacy and paper thin walls. One evening we had been discussing our rent money, knowing the next day we needed to get it to the landlord. That day, while at class, someone decided to help themselves to our rent money. They either picked the lock or crawled over and through the transom window above our apartment door and helped themselves. After class that day, we went to the drawer to get the money to pay the rent. IT WAS GONE!!! Finding nothing disturbed in the room, it appeared that whoever took it, knew right where we kept it. Our hearts sank! How would we pay the rent? We immediately contacted the landlord to explain our dilemma and ask for a little time to scrape up some new rent money. They were very understanding and gave us generous time to do so. In the meantime, some "little bird" had spread the news among our college family, and a day or two later we discovered that the rent had been paid! We have never to this day, found out who and how it was done, but we felt incredible gratitude! The grace and mercy of God had "snuck" up on us when we least expected it, and blessed us in an incredible way!

GORDON AND BETTY SORENSON...AND FAMILY

It was at about this time that God blessed us in another entirely different way. Betty was suddenly experiencing some "queasiness" after waking in the mornings and some significant changes in her body. On a visit to U of M campus clinic we discovered that WE WERE PREGNANT! It was one of those times of mixed emotions we all experience when you are overjoyed at the reality of starting a family, but apprehensive as to how in the world you would pull it off—both of us with a full load of college work, both working at jobs, and now another mouth to feed! I think we felt so elated about it, that we simply dismissed the difficulty factor and placed it all in God's hands.

Then, a very unusual thing happened. Perhaps God sensed that I (we) needed a temporary break from this routine. Early in the spring of 1960, at a Gospel Hour program, Jean Zylstra, wife of Bernie Zylstra, minister of two congregations in Wisconsin, made an appeal on behalf of Bernie and their ministry. He had become hospitalized for a reoccurrence of Tuberculosis and would need a lengthy period of treatment and recovery. She addressed the large Gospel Hour audience and made an appeal for someone who would possibly consider moving temporarily to Hickory Corners, Wisconsin and take over the ministerial duties of both that congregation and the Mountain Church of Christ. For some "crazy" reason the idea of filling that need appealed to me. After discussing it with Betty and getting her approval, the next day we located Jean and offered our services to help with the ministry. She was elated.

We then approached the staff and faculty of the college, appraising them of our intentions and asking their blessing and assistance. Our professors were very supportive and helpful. We did have their blessing and offers to help in any way they could, to help us maintain our degree programs upon returning to MBC. Within a few days we had the Ford loaded and headed toward Suring and Hickory Corners Wisconsin. As we traveled east/northeast through central Wisconsin, I had some fleeting thoughts and apprehensions about what we were doing—about what I was doing. Before going to Bible college I had, I thought, made a deal with God that I would not want to prepare and deliver sermons to adults the rest of my life. And now—I am volunteering to do what I had said I would never do? Hmm..."God works in mysterious ways His wonders to perform!"

OUR FIRST MINISTRIES

So, on we drove—too late now to turn back—through Chippewa Falls, Stanley, Abbotsford, and Wausau as evening began to fall. Then, it seemed like the roads got lonelier and more deserted. As we passed through Neopit, we noticed there were no yard lights but only the dim glow of fuel oil lamps in the windows of the homes we passed. We noticed numerous people out walking the roads in the dark, one or two wobbling along with bottles in their hands, and then realized we were driving through the middle of the Menominee Indian Reservation! As we checked the map, we were relieved to find we were right on course and not far from the village of Hayes, about three miles from Suring, near our destination at Hickory Corners. Late that evening we arrived at the parsonage and were greeted by Jean Zylstra and her daughter. She helped us settle into the attic bedroom we would be occupying for the next few months and after a short visit about the events of the day and a brief schedule outlining the next day's activities, we caught some much needed sleep!

The next day, after getting acquainted with the buildings and grounds, the services and programs and what our responsibilities would be, we began to meet a few of the neighbors and members of the congregations. There were the Stewarts and their hired man Swen; the Colsons just down the road and their boys Curtis and Bruce who later attended MBC. There were the Rasmussens and their girls Charmaigne and Diane; the Russell McMahans and family and the Ted Lartzs and many others whose names now escape me.

In the Mountain church we met Mattie Tate and Mrs Loebner, Wesley and Marcella Kingston and their three adopted Native American boys, Andrew, Albert and Jay. There was the Holmes family and the Bogards with their milk cow. Over the course of these summer months we all became good friends. For me, this was the "best medicine" I could have taken for the panic attacks. They were gone! I was now busy with my new ministerial duties, home calls, hospital calls and of course, the perpetual studying and preparation of my weekly sermons. Most mornings I could be found in the office studying, or at the little desk on the landing outside our attic bedroom, typing my sermon notes. In high school I had hated doing research and typing research papers but by now it was becoming almost second nature. Now, there was not near the volume of work awaiting me each week as in college. A sermon and a lesson each week I could do! The big plus was the support and encouragement of the members of these two wonderful little congregations. They were, as is said, "the salt of the earth", and it seemed a very good match. As the weeks rolled by my spirits lifted, and the burdens of my heart rolled away.

PREGNANCY PROBLEMS

Things seemed to be going just the opposite for Betty. For her, there was the morning sickness, and having to eat apples and crackers before she got up, and some new concerns about "toxemia". Her legs were swelling and her blood pressure was gradually creeping up, requiring special attention by her new doctor in Gillett Grove. He recommended we make a return trip to Minneapolis for a consultation and advice from her doctor there...which we did. He recommended a salt free diet which brought a whole different dimension to her daily diet. We discovered how incredibly bland life can be with no salt! Everything she ate was flat. Salt-free bread and butter was the worst! It was like eating axle grease on cardboard. I tried to suffer with her by eating what she ate...no way!

But I found she was suffering from more than toxemia. Betty missed having her own kitchen, her own home to arrange and care for, her own menus to fix and having her own space. The only space she felt was hers was our attic bedroom and it was closing in on her. For the first time in our marriage, I witnessed my emotionally rock-solid wife suffering moments of depression and crying. I felt so stupid that I didn't see it coming. I felt so bad for her. I was feeling so great—now she was feeling so bad. I wanted to console her. I wanted to make it all go away. I really didn't know what to do except to just "be there for her" and wait patiently for about eight more months. But, trooper that she is, she adjusted to it all, even sharing the domestic duties with Jeanie. There was one other jolt she experienced while living there—falling down the stairs! As concerned as we were, she appeared to have no injuries. She picked herself up, brushed herself off and started all over again!

BACK IN THE CITY

During those months Bernie was orchestrating many of the ministry details from his hospital room in Green Bay. But toward the end of that summer it appeared he would be able to return home. Although he would be back in circulation, he felt he would not be able to resume the full load of ministry duties he had before—ministering to both congregations. Betty and I were planning to return to Minneapolis, me resuming my classes and job at B &C Furniture and Betty waiting out the pregnancy and the birth of our first child. Feeling an attachment to the Mountain congregation, I felt called to continue my ministry there, relieving Bernie of that responsibility. The congregation paid me enough each week to cover the cost of a round-trip bus ticket, plus a small stipend.

Upon our return to Minneapolis, fellow married students Denny and Alys Haugen invited us to stay with them until we could find an apartment. They had invested in an apartment house a few blocks from the campus where they and their family occupied the first floor. It comfortably housed both of our families for a few days until we located a $50 per month up-stairs apartment on First Avenue Northwest, near the furniture store where I worked. It was cheap rent but it was not a good neighborhood. There was a sleazy bar a couple of doors away, with a continual nightly stream of drunk people coming and going, fighting and screaming, sometimes right in our little front yard. From our second floor front bedroom window we saw and heard it all, drunk and jealous husbands and/or boyfriends beating up on "their women", shoving them into and through the hedge along the sidewalk, and fighting with each other. Betty and I would be startled from a sound sleep to witness these violent domestic brawls right below us. Betty was petrified—I wanted to take a ball-bat to somebody! "Take your booze and your fight somewhere else!" We did enjoy some times of peace and quiet there and otherwise endured the days and months until in late spring, a year and a half later, we moved to a new student ministry in Batavia, Minnesota.

A WEEK-END COMMUTER

Until that time, I carried a full load of classes, worked 30 hours a week at the furniture store and for a while, traveled week-ends to Mountain, Wisconsin and back to serve that congregation. I would board the bus in Minneapolis Saturday 8:30 a.m. and arrive in Shawano, Wisconsin around 4:00 p.m. The Kingston's, Wesley, Marcella and the three boys would meet me at the bus station and take me to their farm home to stay through Monday morning, returning me to Shawano to meet the bus for my return trip. I used the Saturday trip out, to study and prepare my sermons, and the Monday return trip, to prepare for class on Tuesday.

THE KINGSTONS

Those week-ends with the Kingston's were a delight! I would play football with the boys until we literally wore the ends off the football and the bladder would pop out. I would help Wes around the farm, milking the cows, putting up hay (with an old loose-hay loader) and the best fun—helping to collect tree sap to make maple syrup. They cooked the sap for hours in a long, flat, open vat, using an old 4-door model-T Ford car body as a "stove" for the fire. They would feed 4-feet to 6-feet long firewood logs through what had been the back window. All of Wes's farm operation was a bit crude and improvised. He just used whatever happened to be lying around, which was often amusing—but it worked!

Another fond memory of the Kingston's was their dog "Rusty", a super intelligent rust colored border collie. It was fun to watch Rusty work the cattle, bringing them down from the pasture above, "rounding up" the chickens, chasing the geese and being perpetually on the prowl for rabbits, skunks, squirrels, balls and bones to chase and adventure. "Chase the ball and bring it back Rusty—chase the stick and bring it back Rusty! Bones, balls, sticks, shoes, news papers—Rusty never tired of those games. Dad Kingston was in verbal connection with Rusty throughout the day. "Rusty—watch yourself!" or "Watch yourself Rusty!" Whenever Wes's brother Sheldon was around, the dog was just "Dog".

The other special thing about the Kingston's was Marcella's cooking. She was not a "Martha Stewart" with her house work and decorating, but she was a fantastic cook. I always looked forward to arriving at the Kingston kitchen when I arrived on Saturday afternoon. I say kitchen, because that's where everything happened at her house! Even before I entered the kitchen door, I could smell the aroma of fresh pies, fresh bread, and cinnamon rolls baking in the oven. What an olfactory delight! As we entered, we were greeted by a big old Monarch wood burning kitchen range, with the adjacent woodbox which the boys kept full. The huge kitchen also contained their kitchen table and chairs where we ate our meals, and a few old style, freestanding kitchen cupboards where she worked up her receipts and dishes. The meat was from their own livestock and chickens, as were the milk, butter and eggs. The peas, beans, beets, and corn came from her own "Ball Jar", home-grown, home-canned supplies.

And, by the way, the life and atmosphere of love for the three adopted sons in their home was so excellent, that as those early years passed, all three graduated from high school with the two oldest boys earning college degrees and the youngest, Jay, maintaining a solid position with a manufacturing company in Appleton, Wisconsin. Andrew, the oldest, is now an attorney with the Oneida Tribe near Green Bay, Wisconsin. Albert is a school principal and teacher in Shawano. All three are outstanding, fine Christian gentlemen.

CYNTHIA GALE ARRIVES
The pregnancy went well, in spite of the dangers surrounding

Betty's toxemia. The doctors both in Wisconsin and Minneapolis did an excellent job monitoring and managing the problem. But as the projected day of delivery neared, her primary obstetrician expressed the desire that she come in to the hospital before labor began. The date was set—I was to admit her to Hennepin County General Hospital on the last day of September, 1960. Earlier, I had wanted to have the delivery at the University of Minnesota hospital, considered one of the best around. This was where her obstetrician practiced. But he advised against doing that. He felt that with the two of us being students the cost at University would break us financially since we had no medical insurance. He suggested rather, that we consider Hennepin County General due to the fact that it would not cost near as much and besides, a close friend of his, a Russian obstetrician doing his residency there, would give her excellent, expert care. We accepted his advice and on that day arrived at the emergency entrance of Hennepin County General. I was horrified at what I first encounter there. There were people screaming in pain from a variety of injuries, another was bleeding from a stab wound and another going crazy from too much booze. I was very uncomfortable and felt very protective of my pregnant wife. But I was even more uncomfortable as finally, an attending ER doctor ushered me into a small room to get our personal statistics. He left no stone un-turned. What is your employment? What is your income? What is your "out go"? What are your assets? On and on and on. I was exhausted and concerned for Betty, as I could look out through the glass window of the cubical to see her patiently waiting in the midst of this sea of sick and injured people. It must have been a bad end-of September day on this afternoon in Minneapolis.

AND HERE SHE COMES NOW!

Finally, he was finished with me and said I could return to my wife. But I no sooner sat down and two nurses came with a wheel-chair and in a flash she was on her way to her room. I followed the nurses, with Betty in the wheel-chair, to see her room and spend a few moments with her before leaving. After seeing her settled in her room and well cared for, I kissed her goodbye and was assured "we will phone you when things begin to happen!" Well, what do I do now? Betty had wanted me to return to the campus to take in the Gospel Hour program scheduled for that same evening. So I did. But during the program I wrestled with the thoughts of that afternoon and what I had seen and about how she was doing. Much to my surprise and hers, as I later found out, we wouldn't have to wait long. That evening, as they were serving her evening meal, her water broke, saturating her and her bed. Her labor began. If they had tried to call me then, I would have been at the college program and unavailable (there were no cell phones in 1960). Rather, I had decided to just return to the hospital for a last minute visit before going home.

I had an enormous surprise when I arrived at her room. "She is not here sir, she is in labor!" IN LABOR? Where? They directed me to labor/ delivery room area. Upon arriving there, I was met by a team of four interns who would be monitoring her around the clock. I was told I would not be able to see her. It was critical that they keep her blood pressure down and wanted absolutely no unnecessary excitement or disturbance. So, I waited and I waited and waited. Finally, late that evening around 10:00 they said I could go in for a few moments to greet and reassure her but would have to leave. They invited me to use their own private lounge to wait and rest, which I appreciated very much. Shortly after 1:00 a.m. the next morning, October 1st 1960, they came in to tell me I was the father of a beautiful little girl—and she was just fine. They also assured me that Betty was fine as well. The delivery went well in spite of being a breach birth! We've often joked with Cindy about coming into the world butt first! My first thoughts, of course, were, "THANK YOU GOD—little Cynthia is fine, and Betty is fine!"

WE WANT TO GO HOME!

Her recovery and the baby's progress went very well. But after the second day I noticed that Betty was not her usual self. She seemed upset and revealed to me that the nurses were not allowing her to see the baby. She could stand it no longer. On the third day, when her doctor came for a visit, she informed him that the nurses were not allowing her to see her baby! When the doctor heard this disturbing news, he "hit the ceiling!" He immediately demanded an answer why—and to have our little Cindy delivered to the arms of her mother immediately! And Betty's spirits lifted immediately! She at last had our baby Cynthia Gale nestled in her arms and nursing. All is well! But then, four days rolled by and then five—no word about taking our family home. Betty was fine, and the baby was healthy and doing fine—day six passed and seven. We were getting concerned. This was very unusual even in the sixties, to keep a mother and new infant in the hospital that long. The word we were given was that they were still concerned about Betty's blood pressure remaining high. Not only was the length of stay becoming excessive, she had to stay in bed twenty-four hours a day. Finally, after ten days, she and Cindy were released from the hospital. It would be the first time her feet had touched the floor those ten days. My next concern was how I would be able to pay this astronomical bill???

MOM AND DAD SORENSON...OUR GUARDIAN ANGELS

A very wonderful and convenient blessing took place at this time, my folks had decided to drive back from California for a visit. I think they had planned the trip to coincide with Cindy's arrival, to be able to help in what ever way they could. And help they were! They had arrived a couple of days before Betty and Cindy were released from the hospital. Mother helped around the apartment, and Dad attended classes with me at the college. For some strange reason I felt I should be faithful in serving the little church at Mountain, so I made plans for another weekend sermon and round trip. The folks said that as long as they were there, they would see to it that Betty and the baby and their things got home whenever they were be released. So Mom and Dad brought my family home from the hospital on a Monday, and I joined them that evening after my return from my ministerial duties in Wisconsin.

As I look back on my decisions, I sometimes wonder if my "dedication" to ministry was a bit excessive, if that were possible? Nevertheless, it is past history—it cannot be changed and besides, "all's well that ends well"! All has ended well in our years of partnership in ministry! The following week, while the women took care of the baby and things around the house, Dad decided to drive me out to Mountain in their car to see what this oldest son of theirs was doing in ministry. We both enjoyed the ride together and the beautiful fall colors. Dad enjoyed meeting the members of the Mountain congregation and seeing and hearing for the first time, his oldest son leading a congregation in worship and preaching a message from the Bible. How proud I think he felt!

We continued to enjoy our fellowship with Mom and Dad until they felt it was time to leave for home. For some reason, those parting moments were some of the most difficult I have ever experienced. As they drove away from our little apartment, I simply came apart at the seams! I began sobbing and crying like I would never see them again—but of course I did see them again, many times. I think that those moments signaled in my heart the beginning of a new chapter in our lives, the final cutting of parental ties and the establishing of a new life together with my wife and daughter.

And God had another blessing waiting for us—it had to do with paying the hospital bill for a delivery, special care, and 10 days in the hospital. I went to the hospital offices to make arrangements to pay the bill. With no medical insurance I would have to work out some kind of monthly payment program with the hospital. I was surprised to find that the office had no account listed for Gordon and Betty Sorenson, nor was there any bill of any kind posted for us. I thanked them and assured them that it must be a clerical "glitch" or delay and that I would return in a few days to make arrangements to pay the bill. I did return, but they again had no success finding any billing under my name and assured me that "there simply was no billing and would be no billing!" THE BILL WAS PAID! We could not believe it! We must have fallen under the poverty income guidelines. We have often joked that our oldest, Cynthia Gale, was a "freebie"! What a blessing—in more ways than one!

FALL 1961—LIFE GETS BACK TO A NEW NORMAL

For me it was back to classes and delivering furniture. The rest of that year Betty stayed home to care for little Cindy and our humble home. As the months rolled by, I could see that the weekly trip and ministry to the Mountain church was too much for me to continue. The experience was great, but the income was too meager and the expenses in time and money too great to continue. In the early spring of 1961, I stopped the weekend ministry with the Mountain church and devoted my full time to school, to work and to my family. Life was busy, but life was good!

ANOTHER STUDENT MINISTRY

In the fall of '61 Betty enrolled again at MBC for her final year. Since I, too, would be enrolled full time for my junior year, we would need child care for Cindy. Mrs. Earl Justice, house mom at Bailey Hall, did an excellent job providing day care for us. That same fall, Ralph Christman, another MBC student who had recently finished his studies and who also had a student ministry with the Batavia Church of Christ in Minnesota approached me about taking his place as minister of that congregation. The Batavia church was a small, rural congregation, meeting in a classic old wood-frame building across the road from Turtle Lake, a few miles southeast of Staples. It was a truly beautiful, secluded spot at least a half mile from the nearest neighbor. The commute each weekend would be three hundred miles round rip, only half as far as the six hundred miles round trip to Mountain. After considering it with Betty, we decided to do it. It would be good to stay in practice. The expense would be less, and the income would be a bit better. We commuted back and forth to Batavia for about a year. Things went well enough, the attendance increased, and there was even some talk by the congregation of finishing the parsonage next door and having us move in. Sometime before our arrival, the congregation had purchased a two-story house, slated to be moved to a new location. They constructed the basement and had the house moved onto the new foundation. As summer drew near, the congregation verbally committed themselves to finishing the house project. It needed a sewer system, a new well, and plumbing system, a new furnace, and a complete electrical rewiring. Since the early summer months were warm, we decided to move our things in, ahead of all the finish work, saving us paying rent on the apartment in Minneapolis and providing a much more peaceful and safe place to live.

After the move and during that summer, we continued a full-time, on-site ministry with that congregation. We became involved with the summer Vacation Bible School program, and summer church camping program at Pine Haven Camp on Long Lake. We even scheduled a week long summer evangelistic meeting, with Professor Earl Grice as the evangelist. Earl Grice was a brave soul. At that time we still did not have a well, a sewer and bath, heat, or electricity. We strung two hundred feet of extension cord from the church building to the house for electricity. We hauled water from a neighbor's well in milk cans for washing, bathing and drinking and we used the outhouse behind the church building for our toilet. We took baths in a wash tub by boiling water on the propane stove and adding some cold. There were no windows or doors in the basement openings and the west room of the basement stood wide open. At night you could hear the rats and mice and raccoon having a "hoot-n-nanny" down there!

While Earl Grice was with us for the week of meetings, a member of the congregation opened their home for his stay. The meetings went well, but as the summer drew to a close, other things were not going well. There had been a draught in the area, resulting in extensive crop loss. This was not a rich farming area to begin with and those losses began to show up in the offering plate. By the end of summer our weekly pay had been reduced to $25 per week, and nothing had been done to the parsonage. And if that were not enough, one day we experienced a minor crisis.

We had suspected the start of another pregnancy and I had cautioned Betty about lifting the heavy water cans. While I was gone from the house for a few minutes one day, she needed water and lifted the heavy can. She immediately began to cramp and hemorrhage. Little did we realize she was experiencing a miscarriage. She "bled" all that night before we realized what was happening. The next morning I quickly got her and little Cindy to the car and raced to the Brainerd Hospital emergency entrance thirty miles away. The ER staff began to administer help immediately. As I filled out and signed papers, admitting her for care, I was informed that I would have to pay whatever the entire bill would be before the hospital would discharge her. My heart sank. We had nothing—not even money for gas. Where would I get that kind of money, having no medical insurance? It was a dark night for me in more ways than one as Cindy and I drove back to Batavia. Cindy wanted to know where "mommie" was, and I wondered where God was!

HE WAS THERE ALL THE TIME

As I drove in the dark driveway, I decided to check the mail box for the day's mail. In the box was a letter addressed to us from the church in Marion, Minnesota. Their youth group, with whom I had gotten acquainted during the summer camping program, had decided to do something with their sizable mission fund. In the envelope was an enclosed note along with a $75-dollar check. The note said, "we know you and your wife are working with a small struggling church as a mission. We want to help you in your work!" WOW! And I wondered where God was—He was there all the time! I hadn't seen that much money in months! I had enough money for gas and groceries and to more than pay the forty-five dollar hospital bill. The next day little Cindy and I returned to the Brainerd Hospital, paid the bill and brought Mommie home.

AND AGAIN!

Having recovered from that episode, we were faced with another major problem. In a few days we needed to be back in Minneapolis to enroll for the fall quarter. Because we had little or no money, to continue commuting for this weekend ministry was out of the question, so we resigned from the Bativia ministry. We had no idea what we would do or where we would live when we returned to the college, nor where we would get the money for me to finish my senior year. All we could do was trust that God would provide the way. So we fueled up the car with the last money we had, and drove back to the city, leaving our few "worldly goods" back at the parsonage. Upon arriving at the campus, we decided to check our mail box to see what mail awaited us. The back side of the mail boxes were adjacent to the college office and familiar friends in the office detected that we were back! Someone quickly came to tell me that I was wanted in the office. I went to see what this request was about and was approached by Merle Maher, the office manager. He wanted to know if I would be able to fill a pulpit the approaching weekend. I saw no reason why not, but would have a problem with reliable transportation and money for gas to get there and back. He sent me to Leverton Hall next door, to talk to a "Dutch" Bueghly, a deacon in the Liscomb, Iowa Church of Christ. He was enrolling his two daughters, Phyllis and Rosalie, at MBC and was moving them into the girls quarters. I immediately found him to be a pleasant and congenial man and felt like I had known him for years. He urged me to come to Liscomb that coming weekend to speak and meet the congregation. How could I resist? It was a date!

Cynthia Gale

Betty and me with Cynthia Gale, 1960

Mom, with
Cynthia, 1960

Pastor, Alvin Geise, Dad, Mom, me
and Jack Barber

The Kingston family
from Mountain, WI

Loads of hay at the Kingston's

The Hickory Church, WI

CHAPTER 18

THE BEGINNING OF
FULL TIME MINISTRY

Our good college friend Mary Etta loaned us her car and some gas money and the next day, Saturday, Betty and I and Cynthia drove to Liscomb, Iowa. We stayed that weekend with Dutch and Clarice Bueghly and had a wonderful time with the congregation! They gave me a speaker's fee of $75! I couldn't believe it—$75! I was in "hog heaven" (pardon the pun)!

"Could I come back next week?" they asked.

"You bet I can!" But not just for the money, also for the great fellowship. This large, active congregation was affirming and compassionate and very friendly!

We looked forward to returning—it was a total boost to the spirit—my spirit—our spirit. And, it seemed, we were a boost to the spirit of this congregation. They had been without a minister for a while and upon our return the next week, we were approached by the board to continue there permanently as their minister! They suggested that we move the family into the parsonage while I continue my studies at MBC, possibly staying in one of the men's dorms during the week. I loved the idea! I loved this congregation! I would be away from my family a few days each week, but my family would be safe in their care, and I could finish my degree. The other unbelievable thing was, on this second visit they gave me an eighty-five dollar speaker's fee and offered me that same amount per week as their resident minister! GOD IS GOOD!

Several of the farmers in the congregation volunteered their pickups and strong backs to get us moved down from Minnesota. In a single day, three or four pickups with six or seven men drove to Batavia, loaded our furniture and household goods, and returned to Liscomb. If my memory serves me, some of those men were "Dutch" Bueghly, Wilbur Gallaway, Lester McKibben, Russ Sword, Ezra Hunt and a few others whose names I cannot recall. They, and several others helped us move our furniture into the parsonage and we were off and running in one of the most pleasant and rewarding experiences of our forty-five years in ministry. God truly provides for his servants!

LIFE IN SMALL TOWN IOWA

In Liscomb we were able to really settle into a rich family and community life. The members of this congregation were so supportive and gracious, I felt comfortable leaving my family in their care while I was attending classes in Minneapolis each week. I would leave the city following the last class mid-afternoon on Fridays, drive the two hundred seventy miles home to Liscomb, arriving around 9:00 or 10:00 p.m. Cindy would be asleep, but I would enjoy the rest of the evening with Betty, getting caught up on the events of the week. What a joy to spend Saturday with Betty and Cindy and to resume getting acquainted with the neighbors and members of the congregation. The only difficult part was taking the time to prepare my sermon for Sunday morning. Most of the research I had done during the week at college. It was just a matter of taking the time to get my thoughts organized and on paper. I would usually spend an hour or two at the office later in the evening after Cindy was tucked in, putting the finishing touches on it.

Sunday mornings were always busy and "nervous" as I prepared my head and heart for the worship service. In my forty-five years of ministry I never got over the Saturday evening/Sunday morning "pre-game nerves". I never had to worry about "regularity"—the weekends took care of that! After the service I looked forward to greeting the congregation and sharing in their great fellowship. It seemed we seldom had to concern ourselves with Sunday dinner. There were many who were generous in sharing their homes and great "down home cooking". There is no fellowship like the fellowship of God's people! Our brothers and sisters in Christ in Liscomb, as in many other congregations, have through the years, become closer to us than our own families. Many of the grandparents in the Liscomb church became grandparents to our daughters. Many of their sons and daughters became our sons and daughters—the Bueghly girls, Phyllis and Rosalie; Karen Hunt; the Harmon kids, brothers Jim and Dave and sister Deanne; the Galloway kids, Rosemary, the twins Rick and Ron, and Dean; the Gifford girls, Linda and Becky and Ralph Norman. The McNair kids, John and Marty, lived right across the street and also participated in church activities. We attended their school activities and sports events. I had the privilege of mentoring many of them into ministry and Christian service.

Many of the older couples became like parents to Betty and me. An incident that characterized the generosity of this congregation came as a result of our car breaking down. The Volkswagen we were driving decided that on one particular very cold morning, (fifteen below zero) it just wasn't going to take it anymore! As I left the house driving east of town on an errand, a valve head broke off inside the motor and totally destroyed it. Lester McKibben promptly towed me and the car to his farm and garage and together we went to work on it. We raised the back end of the VW off the floor, disconnected the wires and cables, unbolted the engine from the transmission and slid it down a plank to the floor. The two of us picked the engine up with our four bare hands and slid it into the back of Lester's truck. The next day we took it to a VW dealership and parts house in Des Moines and exchanged it for a complete new engine. If I recall, the church picked up the cost of the new engine which was, as it turned out, amazingly reasonable. We headed back to his garage, unload the new engine and slide it back up the plank into position with the transmission and bolted it in place! I was soon back on the road again thanks to the generosity of this congregation and good work of this elder—Lester McKibben.

GOD WAS IN THE BACK SEAT.

We led youth meetings and social functions on Sunday evenings. Mondays were for making a few calls and spending the bulk of the day with the family. I would always wait until the last minute, after Cindy was asleep in bed to kiss Betty good-by and make the long return trip to Minneapolis. It would usually be 9:00 or 10:00 p.m. before I was on the road. This would put me in Minneapolis around 3:00 a.m.

Of course it was back to class by 7:30 a.m. Looking back, I've often wondered how I did it!

Many times I made the trip in not the best of weather—especially during the winter months. One miraculous incident took place on a snowy, slushy night while heading north near Osage, Iowa. The snow was coming down in large white flakes which, in the glare of the headlights, had a hypnotic effect on me and I momentarily dozed off. At that hour of the day (or morning) there was no traffic on the highway, thank God, but I had just entered a quarter mile section of girder bridges spanning the Cedar River swampland. Suddenly, clear and loud, I heard someone screaming my name "GORDON, WAKE UP" (my guardian angel)! I did wake up— with a start—just in time to see sections of girder bridge passing by in front of my windshield from right to left! I then realized that the car and I were sliding sideways right down the middle of the road on this girder bridge! The car came to a stop—engine running, windshield wipers still slapping back and forth, heavy snow coming down—but no dents in the car and no "dents" in my body! The car and I were still all in one piece! I looked to see who had screamed at me from the back seat—I found no one!!?? I drove on into the night, now—totally awake!

IT HAD TO BE A GOD THING!

One thing that really helped with these long trips back and forth to the campus was when any of the Liscomb kids attending MBC would hitch a ride with me one way or the other. Their conversation kept me awake and "shortened" the trip considerably.

MY TURN AT A DORM PRANK

My many trips on the highways back and forth to college had their exciting moments, but so did life on the campus during the week at Milliard Hall. It seemed there was always some kind of hi-jinks going on. Some of us always seemed to be the victims of these practical jokes because we either had a late night work shift or were traveling to or from ministries to the campus. One early morning I arrived back on campus from Liscomb in time to meet a fellow resident just getting in from his night shift. Together, we discovered our rooms had been "rearranged" and major items hidden all over the dorm. We were fed up! We were tired but had to spend the rest of the night locating our beds, clothes etc. So we decided to give all these sleeping pranksters some of their own medicine.

I just happened to have a large bundle of clothesline rope in my car. We spent the rest of the early morning hours filling both bathrooms to the ceiling with all the luggage we could find. We then tied all the dorm-room doors together criss-cross, up and down the hallways. We then went down to the campus dining room to have an early breakfast and watch the fire works. We had breakfast, went to our 7:30 classes and continued to wait for the excitement. Midway through our 7:30 class (with many conspicuously empty chairs) in they came—fussing like a bunch of wet hens! They were late for class, having had to leave their rooms by window or fire escape. They had no bathroom time, with no time for breakfast and totally puzzled as to who would have pulled off this dirty rotten trick. Dennis Young and I have been laughing ever since! AND—they never figured out "who dunnit"! My one last opportunity to make my mark on dorm life and have a little payback was a roaring success! One side note—this was my one and only prank at MBC! Really, it was!

SPRING 1963 COLLEGE GRADUATION

I made those long trips through the fall and winter of 1962 and into the spring of '63 when the "grueling grind" finally came to an end. I was graduating! On the 29th day of May, 1963, at Minnesota Bible College, I walked the walk across the platform and received my Bachelor of Theology Degree! Six long years of stress—finally over! Yet, at the same time, six wonderful years of Christian fellowship and camaraderie ending all too soon. But that great camaraderie has continued through the years. We have been able to stay connected and reconnect with many of those college friends even though hundreds of miles have separated us. We are grateful!

GORDON AND BETTY SORENSON—AND DAUGHTERS

Lots of big things happened in 1963. Yes, I did graduate, but earlier that spring we discovered we were pregnant again! This time the pregnancy was quite normal from the standpoint of toxemia. Betty had no swelling or fluid retention, nor blood pressure problems until the last month. It was then, some toxemia began to show, prompting the doctor to hurry things along. He felt I should bring Betty to the hospital for delivery prior to waiting for natural labor to begin. We admitted her to Grundy Center Community Hospital, where he began a procedure to induce labor. After a full day, nothing was happening so we returned home. A week later we admitted her again, at which time her obstetrician broke her water, and Sherry was on her way. On September 26, 1963, Sherry Lee entered this world. At Sherry's delivery I was allowed to stand in the doorway of the delivery room to witness her birth. In those early days, doctors were very cautious about allowing fathers into the delivery rooms for fear of them fainting, or creating some problem. But, after requesting to be present, they allowed me that far. It was a wonderful experience! I vowed that if we were to have other additions to our family, I definitely wanted to be there. AND—twelve years later, long after we thought we were finished having children, we were in for a REALLY BIG surprise! We were "expecting" again. We felt sort of like Abraham and Sarah. This time I would be there—in the delivery room—standing next to Betty, holding her hand when our youngest, Shannon Carol was born. But, more about her later.

Liscomb was a wonderful place for the girls to grow up. Liscomb was a wonderful place to minister. We continued our ministry with that congregation for two more years. There was no more commuting, no more living in the boy's dorm, no more being away from my family four and five days every week. It allowed me the pleasure of getting to know my girls, my congregation and my community. I could be totally involved in what was going on in the area. I had their weddings. I had their funerals. I called on them in the hospitals and in their homes. We sang together in their choir. We enjoyed their pot lucks and barbecues and community celebrations. It was there we shared in a national tragedy—the assassination of President John F. Kennedy. We were watching the news coverage of the Dallas motorcade as the whole event unfolded. We mourned with the community and the nation.

MY VERY FIRST WEDDING

Earlier that summer, actually immediately following my college graduation on May 29, I performed my very first wedding. It did not even involve anyone in the Liscomb church. I "tied the knot" for two of my college classmates. Sometime before classes were out, several of us were "hanging out" in room 200, a favorite gathering spot between classes. Bob

Eckman and Arlene Frick came in and made the announcement to me that they were planning to get married right after graduation. I said, great and asked when and where and then—"who was going to perform the wedding?" And without blinking an eye, and in unison, they said, "YOU ARE!" "Wait a minute, wait just a minute—stop the music! I thought I just heard you say—you are! What do you mean you are? How could that be, I have never done a wedding, and I'm not even "degreed" yet and certainly not ordained! But they had already researched it and informed me that all I would need is a letter of recommendation from the Bible College and to register at the Rusk County courthouse in Ladysmith, Wisconsin where the wedding would take place. It was a "done deal", the Eckman's would be my first wedding!

MY LIFE IN THE HANDS OF A BUSH PILOT

A few days later I had the letter of recommendation from the college but was faced with a three hundred mile round trip out to Ladysmith and back. I hardly had the time and barely had the money. I was discussing this dilemma with them, again in room 200, with fellow classmate Paul Williams listening in. Paul immediately spoke up and informed me that he had his own plane, a little Areonca Champ two-seater, and he would fly me out there that very afternoon— "get your hat...lets go!" We drove out to a little grass airstrip near Circle Pines, Minnesota, gassed up the plane and we were on our way! It was a beautiful, bright, and calm afternoon. After about an hour we landed on another grass strip on the west edge of Ladysmith. We hitched a ride into town to his home; his dad was the pastor of the Church of Christ there. I walked to the courthouse and registered, and after spending a few minutes with his parents, we were on our way again. They drove us to a service station to buy a can of aviation fuel, then headed to the air strip. We gassed up, checked out everything and boarded the plane.

Paul wanted to make one "minor" change—he wanted me to sit in the forward seat, behind the gages and forward controls. There were two sets of controls and he informed me he could fly it from the back seat. Since I was heavier the plane would "trim" better with me in the front seat—yeah, sure it would! The return trip would a bit more exciting than the trip out—to say the least! First, we had a wind change while we had been doing business in town and that would make it a little "dicey" getting off the grass strip and over the stand of cottonwood trees at the end of the runway. We made it above the trees—barely—with a few cotton wood leaves in the landing gear. Then, after we had been in the air a few minutes, Paul informed me he was sleepy and would later have to go to work on his "night shift" at the Clark station and would I please fly the plane back to Minneapolis and the airport at Circle Pines. He assured me that because I had watched the geography below us on the way out, I would be able to find my way back. He told me to just wake him up as we neared the airport—he would land the plane. "Well that's good!" I thought! Hmmm—"sit in front so the plane will trim better!" So I would not only have my first wedding in 1963, I would also fly my first airplane in 1963—just so I didn't have my first mid-air collision in 1963! I had never flown a plane before—ever, but I flew us back to the Circle Pines air strip, I woke Paul up as we made a pass over the run way and he landed the plane. I noticed though as he exited the plane, he looked a little "green around the gills". He had become airsick while sleeping that hour in the back seat and was about to "up-chuck" everything. Except for that, it was a great experience!

A WEDDING AND A WEDDING "BOOBOO"

The wedding was also quite an experience! We had a wedding rehearsal the day before where I spelled out how the service would go and who would do what. That sounds easy, but it was not. I had never performed a wedding! I sweat blood the weeks before, putting together what I thought should be the right Biblical focus in the message, and the right symbolic things to include in the ceremony with the approval of Bob and Arlene. I put everyone through their paces, starting with the ushers, the bride's maids, the male attendants and groom, then the bride and her father. Her father was to usher her in on the wedding march and after the invocation, respond to my question, "who gives this woman to be married to this man?" He was respond with "I do", step back to his seat, just one or two steps away and be seated. His being seated would signal the audience that they too could be seated. The evening of the wedding, the singers sang, the players played, the groom and I, and groomsmen took our places on the platform, and the wedding march went perfect. But there was one big difference—this was an evening wedding. Not only was it dark outside, unexpectedly it was dark inside because the ushers had doused the house lights, except for those just above us in the wedding party. Due to the glare of the spot lights directly above us, we in the wedding party could not see what was going on in the audience. I gave the invocation, then asked the question "Who gives this woman to be married to this man?" Her father responded with "I do", stepped back to his seat in the darkened auditorium—and stood! And stood and remained standing for almost the whole service. One of the bridesmaids, suddenly noticing this, tugged on my sleeve just as I was about to tell the groom "You may kiss your bride" and informed me that everyone in the audience was still standing! As I peered out into the darkness, I couldn't believe what I saw! I immediately apologized, seated the audience and finished the ceremony. I was embarrassed! Earl Grice, one of my professors, after congratulating Bob and Arlene in the reception line, "congratulated" me with the comment, "Gordie, I am aware we are to show due honor and respect to the bride and groom during a wedding ceremony, but this is ridiculous!" This brought a roar of laughter from the crowd, and put me at ease. These are the things we remember and cherish as the years roll by. Ah yes, my first wedding! We are still retelling the story.

OUR FIRST FAMILY VACATION 1965

After the fun of the Eckman wedding, it was back to Liscomb, Iowa and really settling into family life and ministry there. Graduation was over, the load of schoolwork was a thing of the past and we could plan some relaxing family activities. So, we planned what would turn out to be a very interesting vacation. Even though money was always short, we felt it was important to take vacations with the girls, to travel to famous scenic places and visit family. The plan this time was to drive to California in our 1958 Ford station wagon to spend a week or two with our families. The first part of the trip went fine. We saved money by sleeping in the station wagon and fixing meals from food we had brought with us. The first night was spent in North Platt, Nebraska in a city park. For curtains, we smeared "Glass Wax" on the inside of all the windows. We slept the night, and the next morning ate a breakfast of juice and cereal. We wiped the glass wax off and went on our way. We had the cleanest windows on the highway! Things went well as we drove on into Wyoming and through Rock Springs and Green River.

TROUBLE, AND ANOTHER HEAVENLY VISITOR

About fifteen miles west of Green River, Wyoming I noticed the red oil pressure warning light glowing on the dash. As I slowed up to find a pull-off, I also noticed that the engine seem to be loosing power, as if it were under a load. I found a place to stop, so we pulled over and shut off the engine. It was a very hot day but the car was not over-heating. I let the engine cool down for a while, tried to sort out what the problem could be, and decide on a plan of action.

In those moments my biggest concern was deciding what to do with Betty and the girls and figuring out how to get help. I didn't want to leave them while I went for help nor did I want Betty hitching for help. I decided to see if the engine would start. It did—and it seemed to run well. I would try to drive back to Green River with the family. I drove slowly, not overtaxing or overheating the engine. As we got within seven miles of town and I could feel the engine tightening up. It seemed the best action would be to shut it down immediately before it seized up completely.

I stopped, got out to raise the hood, and immediately saw off to the south, a big "dust devil" swirling its way our direction, blowing tumbleweeds, sagebrush, sticks, and dirt. It crossed the highway about one-hundred yards west, behind the car. But I was surprised to see coming out of the midst of the dust devil onto the highway, a pickup truck! The pickup had not been on the highway, but came out of nowhere! It just appeared out of the dust devil! The driver pulled up just ahead of my car and was immediately walking back toward my car carrying a tow chain. Without a word, he quickly had the chain hooked to the front of my car, and the back of his pickup and was quickly ready to go down the road. I had to step fast to get back into my car and release the brake! We were going! Where, I had no idea—but we were going., and fast! "What is happening here?", we asked each other.

Quickly he pulled us into Green River and right in front of a small Ford garage. I was amazed! As I exited my car the shop foreman was on his way out to see how he could help. I quickly explained what I thought the problem was, at which time he paused to look around and then asked, "How did you get your car in here"? I looked around to introduce the gentleman and to help unhook the chain, and thank him for towing me in. I saw no one! He was gone—the tow chain, pick-up and all! He came out of nowhere and simply disappeared into thin air! I've reviewed that incident in my memory a hundred times and I am certain we were visited by a guardian angel—but there was more to this story!

THE "FONZE"

The shop foreman informed me that it might be the next day before he would have a mechanic available to work on my car. Then he paused and said, "Wait a minute, let me make a phone call", and walked to the office. Soon he came out to inform me that he had found a mechanic who would be right over to see what he could do. Fifteen minutes passed and around the corner came the sound of duel exhausts and a hot rod—a little black "duce coupe".

Out of the car stepped "The Fonze"! He had a duck-tail haircut, was dressed in Levis, black engineers boots and T shirt with a pack of "Camels" rolled up in the sleeve. My first thought was—"Oh no, this shade-tree mechanic is going to work on my family car!" In no time he had the car in a stall, front-end hoisted in the air, and on a creeper with an air wrench in his hand. Zip, zip, zip, zip! Off came the oil pan! Off came the oil pump! Within 15 minutes had the problem diagnosed.

"Your oil pump shaft broke—a common problem with this year Ford engine", he said. He then said he would have to replace all the bearing inserts. However, the rod and crankshaft journals appeared to be in good shape. He would get on it right away. I was pleasantly surprised he could repair it so soon. I didn't even ask what it would cost—I really had no choice. I would pay for it some way. It was the only show in town. I was sick—relieved, but sick—sick about what it would cost.

But I was also hungry, as were Betty and the girls. We found a little Bed and Breakfast diner down the street from the garage. We enjoyed a good meal (I would have enjoyed it more under different circumstances), and then looked for a motel. A little further to the east, within walking distance, was a motel with a swimming pool. The girls were ecstatic! I was still sick, not "sick" sick, but worried sick! I didn't sleep well that night. I tossed and turned until six a.m. so decided to get up and go for a walk. I walked the two blocks back to the garage and in the morning light, noticed the little black duce coupe sitting by the side door to the garage. I could hear the sound of an impact wrench coming from inside! The Fonze was already at work on my car, skillfully, painstakingly fitting new bearing inserts to the crankshaft mains and rods! As I watched, I could see that the kid was good—really good! Betty and the girls enjoyed the day at the motel pool and by four p.m. that day the car was ready. The whole bill came to only $185, almost the entire balance of our vacation money. We had just enough for gas money to get to California, but then what? I was pleasantly surprised the bill wasn't more—but still feeling the pain. How in the world could we finish the trip? Answer, Dad to the rescue! After arriving in California and explaining to my family what had happened, Dad offered to loan me the money for the rest of our vacation (actually, the return trip to Iowa).

After paying the bill at the little Ford garage in Green River, I went to thank the young mechanic for the work he had done, but he too had disappeared! I asked the shop foreman who that "kid mechanic" was, and he informed me that I had lucked out—I had gotten the best! He was a crack mechanic for the Parnelli Jones Indy racing team. It was the "off season" and he just happened to be home for a few days and wanted to make a few extra bucks. It's a "God" thing! We were able to continue the trip and enjoy the vacation, and do it in one of the best running family station wagons in the country! I sure wish I knew his name!?

UP TO MY EARS IN MINISTRY

It was at Liscomb, I had one of my first emergency intervention/counseling experiences. I received a desperate call from a local teenage farm boy, urging me to get out to their family farm as fast as I could. He gave directions and said I could find him and his dad out in the corn crib. I hurried to their place, drove past the house to the corn crib and there they were. The young man and his dad were hiding in the corn crib from the wife/mother. Right away, I noticed bruises and bleeding lumps on their heads, arms and faces. The story was that "Mom had gone berserk for some reason, and had grabbed a heavy hob-nail glass lamp and was beating up on them—would I confront her, calm her down, and get that lamp out of her hands?" Suddenly, the thought occurred to me that this could be a case of a woman going through her change of life. It had to have been providential for that insight to pop into my head. Twenty-six year old, fresh college graduates are not that knowledgeable on such matters! I made my way to the house and in a voice loud enough for her to hear inside, announced who I was. "I am the minister of the Liscomb Church of Christ—I would like to talk to you". My being a clergyman must have had a calming effect on her for she immediately invited me in and was very willing to talk. She gave up her "bludgeon", and soon seemed restored to her right mind. I then called the men in to share in the conversation and after raising the probability of this being her change of life, the lights seemed to come on for all three of them. As the days went by, I stopped in a few more times to see how things were going. It appeared that with the new "revelation" they were coping just fine. Again, "Thank you God—it had to be you". I never would have guessed this to be the problem on my own.

One of the things I enjoyed about this ministry was my involvement with several of the farmers in their farm operations. At different times of the year, I would hire on to help with their field work and harvests. Most often, I worked for and with Russell Sword, whose farm was three miles west of town. Mainly, my help came in the form of shuttling loaded wagons to and from the fields where Russell and the corn picker were working and to the corn crib, where I elevated the ear corn into storage. I always enjoyed being outside, operating machinery and doing manual labor. I looked forward to being out of the office and active. It was great working with Russell. Our families soon became close friends, as with so many in the Liscomb congregation. I had several "temp" jobs with the farmers in the area—from operating machinery, to plowing and bailing hay. I recommend it to every minister. It allows you to truly identify with the people. Someone has called it "incarnate" ministry".

A young Sherry

Cynthia with our Beagal

Church of Christ
Liscomb, IA

CHAPTER 19

1965

ANOTHER MOVE
FORT DODGE, IOWA

As a minister in Iowa, I became involved with area church fellowships, summer camps, area evangelism, and men's meetings. The state evangelism ministry, the Iowa Christian Evangelistic Mission, had been involved in a new but struggling church in Fort Dodge, Iowa. Seeing that the few ministries Betty and I had been involved with were successful and growing, they issued the call to us to move to Fort Dodge and work with that congregation. We were somewhat reluctant to make such a drastic move, since we loved the Liscomb area and church as we did. But with the two of us, "duty" always came before personal desires. We accepted that call and moved to Fort Dodge. There have been many times since, we wished we had not. We missed the loving and stable atmosphere of the Liscomb congregation and community. Helmer Peterson and family were called there to continue with the work after we left and did a wonderful job. He stayed with the Liscomb congregation from 1965 to 2005 or 06 when he retired. The Peterson's kept us up to date on the congregation and events in Liscomb.

God had something different in mind for us though. Little did we know the variety of experiences we would have living in the Fort Dodge area. We served the church in Fort Dodge for two years, from 1965 to 1967. Although supported by the state evangelistic mission, the work soon had difficulty. One of the problems was the church building and its location. The congregation had, at an earlier time, purchased an old downtown Lutheran church building which had no off-street parking, as well as many design problems. It was built to accommodate an outmoded concept of church and evangelism. It did not invite church growth. The same was also true for the leadership of the congregation. They lacked a real vision for church growth. Churches are often threatened by change and growth, because they fear having things "get out of their control". This, along with some family dysfunction among the leadership, meant stymied church growth. If evangelism were to take place in this city, with this congregation, it would have to happen some other way—perhaps apart from the local church.

A DIFFERENT KIND OF MINISTRY

We had become acquainted with the Jerry Rabiner Boys Ranch, a 40-acre residence facility for troubled boys, located west of Fort Dodge. The Iowa State Policeman's Association sponsored this care program and had one house of fourteen boys already in successful operation and wanted to open a second home. Betty and I felt called to become house parents with this operation and to allow troubled boys to feel the atmosphere of a Christian home and the impact of Christ in their life. The Ranch guidelines not only "allowed" for the boys to have a "church experience" on a regular basis, but the leaders insisted on it. The boys were all to attend church somewhere on the weekends. Guidance and counseling was provided by local social services, but the house-parents were also allowed to provide Christian counseling. We felt that if we could not reach those most in need of the Gospel through the church, then we could do it directly through the Boy's Ranch program.

In 1967 we moved our family, Betty and me and the two girls, from the church parsonage in Fort Dodge, to our own personal apartment in residence #2 at the Jerry Rabiner Boy's Ranch. In no time our family increased from two young daughters to two young daughters and fourteen teenage boys—many of whom had police "rap sheets" for minor offences such as truancy, petty theft, shop lifting and running away. In many cases the situation at home was so bad, this had become their way of surviving. We ministered to these boys for a year. It was very rewarding in many ways—but very trying as well. In this kind of care, it is your job twenty-four hours a day, seven days a week. You don't go home at the end of your shift. We had to deal with it all; when they were sick; when they had picked a fight at school; finishing their home work; seeing they did their assigned household chores—the dishes, their rooms, the wash, helping with the cooking —and crying with them through the hard times. Often we had to comfort and calm them when their parents had promised a visit but didn't show. In their minds that hypocrisy translated into "I don't count for much" or "they don't really care" or "they have more important things to do". The burnout rate for house parents is high. Having to deal with this subtle abuse took its toll on the boys. Having to help the boys deal with it takes its toll on even the strongest house-parents.

We had many great times with the boys—basketball in the back yard, softball and football in the front yard and a stubborn bunch of Shetland ponies to train down in the pasture. The ponies were great for the boys to work with. They enjoyed riding out across the pasture and down along the creek bottom, but they also learned some great lessons about life from having to deal with a pony's stubbornness. They began to experience the frustration of having to deal with something wild and rebellious. At times they would come back to the house angry and frustrated because the pony would not cooperate but just run off, bucking the saddle and gear and sometimes them, into the creek. Many times my reply to them was in the form of a question— "does that remind you of anybody you may know?" They quickly got the point!

TORNADO CLEANUP WITH TROUBLED BOYS

One of the great experiences we shared together with the boys was a mission of mercy in the aftermath of a tornado. A tornado had just devastated the Charles City, Iowa area, and there was a great need for workers to go there to help with the recovery and cleanup. I challenged the guys with the idea of going there for a day to provide cleanup assistance. Immediately, it was unanimous—they all wanted to go and help!

I cautioned them that this was not going to be a vacation nor an excursion to "gold-brick". They assured me they wanted to go and to go for the right reasons. So we went. We got up early and had a hearty breakfast, packed the hand tools in the van and headed for Charles City. Once there, local officials assigned us to a particular street and section of devastated homes. Our first assignment was to help an elderly couple clean up the debris of their ground up house. They especially wanted us to locate as many pictures and keepsakes as we could find. But before I could ask about other particulars concerning their home site, the couple began to tell the boys about a bunch of money they had hidden in the house which was now obviously scattered everywhere in the ruins. I thought to my self, Oh no! These guys didn't need to hear that! I feared that during the course of the day some would be tempted to pocket whatever money they found. Miraculously, that was not the case! Suddenly, seeing the plight of this elderly couple, their compassion kicked in! Most of the day they were recovering dishes and pictures and "knick-knacks"—but also pennies, nickels, and dimes in one place, and quarters and bills over in another. The boys were all so excited that they were able to help get the money and keepsakes back to them! It was as though this elderly couple had suddenly become their own "Grandma and Grandpa". In my mind, they had passed the extreme test—especially knowing several of them had been in trouble for stealing, purse snatching, and shop lifting. For Betty and me, this was a reward beyond measure!

MORE CHANGES: "BACKBREAKING" WORK!

Since the burnout rate was high and the monetary payback low, after a year we needed to move on to something else. Most important, our girls needed the full attention of mom and dad and not have to share us with 14 teenage boys. I looked for work elsewhere in the Fort Dodge area. Our bank account also needed a major transfusion! I kept noticing an ad in the employment section of the local paper. Iowa Beef Packers needed "beef luggers" and the hourly pay was phenomenal! I stopped at the plant to inquire as to what a beef lugger was and if I might qualify. The personnel guy tossed me a hard hat and took me to the loading dock next to the meat coolers. There, I got to see first hand what a beef lugger did—carry one hundred seventy five to three hundred pound beef quarters out of the cooler and load them into semi trailers and rail cars. A seven man crew would load twenty cars and trailers a shift, or nearly eighty tons of meat per man! Seeing I was still in pretty good shape and stood six foot three, before I could say NO they hired me on the spot! But, the first two weeks—what agony! My back was killing me, my shoulders were "raw meat" and I couldn't get enough to eat. But, I stayed with it! I toughened in—ate everything in the house and still lost weight. But, I made some great money! We had recently purchased a small house—a very small house in Fort Dodge to serve as an investment—a "get-a-way" and a place to put our personal stuff. But we now had the desire and financial ability to own something bigger.

DOWN ON THE FARM

We sold the "mini" house in Fort Dodge and bought a five-acre acreage near Rockwell City, Iowa to be our real family home. We bought a Ford 9N tractor with a front-end loader, a plow, a cultivator and mower. We had twenty-four chickens, twelve head of sheep, an orchard of apple and cherry trees and an acre of garden. The girls have often said of those years on the farm, that they were the best years of their youth. Their daily chores included; feeding the chickens, collecting the fresh eggs, working in the garden harvesting the tomatoes, fresh sweet corn, string beans, and peas. They helped pick cherries and apples when ripe. They also got in on butchering chickens and freezing and canning vegetables and at the end of the summer, digging and collecting potatoes. It seems we all got in on "lambing time"—in some cases (Betty) helping the ewes give birth (i.e. pulling lambs). Most of the ewes would have at least two and sometimes three lambs. What a joy to watch the barnyard jumping with activity as all the new lambs would cut loose, frolicking around their mothers!!

KIDS SAY THE DARNDEST THINGS!

It was also a joy to see the girls growing and developing personalities and vocabularies of their own. This actually began while we were still living in Liscomb. We overheard Cindy talking about "Oxcream on a stick". We couldn't figure out what that was. She revealed that she had heard "Grandpa Sorenson" talk about it. It was an ice cream bar—ice cream on a stick! On another occasion we heard another new phrase after she came home from playing with the neighbor kids— "go-din-it". We kept hearing her repeat this curious phrase. We finally realized it was her version of god damn it! She had no idea what she was saying—just repeating what she thought she heard the neighbor kids saying.

An incident with a bit more trauma was "the bunny". While in the yard mowing the lawn, I uncovered a nest of new born rabbits with the wheel of the mower. None were injured, but as they began to scatter and run all different directions, Cindy gave chase trying to catch one. Suddenly the bunny she was chasing stopped—but she didn't. Her foot came down on the bunny and squished it, like slipping on a banana peel. Seeing what happened, Betty exclaimed, "Oh, poor little bunny!" But Cindy looked up from the squished bunny and replied, "Oh, but we can get another one mommy!"

With Sherry it was strange words like "hoptikeller" and "papina babut". We later discovered these words were *helicopter* and *peanut butter*. How could we have missed that? Her coining of new words went on even into her teen years. On one occasion while living in Show Low, Arizona, she was prepping a load of laundry and wanted to know what to do. Questioning her mother, who was in the back bedroom and almost out of ear range, she yelled, "I put the water in...and then I put the soap in... and then put the clothes in...and then I set it on *regurgitation*?"

On another occasion, Shannon, after looking in the mirror, came to Betty holding her eye open wide and pointing to her eye with her index finger asked, "Mom...do you see this black fleck right here on my *uterus*?" Needless to ask, how do you keep a straight face and keep from roaring in laughter at such times? The girls were a delight!

SNEAKING HOME FOR CHRISTMAS

We had many great times as a family. One of those great times was a surprise Christmas trip to California. Our family made plans to "sneak" in on our relatives on Christmas Eve without a hint we were coming. Of course to make arrangements to do that we would have to tell someone, so we plotted with my brother Gary to pull off this surprise. We would take the train from Perry, Iowa to East Los Angeles on Christmas Eve, and he would take us from the station to his home. They had planned a Christmas Eve dinner to get everyone together in one place. That part of the plan turned out to be harder than we expected. No one could figure out why they were having Christmas Eve dinner when we would all be getting together for dinner on Christmas day. Nevertheless, our family loved to eat and if anyone wanted to prepare it, they would come. That evening Betty and I and the girls sat together in Gary's living room next to the Christmas tree and waited. I think that was the longest wait I had experienced in a long time—the anticipation of once again seeing loved ones whom we hadn't seen for a few years, face-to-face!

The moment came. We heard a car door slam—it was Dad and Mom and Peggy They were casually making their way to the front door—then the knock. Gary opened the door and as they walked in the sight of us sitting there did not hit them at first. Peggy said casually, "Oh, hi, Gordie". Then it hit her— "Hi, Gordie"? —something is wrong with that statement! Gordie is not suppose to be here—he and his family are in Iowa. Mother stood in the doorway in utter shock! Dad, also in shock, had to make his way to a chair and sit down. This Christmas surprise was a total success! We were all thrilled to be in each other's company once again. We immediately began sharing information on how everyone was doing back in Iowa and mainly how we were able to pull off this sneaky trip with no one knowing about it. Of course Dad wanted to know all about the train trip, being a great train enthusiast. As other friends and family arrived, they too, were shocked to find us there in California. It was then that everyone figured out why we were having a Christmas Eve dinner.

Actually, the train trip was not without incident. As we boarded the train in Perry, Iowa, we noticed that our passenger car was stone cold, with passengers wrapped up in blankets, shawls or whatever they could find to keep warm. This was a very significant observation due to the fact that the temperature outside was only ten degrees! The railcar had no heat! As it turned out, the train crew could do nothing or would do nothing to solve the heat problem in the train. As other passengers from the rear of the train came forward to see if there was heat, we realized that the whole train was frozen up. There would be no heat during that night and all the next day. It was twenty-five below zero in Ogden, Utah and still no heat. The cars didn't warm up until we neared Las Vegas. We wrapped the girls in every blanket or piece of clothing we could find and just endured the hours of cold. We figured it was just one of those unfortunate, rare glitches that happen.

Little did we know we were to face the same dilemma on the return trip. The ride from East Los Angeles to Las Vegas was perfect. The temperature through the desert was a dry 70 degrees. But as we traveled north into Utah, toward Ogden and Salt Lake City, the temps inside the car began to drop. "No," I thought, "This couldn't be happening again! NO WAY!"...WAY! Indeed, the car was frozen up. Later, we discovered the whole train was frozen up again, as passengers from the rear of the train came forward to see if there was heat in the forward cars. No heat anywhere! Again, the temps in Ogden were minus twenty-five degrees!

We had no choice but to endure it again, all the way to Omaha. We had a layover at the Omaha station before rolling eastward to Perry. The train was an extra long one due to holiday travel. They let those of us in the front cars exit into the warmth of the huge depot. We had been in the station for half an hour warming up when we met fellow passengers from the rear cars of the train just entering the station. They were angry! Instead of pulling the train ahead so those on the back half of the train could exit, they simply left them sitting on the train in the sub zero cold. Had they known, they could have walked through the forward cars to exit on the train platform, and then into the warm depot.

After a few more moments warming in the station, we all boarded the train for the final leg to Perry, expecting to continue freezing to death in those unheated cars. Here at Omaha the Union Pacific service and jurisdiction ended and the Milwaukee Railroad took over. To our surprise, as we entered our rail car we found everything warm and toasty. "What happened?", we all asked. The new conductor and train crew did not understand the reason for the question.

"Nothing", they said, "We are with the Milwaukee line and have just hooked our engines to the train. We'll be Milwaukee Line from here east to Chicago. Why do you ask?" When we explained that these same cars were frozen up all the way from California to Salt Lake City and here to Omaha, he said that there was no excuse for that. The heating systems in the cars were just fine. Obviously! We discovered that the "train freeze up" was deliberate on the part of the Union Pacific. They wanted out of doing passenger service. There was no money in it, but the federal government mandated it. They wanted to discourage ridership until there was no more. Amtrack could then take over. I lost my respect for Union Pacific from that point on. We never road the train again. So much for another corporate giant!

1972 THE ROCKWELL CITY CHURCH OF CHRIST

Since we were living in the Rockwell City, Iowa area during the years at the acreage, we enrolled the girls in that school system. Since we were becoming involved there, it seemed natural to become involved with a local church. We began attending the Rockwell City Church of Christ. We knew some of the members and we knew it to be a long-established and solid congregation. We were not disappointed. We had a wonderful experience with that congregation Not only did we attend, I became interim minister after a short time. The minister they had resigned and moved on, leaving me as the obvious choice to "fill in". I was glad to do so. Church Elder Tom Stearns and wife Barb and their four boys, who owned and operated a beef farm on the west edge of town, became very special friends to Betty and me and our two girls. Tom, being an elder in the church, also brought us together in a working relationship in leadership ministry.

"HE'S AN OLD COWHAND FROM THE RIO GRAND"

As I had done before, I helped Tom and the boys with his farm work; the usual bailing hay, harvesting the corn and beans and on another occasions, help to vaccinate, medicate, and de-horn about 250 head of western feeder cattle. Tom decided to save some money by not hiring a vet for the job. The one advantage of having the vet, was having the use of his head gate, allowing good control of each steer. Instead, we improvised a narrow wood fence "chute" next to the barn. The idea was to run them down this narrow chute to corral them, then grab them by the snout, shove the worm bolus down their throat and jab them with the needle. It went as planned with about half of these 250 pounders. The rest were not that easy. They had somehow "grown" to five hundred pounders and wild as bed bugs. They had been calved and raised in the remote and vast range country of Wyoming and western Nebraska. We were probably some of the first human types they had seen since the sale barn in Valentine, Nebraska. They were not about to stand still for a shot and a medicine bolus shoved down their throats.

Since I was big and strong, I was elected to get down in the chute with them and put a headlock on them. Talk about ballistic! I got grand slammed into the side of the barn, slammed right through the two-by-six wood rails of the chute—broke them right in half—with me in between them and the fence! This went on into the evening. It was nearly 7:30 p.m. when the agony stopped and we had nailed the last one. I felt like I had played middle guard in an NFL football game! I was covered with bruises, cuts, and abrasions and cow snot. And on top of this, a few days later, developed a nice case of ringworm. The medicine I had to take to knock out the ringworm knocked me out. It gave me the worst headache I had ever experienced—and I don't get headaches. As Tom and I and the boys sat around the supper table that evening, we decided that—"maybe a head chute would be better next time!" What a day! Yet, when we get together all these years later, this "cattle punching" experience is one of the things we talk about and again, enjoy many laughs.

THE JOYS OF FAMILY CAMPING!
Camping was one of the other things we and the Stearns shared and enjoyed together as families. On one 4th of July holiday we decided to go camping at Lake Okoboji, in the Spirit Lake, Arnolds Park area. It was an easy and enjoyable trip to the campground. Tom and Barb and family set up three tents, two for the boys and another for themselves. Betty and I had a small, cheap, pop up tent camper. We wisely picked a high, wooded spot in the campground where we all set up our tents. We fixed supper, sat around the campfire for a while spending some quality time with Tom and Barb and all the kids. Later that evening we all went to bed and enjoyed what started off as a peaceful, restful night.

Then, things began to happen! I was suddenly startled from a sound sleep by a strange noise. In my half awake, dazed condition, I fumbled around for my flashlight, which turned out to be my can of aerosol shave cream and pressed what I thought was the "on" button and promptly filled my shoe full of shave cream! I went to see what caused the noise and found Sherry, still sleeping, on the ground outside the camper. She had rolled over so tight against the side canvas wall of the camper that she actually rolled off the bed pull-out, under the "bungied" side canvas, and dropped out onto the ground. Coming to my senses, I opened the camper door and carried her back her in and got her snuggled back in her bed. Next morning, she didn't remember a thing. But that was not the end of the nights excitement.

WEATHERING AN EXTREME STORM IN A TENT
Sometime, very early in the morning, a violent storm came up. Lightening strikes were hitting all around us. High winds were snapping limbs off and the torrential rains flooded everything—everything except our little high spot in the campground. By the time the storm passed on, dawn was breaking, and it was time to get up and see what damage had been done. We knew we were alright, but we were concerned about the Stearns family in their tents. We looked out the door to view the soggy

morning and dripping trees and vegetation and found Tom, Barb and the boys still where we left them, still in good shape—very wet, but in good shape! The wind and driving rain had forced water through the zippers of their tents and gradually filled the slightly lower parts of their tents with water. Its like, they were sleeping in giant water balloons. They found the boys lying in water up to their waist. Tom and Barb couldn't figure out why they were wet and lying in water also. Tom accused Barb of wetting the bed...big time!

Everyone dried off and dressed and exited their tents to survey the rest of the camp ground. We were shocked! We found we had come through in great shape! But we saw where whole camp sites had been swept down the hill with the people and contents, to who knows where. There were sleeping bags and camping gear half buried in the mud, clothing and personal items hanging in trees—not just in one site, but in many, many camp sites. What a mess! We felt sorry for so many others who really had a rough, dangerous night. Everything was just too wet to try to fix breakfast so we voted to find a good restaurant and buy breakfast. So did everyone else in the campground. Every café and restaurant in the Arnolds Park, Spirit Lake area was full, with a waiting period. We had no choice, so we waited and waited and finally ate a good breakfast.

ALMOST LOST SHERRY

That morning the weather continued to clear, giving us a beautiful, warm afternoon to spend enjoying the beach and water. While the kids were playing in the water, the adults were "just chillin out" on the lake shore. As we all know, at times things can be going along too good to be true. Suddenly, a young father was walking toward us with our daughter Sherry in hand. She had been having a great time floating in the light surf on an air mattress. But now she was crying and seemed frightened. The man explained that evidently she had strayed out in water just over her head, had fallen off the air mattress and couldn't get back to shallow water. He saw her bobbing up and down on her tiptoes trying to get air. He immediately saw what was happening and easily took her by the arm and brought her to us. She calmed down and we thanked him for being so observant and taking action. We considered ourselves very fortunate and also very forewarned. Kids and water—parents pay attention!

ALMOST LOST SCOTTY

But no sooner had we calmed down from that incident, suddenly the Stearn's could not find Scotty, their youngest. Our family joined the search. We could not find him anywhere. Somehow, he thought he saw Tom and Barb and his brothers leaving for the parking lot and decided to follow them. His parents were not leaving for the parking lot at all, they were looking for him. He was mistakenly following another family with children about the age of his brothers, thinking they were his family. This family, realizing they had some strange kid tagging along, began looking for his real family. Eventually, after a dozen people had been looking in a half dozen places for the right parents and the right youngster, we all found each other and got reconnected. What a day at the beach! Later that afternoon, we loaded our camping gear in our cars and headed back to Rockwell City and home.

THE CAPTAIN OF MY OWN SHIP

We also enjoyed boating together on Twin Lakes. Tom and Barb bought a boat, and about this same time Betty and I found a great boat we could afford and headed for the water. I had always dreamed of owning an inboard ski boat but never figured I would be able to afford one. While driving through Humbolt, Iowa one day, I saw a genuine wood hull, inboard, speed boat. I stopped to check it out and fell in love with it right away! It was an older *Correct Craft* that had been used in Florida in the Cypress Gardens water ski shows. It was powered by a big Ford V-8 engine, and came equipped with a tow mast. This boat was designed for water skiing! I couldn't believe the price—$1,200! I quickly put together the money and brought the boat home for some servicing, cleaning and a little touch-up here and there on the marine finish. I couldn't wait to get it in the water! This boat did not disappoint us in any way. It could pull as many as four to six skiers at a time!

We had many exciting summers of boating and skiing with that boat. I once took it to Canada on a fishing trip and took it places on Signet Lake I still cannot believe! Slowly going through one very tight channel with huge boulders submerged everywhere and even with Betty up front on lookout, I still managed to "nick" a boulder with the prop and later had to send it to a prop shop to true it up. It came back from the shop straightened and polished so beautifully that I didn't want to put it back on the boat. I wanted to hang it on the wall! Needless to say, I bolted it back on the shaft and enjoyed many more hours of fun on just about every lake in northwest Iowa. Later, after a move to Arizona where there were no lakes for a hundred miles, we sold it. No sense having it sit and dry-rot in our front yard. We had taken it to a small reservoir lake over one hundred miles east of Show Low and spent a wonderful afternoon water skiing and sightseeing in the boat. As I was loading the boat for the trip home, the gentleman who operated the only concession stand on the lake ran down to look the boat over. He exclaimed that it was the greatest boat he had ever seen perform on that lake. He was amazed at the power and performance and asked if I would ever be interested in selling it. I told him I was considering selling it and quoted him a price of $1,200—what I had paid for it. He wanted my address and said he would see me sometime later.

Several months passed and I was working in the front yard around the boat and saw a pickup parking in front of the house. The driver was walking toward me and then announced that he had come to buy the boat. For a moment I had forgotten the conversation at the lake. As I recognized who the man was, he was pulling a large wad of one hundred dollar bills out of his pocket and started pealing them off and laying them in my open hand—exactly $1,200 in cash. I could hardly catch my breath! It was the fastest deal I had ever made. But he was happy, and I was happy and just that quickly—he hooked her up to his pickup and was driving off down the street. No more boat. I am seventy now, but I wouldn't mind having another one like her!

Church of Christ,
Ford Dodge, IA

Jerry Rabner Boys Ranch
at left and below

The Family Portrait

Happy, our St. Bernard

Life on the farm

The Stearns Family

CHAPTER 20

MINISTRY COMES IN ALL SHAPES AND SIZES

Shortly after moving to the acreage, another change came into my life, a change of employment. A minister friend who had followed my ministry with the Fort Dodge church, who knew my desire to take ministry to the streets of the city, informed me of a move by the residents of a depressed black neighborhood in Fort Dodge to establish a Neighborhood Opportunity Center through the local Community Action Agency. They were looking for someone to direct and oversee the program. I hesitated to apply for that job, thinking they would certainly want one of their own black residents to fill the position. After being urged by my friend, I halfheartedly applied and then waited for the vote of approval (or disapproval) required by the black community. To my utter astonishment, I got the vote! I couldn't believe it! They wanted me, a white man, to develop and operate their opportunity center in their black neighborhood...Wow! That had to be another "God thing"!

A WHITE FACE IN A BLACK NEIGHBORHOOD

My daily commute was now to the "Flats" neighborhood of Fort Dodge, a predominantly low-income, black neighborhood. My first duty was to locate the biggest house we could find, in the most central location and set up our offices and opportunity center operation there. We found the perfect, large two story, multi-room house with attached garage, next to the neighborhood grocery store. We made the kitchen the central office. The other adjoining rooms we turned into an art room, a music practice room with a piano etc., a study room for doing homework and a library room with a good selection of books, which impressed the downtown public library folks. They were so impressed, they adopted us as an "outpost" or neighborhood branch library and helped us maintain a constant flow of new books. The four large rooms upstairs we turned into a free clothing exchange and food pantry. We used the attached garage for collecting, storing and distributing used furniture, appliances, and hand tools.

In no time, the place was humming with activity. We had funds available to hire women from the local neighborhood to serve as secretary/receptionists and as neighborhood outreach workers. The outreach workers literally went from door to door to check on the people's personal needs—especially the elderly. We also tapped into Neighborhood Youth Corp program and funds to put several teenagers to work doing neighborhood clean-up and beautification. One of their projects was turning a large overgrown, and abandoned, vacant lot into an attractive and exciting playground for all the neighborhood children. Another large overgrown vacant lot owned by the local electric power company, which had been used in past years as a ball diamond, was, with their permission, reclaimed by the teen work crews. They manicured it into what was again, a very active ball diamond with a backstop, outfield fence, and team benches. These two formerly wasted pieces of ground were now humming with meaningful neighborhood activity. To inaugurate the new ball diamond, we organized a neighborhood celebration and invited Al Williams and Dolph Pulliam to the "Flats" to help us celebrate. Al and Dolph were basketball stars with the Drake Bulldogs college basketball team who had won the N.C.A.A. playoffs that spring in a big "David vs. Goliath" upset. The two of them really put the spotlight on our corner of Fort Dodge, Iowa.

THIS IS FUN!
Our office also served in an advocate role in cases of discrimination in real estate and employment matters. I also served as a bus driver for

the privately operated school bus service to and from the high school, as well as an advocate for the families having problems with the schools. Our office also served in an advocate role in matters concerning law enforcement. In one very important case, during a neighborhood town-hall meeting, we discovered that many local residents were often arrested for driving without a valid license. In most cases the underlying reason was illiteracy. They simply didn't know how to read the driver's manual or the test questions. I asked to meet with the Iowa State Highway Patrol officials and shared that information with them. They were surprised that that root cause to the problem hadn't occurred to them. In discussing a possible solution, I suggested the possibility of their own officers holding periodic "ground schools" at the neighborhood center. Remedial driver education classes became a reality and a great success. The turnout and participation was exceptional and the program solved the problem of many locals driving without a valid driver's license. A great side benefit was the opportunity of having the local residents and local law enforcement working and associating with each other "up close and personal". Attitudes changed and were very positive and long lasting!

We offered other classes at the center, such as G.E.D. and classes in home management. Remembering that most of the beef luggers I worked with at Iowa Beef Packers had not completed high school, I made a return visit to the plant and met with several of the luggers I knew and with plant officials to propose establishing a G.E.D. completion program right at the plant. Agreeing that it was a great idea, a classroom was dedicated at the plant and a period during the shift change was set aside for class time. Teachers from Iowa Central Community College offered to do the teaching. The program was a roaring success! Several workers enrolled and earned their high school diplomas. The Neighborhood Service Center was "rockin and rollin" and I was having a great time in this new kind of ministry.

FROM A NEIGHBORHOOD, TO FOUR COUNTIES

But again, with the passing of time comes change. The Community Action Agency overseeing the center program and all other CAA programs in the four-county area wanted me to turn the center operation over to others and begin managing all manpower programs in the four-county area. The change put me in charge of 350 Neighborhood Youth

Corp teen workers during the summer; 150 during the school year and 25 hard core unemployed adults annually on Operation Mainstream. The job sites included public libraries and schools, doing clerical work and working with maintenance crews; working in city and county offices doing clerical and maintenance work and in state and county parks and camp grounds doing the same. My duties included developing those job sites, writing new programs, reporting on programs, and providing employment counseling for all enrollees. I supervised a staff of three during the year, which increased to seven during the summer months, due to the increase in summer job slots. I hired four returning college students to help with the added counseling. As the months and years rolled by, I found this work to be very agreeable and rewarding due to the fact that I could see lives changed and life made better for so many teens and adults.

Cynthia, Jon Mathiason and Sherry

JON...NEEDS A HOME

A very meaningful experience came from my involvement with these young lives. One of my summer counselors revealed to me a personal crisis looming in her life. Her younger brother was being sent home from living with an uncle in Oregon. Their mother and father were both deceased and she would be the only one responsible for his care. This would be nearly impossible since she was a single student at Iowa State University. She did not have the money nor room to care for him. Having discussed it with Betty and the girls, we decided that we would take him into our home. We had cared for many foster kids in the past and living on the acreage gave us the room and a perfect environment in which he could thrive.

So Jon Mathiason, a 13-year old teenager came to live in our home. Jon helped with the chores, enjoyed the animals and the family dog, rode the bus to school with the girls every school day and became involved in church activities, which was something new for Jon. He seemed to fit into the school life and discipline very well. Having arrived in the fall during

184

football season, he decided to try playing football. He found that he was a bit too light for football, so chose not to try out again in future seasons. Later, upon our moving from the Rockwell City school system to the Webster City area schools, Jon felt he wanted to try playing basketball. He enjoyed this much more but still felt he didn't quite "fit"—since he didn't have the moves for basketball. Next, was track.

This was all new to Jon, but he wanted to keep trying to find his niche in sports, so track was next. After a few days of workouts and endurance running, I asked him what he thought he might be doing in track. He said he didn't really know for sure yet, but it looked like the coach may have him running in the mile. Jon was never very talkative, so I had to pull out of him any particulars of what was going on. I asked if the coach had held any time trials, to which he responded only...yes!

I continued to pump him, "Did they time you on the mile yet?"

"Yes", was his only response.

"Well, what was your time Jon?" I asked.

"Oh—five".

"Five what Jon—five minutes, five-three, five-four, five-five—five what Jon?"

"Five flat" he said with no emotion. I couldn't believe that time! My own high school's miler, who had the best time in the conference, ran a five flat mile as his best ever time. "Are you sure Jon—a five-flat mile?"

"Yup, I am sure". And Jon was absolutely right! I attended his very first junior high track meet at Clarion, Iowa. He ran a four minute, forty four second mile the very first time he ran and blew the rest of the field off the track! The coaches couldn't believe it! They wanted a conference with me to discuss his phenomenal ability and the possibility of running him with the high school track team. The coaches admitted that with his exceptional ability at running, they didn't know how to coach him! Besides, he would break every junior high track record so badly they would be unreachable to succeeding milers. We did run Jon, a 7th grader, with the high school track team. Even this had its problems. At the first high school meet, which was a dual meet with St. Edmonds high school of Fort Dodge, he again blew all the other runners off the track—even his Webster City miler teammate, who was the best in their conference. Jon ran a 4:23 mile and broke the school record. Then later, at Humbolt, Iowa, he ran a 4:19 mile and broke still another record and did it not even breathing hard. We knew we had a running genius on our hands!

Unfortunately, Jon had trouble in the track off-season. He began running with some shadier kids at school and cutting classes, joy-riding around the back roads with his cronies, smoking, drinking and doing a few drugs. After being picked up for the third time, and not heeding any warnings from the law, school officials, and from Betty and Me, it was time for him to leave—to be with his sister and her new husband. They were still students but were living in an apartment with the needed room and had access to the university health care and counseling facilities at little or no cost. It broke our hearts to see him go, but it turned out to be the best move. He cleaned up his act and continued his running with Ames High School. He continued to set records, although the competition was stiffer in AAA schools. When we last heard from him, he and his family were living in Fort Madison, Iowa and he was continuing to set mile track records. His best time as a junior in high school was a 4:14 mile. Oklahoma State University offered Jon a full ride scholarship upon graduation. He finished his program at OSU, and our last news of Jon was that he was managing a restaurant in Stillwater, Oklahoma. Our ministry with Jon is proof that ministry can happen even in our own homes and with our families!

Working daily in the environment of this community action agency gave me endless opportunities to meet people from every walk of life—the homeless, the poor, the disadvantaged, the abused, but also the affluent, the educated, the "movers and shakers". Christians have opportunities for ministry everywhere they turn—inside and outside the church. The church is not the church just on Sunday morning when it meets. The church is still the church when its members are at work or at school or being a good neighbor. I often ponder the question, "why is the church not more involved in these kinds of enterprises?" Too often the church excuses itself from social ministries, taking the position that it's the government job to help these people! The church's work is "spiritual".

That is not what Jesus modeled and taught! That is not what the early church practiced. The early Christians, without armies or armament, shook the Roman world and culture precisely because of their generous and compassionate ministry to those around them and to each other. God told Abraham, the great man of faith, He would bless him and he in turn, was to "be a blessing". Abraham was a blessing. So must we be! Only then is faith really faith!

CHAPTER 21

1973-1975

BACK TO CHURCH MINISTRY

By 1973 there were rumors of major changes coming to Community Action programs nation wide, changes that could make it not as effective as it had been. At this same time the Webster City Church of Christ approached me with a request to consider coming on staff as their associate minister, overseeing their Bible school, vacation Bible school, and youth programming. It seemed like the right time and right change to make at that point in our lives—we accepted the call. Because of my years of social work in the community and acquaintance with hundreds of youth and adults, available to me was the opportunity of an expanded outreach for the church. That outreach resulted in increased numbers of youth and adults becoming involved in the church, many of whom found a new walk with Christ as Lord and Savior!

Our summers saw large Vacation Bible School programs with many new adults becoming involved in teaching and crafts. We took a bus load of teens to Indianapolis, Indiana for four days to attend the North American Christian Convention. We took adults and teens on Canadian fishing trips and canoe trips into the Boundary Waters and to still more summer church camp experiences. During the football and basketball seasons we instituted a new "Fifth Quarter" social event held in the church fellowship hall. It was to provide for all teens in the community an alternative social activity after the games, rather than getting in trouble with the law by fighting, drinking and vandalizing. This became a popular event on Friday evenings for teens and parents. Also, very big with the youth program at Webster City and youth programs in all our neighboring sister congregations, was the Summer Church Camping program at Dolliver State Park. By this time I was not only the associate minister at Webster City, but also the dean of our high school weeks of camp—as I had been for several previous years while ministering in northwest Iowa. I remember some exceptional weeks of camp with some exceptional speakers and staff.

CHURCH CAMP AT DOLLIVER STATE PARK

In 1965, one week in particular stands out in my mind. I somehow managed to secure Professor James Strauss of Lincoln Christian College as our speaker. I couldn't believe a man of his caliber would come to our little camp! It was like getting Billy Graham for the week. For our music, I acquired the great combo of Boyd Sibley and Dave Klug, who were students at MBC. I had what I thought was a solid commitment from another person to be our athletic director. All was proceeding smoothly toward the start of camp, when my athletic director called to say he couldn't make it that week. Someone mentioned approaching a college student by the name of Jon Ford from the Webster City area, who would be home from studies at the University of Northern Iowa, at Cedar Falls. He had gone through a few rough times in his young life but was doing well in college. Jon Ford would be an unknown to me, but I trusted the word of those recommending him and got an affirmative from Jon when enlisting his help.

JON FORD

It turned out to be one of the best weeks of church camp I have ever experienced. The music captured the kids, the recreation was superb, and James Strauss mesmerized the one hundred twenty teen campers that week! Several teens made a decision for Christ, but many also committed their lives to Christian service. For me, it was great making new friends with this great staff and seeing so many teen lives changed! In particular, it was great getting to know Jon Ford and professor James Strauss. As the next few years rolled by, we maintained our friendships with them and then with Jon's new wife Vicki as well. Jon had become the school psychologist for the Waterloo-Cedar Falls school system and during a very difficult time for our Cindy, in third grade, volunteered his services to test her for possible learning problems. His conclusion was that she was fine, she had no learning problems, but one particular teacher was a problem. About this same time we were making a move to a different city and a different school system. That move solved Cindy's school problem.

WEBSTER CITY....NOT A GOOD FIT.

Unfortunately, at the Webster City Church of Christ, along with the increase in new youth, came an increase in the dissatisfaction of some board members and elderly. All the new faces and activity and sometimes noise and rowdy behavior, made some of the "comfortable" uncomfortable. I began hearing complaints at board meetings from those who were uncomfortable. As one deacon complained at one meeting— "We didn't hire you to bring all this riff-raff into the church, we hired you to work with our kids!" Since no one spoke up to object or come to my defense, I assumed that most of the board was in agreement. As with too many long-established and comfortable churches, they saw the Great Commission as not applying to them. The Church was their private club to do with as they pleased "Don't bother us with the lost world". I began wishing I were somewhere else! It wasn't long before God gave us an answer to that wish and a graceful exit from this congregation.

CHAPTER 22

THE AMERICAN INDIAN CHRISTIAN MISSION

Early one morning a long distant call came for us from an Ellis Back. We had met Ellis years before, while working at the Angeles Crest Christian Camp. He and his family had been doing missionary work in Tibet and China until the Communists took over. They had to return to the U.S. and continue in some other type of Christian work. He was serving as the head cook for the church camp, where I was employed as a lifeguard, and Betty as a cooks assistant. As we became acquainted, he discovered our desire to serve in ministry and of my ability and experience in construction work. Now, this many years later, he was inquiring to see if we might be ready to accept a call to come to Arizona and begin construction on a new Christian home and school for Native American children. By this time he was directing this mission, which had purchased 160 acres of land near Show Low, Arizona and wanted to put together a team of families who could develop the facilities and program for the mission. This seemed like a providential call to yet another new ministry. I knew we would fit just right in this new work. I knew how to present the Word of God and I also knew how to operate machinery and build buildings. We accepted the call.

It was not an easy decision to make. Some six months before we received this call, we discovered we were pregnant again. It is difficult enough to make a major move clear across the country but even more difficult when you are expecting an addition to your family. With all the packing necessary for making a move, the weightiest part of this move would rest on Betty. But, as usual, she was unflappable and fearless. She was ready to make the move. Another challenge to accepting this call was that the director wanted me to come to Show Low as soon as possible. I would need to leave my family in Iowa for two months while I looked for housing for the family in Show Low and get started removing trees, grading roads, and readying things for the rest of the crew. I would be living and working alone for two months. The plan was for me to load my tools and basic necessities and head for Arizona immediately. I would do this necessary prep work, then return by the due date for the baby's birth. Betty seemed to have no problem with this decision and felt this would be a good time to start packing boxes for the move, and yes—I would need to find a place for us to live.

LONELINESS

One of the hardest moments for me was saying good-by early the morning of my departure. On February 15, 1975, I kissed Betty and the girls and headed for Kansas City, Wichita, Albuquerque, and Show Low. I felt so bad leaving my family, I found myself quietly crying for the first hour or so. Leaving early that morning, I would have a long stretch of miles covered that first day. I stopped to see a church family friend in Wichita and stayed at a motel there that first night. The next day I finished the trip to Show Low, arriving there around 7:30 p.m. I called Mr. Back the director, who lived in Strawberry, Arizona and informed him I had arrived in Show Low and asked what the plan was for housing. He was surprised I had arrived so soon but said he would leave for Show Low immediately and meet me there to locate a house. It was over one hundred miles from Strawberry to Show Low, so I would have some time to eat a meal and look around the town. Ellis arrived about 9:00 pm, and located a realtor he knew there and made a quick deal on a small five room cottage. Within half an hour I was moved in and had a fire going in the fireplace. The next problem was money. I had brought just enough money to get to Arizona, leaving as much as I could with Betty and the girls. Ellis gave me enough money to get by for a few days with more promised later. But money would always seem to be a problem for us at the mission—but not because it was not available. Ellis seemed to continually forget that our families needed money to live on and the crew needed money for materials. Nevertheless, I was there, settled in, and ready to go to work

Ellis left for the evening and then arrived the next morning to show me around Show Low and then the mission grounds. We looked over the areas of proposed roads and building sites and checked out what machinery and tools were available (not many). The '54 GMC pickup and '55 Chevy dump truck were running well, but the Dozer/Backhoe was not. The main bearing on the large bull gear shaft which turned the track sprocket was shot and had to be replaced. So, my first job was doing mechanic work on something I had never worked on before. I had to take the track apart and remove the sprocket and bull gear to replace the bearing. But, with a little advice from a new mechanic friend and the borrowing of some special tools, she was running again. My next task was removing trees where the roads and building sites would be laid out.

One of the things I hadn't counted on was the loneliness of working all day alone out on the land and then being alone at the cabin evenings and nights. There was no TV or books, only a little portable radio to listen to. As the first days rolled by, I noticed at times I was beginning to imagine hearing Betty's voice. I would be working away cutting down trees and cutting brush and would suddenly turn, expecting to see her standing there. She was not there, of course. As the first Sundays approached, I longed to find a church! I needed fellowship, I needed to talk to someone—another human being, I needed to see another face! Our particular church denomination was not yet represented in the Show Low area, so I decided to attend a Community Church there. What a joy to see and hear people and singing—singing some of the dear old hymns I was used to! It was a moving moment for me! It was a joy to hear the Word being preached! I didn't want to leave after the service was over,. I wanted to talk to everybody.

Another thing that fed that loneliness was not being able to phone Betty and the girls but once a week. She didn't have the luxury of money for long distant calls and neither did I. Besides, I had no phone. The best we could do was set one regular evening of the week, and time, where I would stand outside the phone booth in front of the Red Rooster

Restaurant in Show Low, AZ, and wait for her to call...and that, only for a short visit. Because of the long distance costs, it had to be short. But I longed for that evening and that phone call no matter how short. I was comforted in knowing that she and the girls were fine and the pregnancy was going well. They were busying themselves with packing our things for the move after the baby was born.

UNEXPECTED BLESSINGS

Several encouraging things began to happen during these two "prep" months in Arizona. With no announcements that they were planning to do so, Mom and Dad decided to make a trip from California to Show Low to see me. They suddenly just "showed up" one day! I was totally and pleasantly surprised! We had a great visit,! Mom fattened me up a bit, since I was never much of a cook and lived mostly on cereal for breakfast and soup and sandwiches for the other meals. I, of course, gave them the grand tour of the area, including Show Low, Pinetop, Snowflake and the Indian Mission grounds. They stayed for the week and for me, this was a God send! These guardian angels couldn't have come at a better time. Mother confessed that knowing me so well through the years, she was concerned with my working and being alone for two months—that I might be needing company and that "mothers touch". They enjoyed the visit as of course I certainly did and they were thrilled that Betty and I would be involved in the establishing of this mission. They were also thrilled that we would be much closer to California—one day's drive instead of three. In later months they made other visits to us, on one occasion bringing two of my nieces with them On another visit Dad helped remove the forms from the new bridge, which was our largest and most ambitious construction project. More about that later.

Another encouragement that came to me during those two months was a surprise phone call from an acquaintance in the Webster City church back in Iowa. Dennis Short was on the line telling me he had some vacation time coming and was wondering if he and a friend could come out and help as volunteers with the mission work. When I asked him what sort of work he did, he responded by telling me he worked for the State of Iowa, Department Of Transportation, in highway and bridge construction. I couldn't believe my ears! This had to be still another God thing! My work had progressed to the place where I was wanting to get the footprint of the buildings and, most important, the bridge, staked out. Although I had worked out in my mind what needed to be done and how I would do it, I did not have all the tools nor the help necessary to get this job done. I wanted to have this preliminary work done before the rest of the crew and their families arrived, allowing us to immediately launch into construction. What a God-send this offer was! I obviously invited them to join me for whatever number of days they could spend. Two days later they arrived with a surveyor's transit and tools, AND a large detailed blueprint copy of a standard steel-reinforced, concrete, double-box-culvert—used in Iowa as bridges on state highways—perfect for what we needed! We had a great time of fellowship, spending those few days working with the transit and driving stakes. We set the lines and elevations for the first buildings, as well as for the roadway from the main highway. And, we staked out the elevations and lines of where the bridge was to be built. God certainly provided the right people at the right time! His timing was perfect!

Finally, with much of my preliminary work finished, I was ready for the crew to arrive. Even more important, I had a small, five room cottage ready for the family to live in and I was more than ready to head back to Iowa to get them. I dearly missed Betty and the girls and I was on pins and needles wondering if I would make it home in time for our third daughter to be born. In communications with my folks in California as to when I would be driving back to Iowa, my dad and sister volunteered to meet me in Show Low to help with the drive back to Iowa and then, with the move of my family and furniture to Arizona. Another God-send! As soon as they arrived from California, we left for Iowa. I was so excited about seeing my family, I think I could have driven day and night, non-stop. Actually, we did drive non-stop except for meals and refueling, with Dad and I taking turns napping and driving. We arrived in Webster City at our home, sometime between 3:00 and 4:00 a.m. and, most important, a few days before Shannon Carol was born.

MOVING AGAIN—NOW, A FAMILY OF FIVE

After a few hours rest, we started the next day taking care of the remaining packing, renting a U-haul truck and loading it. But the big event was experiencing the birth of our third daughter, Shannon Carol, at the Lutheran Hospital in Fort Dodge, Iowa! This time I got to experience actually being in the delivery room by Betty's side for the birth. What an incredible experience! After a few days recovery at the hospital and then at home amidst all the boxes of stuff, we readied ourselves to bid good-bye to friends and neighbors and make our way to Show Low, Arizona.

Leaving early in the morning, we made our way south and southwest through Wichita, Kansas, where we moteled it for the night. Early the next morning, our little caravan with me in the U-haul truck in the lead, hurried off to finish the trip to Show Low. As we traveled on southwest, we were met by a change in the weather with very strong head winds. As we bucked the high winds of western Kansas, I discovered the U-haul truck would not make over twenty five to thirty miles per hour. I had an idea! Drafting! Race car drivers and bikers do it all the time! So I put Betty and the girls in the lead in our low slung '65 Chevy hard-top; I had Dad and Peggy in my loaded (and taller) Chevy pick-up following them as close as possible—one car length or less; with me in the U-haul truck tucked up as close as possible behind Dad. Amazingly, we were able to pick up another twenty five to thirty mph. We were able to draft together at a steady fifty-five to sixty mph. It was surprisingly easy to travel this way because of nearly zero traffic, flat, smooth and straight highways, no trees and very few towns or cities to go through. Had I not thought of doing that, it would have taken forever and an enormous amount of fuel to finish the trip. The further west we traveled into New Mexico and Arizona, the winds died down and travel was back to normal.

I must note here, the best traveler of the whole group was two week old baby Shannon. We had purchased a case of bottled formula—which kept her satisfied, healthy, and sleeping the whole trip.

After arriving in Show Low, and getting things unloaded and in their places, we settled into the daily routine of the new community and neighborhood. My work continued on at the mission with yet another task, that of helping the new mission families move from where they were living to the Show Low community. The first ones we helped move were Bob and Vicky Adams and their two boys from the Montrose, Colorado area. This was a trip I looked forward to due to the fact that our dear Bible college friends, Robert and Arlene Eckman lived in Montrose and we always looked forward to visiting them. I made the trip to Montrose and after a visit with the Eckmans, we loaded all the Adam's household goods into our two pick-ups and made our way back to Show Low. Bob brought his mechanical skills to the mission, as well as carpentry and general labor. He also had some Bible college education and he and Vicky had been involved in ministry.

Later, we helped Andy and Kathy Cawalti and family move to the mission from Ventura, California, where they were involved with a congregation there. Andy also brought mechanical skills to the Mission, plus two extra hands to help with the digging and building. Harlan and Marj Kincade and family of four children came from a ministry in Jamestown, Indiana. With lots of hands to help from their congregation there and a rental truck, they were able to make the trip to Show Low without our assistance. Our crew, on the Show Low end of the move, helped with the manpower and women power for unloading and carrying boxes and furniture. Harlan was also a brick mason, as well as an ordained minister.

We made quite a formidable crew. We could not only build a mission, we could also form the core of a new congregation, which we did in quick order. We began holding services on the mission grounds in an open-sided "brush arbor" shelter. In good weather this was a great place to hold services, but with the barbed wire gates to pass through and often bad weather during the winter months, we needed a more convenient, enclosed building in which to meet. We began meeting in our homes, then in a rented Seventh Day Adventist building in Show Low. The outcome of this growth was the development of a new congregation. That congregation now owns property and a new church building in the Pinetop area. They now have their own full time minister and are self supporting. The Pinetop church holds regular services and is involved in ministry in the Show Low, Pinetop area, as of this writing.

BUILDING BUILDINGS...BUILDING A BRIDGE

With a full crew, the work at the Mission moved full speed ahead. With the grade stakes in place for several of the buildings and the bridge, we were able to proceed immediately with digging and pouring footings and floors. Our first "pour" was the well house and shop. The well had been drilled and the 1,500 gallon pressure tank was in place. What was still needed was a building to cover these components, along with an access pit under the tank for water lines coming from the various buildings yet to be built. This building would also house a shop, with an arc welder, cutting torch, vise, and many wrenches and hand tools. Another smaller building was needed to serve as a electric power sub-station where underground lines could be dispersed from a central power panel. It would also house electrical tools and supplies. But these first two smaller buildings would be just the beginning. Later, there would be a dining hall/kitchen, boy's and girl's dormitories, a large chapel and—a major project, the bridge!

OUR OWN READYMIX PLANT

As we began planning for all this concrete to be poured, we realized it would be next to impossible to get commercial ready-mix trucks onto the property. There was no adequate road and no bridge from the main highway. We had gained approved access through two neighbor's private driveways and properties by taking down their "barbed-wire gates" and crossing their cattle guards. This worked acceptably for smaller cars and trucks but not for large and heavily loaded ready-mix trucks that would crush the cattle guards. Since we wanted good relations with our neighboring ranchers, we decided to build our own ready-mix plant, using our own trucks and equipment. This would eliminate most of the heavy truck traffic through the neighbor's property, cattle guards and gates. The Mission already had a small two and one half ton Chevy dump truck, adequate for hauling sand and gravel, bag cement and steel re-bar from suppliers in Phoenix and nearby Snowflake and Clay Springs. The Mission's combination dozer-backhoe-front end loader had served a multitude of uses and would now be a key factor in our ready-mix plant. We measured and calibrated the loader bucket for proportioning the sand-gravel-cement ratios. What we still needed was a small transit-mix truck. God always provides!

OUR OWN READYMIX TRUCK

One day I was in downtown Show Low at a tire dealership. Out back of the shop my eye caught a glimpse of something very interesting. Rusting away in the weeds was a smaller three to four yard transit mix unit on a 1947 Ford cab-over truck chassis. Immediately, I dropped what I was doing at the tire shop and began asking questions about that mixer truck.

"Would it run?" I asked the guys in the shop.

"Yes" came their answer!

"Would the tires hold air?" I asked.

"Yes, we guaranteed it", was their reply!

"Could I buy it?" I asked.

"You bet. We want to get rid of it", they replied.

"How much?"

"How-about $200." they responded!"

"You've got a deal!", I said. I paid the money; they aired up the tires (all six tires faithfully held air for the next two years). I "borrowed" the six-volt battery from the Mission pick-up, got a gallon of gasoline and went to work with a hot wire to the starter and ignition (they had no idea where the key was). I removed the air cleaner from the old Stromberg carburetor, poured a little gasoline down its throat and hit the starter button. *Varooooom!* Dirt and spiders and cobwebs were flying everywhere! It totally startled me! I had figured it would take a miracle for the old girl to start after sitting idle for twelve to fifteen years. I was wrong! I had not been thinking—I had witnessed many miracles like this! There she sat—running as smooth as a sewing machine! Just like the old flathead V-8 in my '41 and '46 Ford hot rods. My experience as a shade tree mechanic served me well. I poured a couple of more gallons of gas in the tank and actually drove her to the mission compound some ten miles away. We had our own ready-mix truck! In the two years of steady use that followed, she never once failed to do her job.

EQUIPMENT FROM HEAVEN

Before we could begin mixing concrete we needed a few more pieces of equipment. We needed a hopper with a bottom gate to hold the dry mix, under which we could back the mixer truck and load it with the ingredients and water. I found this item on my very next trip to the gravel quarry at Snowflake, Arizona where we had been buying our sand and gravel. While at the quarry I spotted a four legged steel hopper with a bottom dump gate out in their "storage" (junk) yard and a set of six detachable mixer chutes that would fit on the back of our transit mixer! Upon asking about these items, I was told to "help myself"! They wanted to get rid of it all. "Haul it out of here!", they said. So I did—promptly! For free!

We discovered on the mission property itself, in a secluded wooded patch of Juniper trees, a junk yard of our own, consisting of several old

Chevy Novas, a large abandoned one hundred gallon commercial water heater, pieces of steel and steel pipe and other odds and ends. We built a wooden stand upon which we set the water heater. It became the water tower, supplying water for the ready-mix plant. Out of those six old Novas (all with identical engines) we found enough good parts for one good engine; one good block and crankshaft, one good head, and six good pistons and rods. Betty's brother, Chuck Smith, who owned his own auto repair shop in Longview, Texas, sent us an overhaul kit which Bob and Andy promptly installed in the engine. We welded our fresh engine in place to turn the mixer drum. We were in business! We had the ability to mix and deliver all the concrete we needed for any job, right there on the mission grounds. And it all cost us little more than the $200 we spent for the mixer truck! What a miracle! Over the next two years the old mixer truck allowed us to mix, deliver and pour hundreds of yards of concrete for all kinds of projects, the largest being the Bridge! As a good neighbor gesture, we also used it to pour the concrete for one of our rancher neighbor's new backyard swimming pool. He provided the materials and labor and we provided the mixer truck and a few good hands to help. It was the Mission's return favor for allowing us to cross his property and cattle gates.

THE BRIDGE

During those first two years we were able to build, in addition to the well house/shop and the power substation, a large dining hall/ kitchen— and the bridge! The bridge was the largest of the projects, taking the longest to complete. The bridge had to be poured in several stages. First, there was all the extensive foundation work to support all the walls, wing-walls and lower and upper floors. We attached all those footings to solid rock, eight feet below the dry stream bed. We then formed and poured the lower floor at stream-bed level. Next, we formed, installed the re-bar grid and poured the eight foot tall by seventy foot long outer walls and wing walls. We built forms from 4 x 8 standard plywood and 2 x 4 studs. Building and setting the forms in place with necessary snap ties and steel grid was a major building project in itself. After pouring the concrete for first one wall and then the other, we allowed the concrete to sufficiently cure. We then back-filled the roadway dirt against them and carefully packed the fill up to the level of the top of both walls. Doing this, allowed us to back the mixer truck up to the outer walls on either side and with our mixer chutes, reach the forms for the center wall pour eight feet away.

Of course, all of these sections of walls, wing walls and floors had to be reinforced with one inch re-bar, which had to be bent and wired in place in twelve inch grids, as per design and blueprints. We bent all the re-bar by using an old blacksmiths forge with a hand cranked blower. We laid all the re-bar across the forge with several saw-horses for support. We marked the bars with a soap stone where we had to make bends. We bought several sacks of coal and began cranking. After a few minutes in the hot glowing coals, we could make any bend we needed. We then wire-tied the re-bar grid together.

The final pour, the upper floor/driving surface of the bridge, was the largest and most difficult pour to make. All forms had to be braced extensively to carry the load of concrete, which was twelve inches thick, by eighteen feet wide, by fifty feet long, with twelve inch by twelve inch curbs added on top on both sides. All floor forms were supported by four inch by six inch by sixteen foot long temporary timber joists, supported in turn by temporary four inch by six inch timber pillars spaced four feet apart. With all forms and supports in place, the double eight foot by eight foot culvert "forms" looked like twin mine tunnels. With the help of a group of teens from California and beginning early in the morning, we poured the entire top floor of the bridge including the curbs, with one continuous pour of over one hundred cubic yards of concrete. The teen crew helped "vibrate", and work the wet concrete into the forms and around all the re-bar by donning boots and walking back and forth through the wet concrete. Finally, THE BRIDGE WAS FINISHED! We were one tired crew, but so excited that it had all gone so well—and was finished! Later, after the concrete had cured sufficiently, we removed the forms. We were doubly delighted! There were no voids, no cavities, no cracks and has stood as solid as the Rock of Gibraltar! Inspecting the bridge after many years of use (as late as the Spring of 2008) and raging torrents, I found it as strong as when we first built it! I must say— "GOOD JOB!"

ON THE RESERVATIONS

The four families, along with some young interns who came for short mission terms, were also involved in face-to-face, contact and ministry with the Native American families on the Navajo and Hopi reservations. Through contacts made at the villages of Dilkon, Old Aribi, Hotavilla, and Second Mesa with tribal leaders, we were given permission to hold weekly Bible school programs in those communities. On Bible school days we would drive to the locations, drive through the sand and sage brush, perhaps down a dry wash and into the midst of a clump of Hogans. We would shut off the engine, take a nap and in twenty to thirty minutes awaken to the sound of children playing outside, waiting for Bible School to begin. The mission men would each take turns going with the family teams of our wives and children. Betty and I were also involved in speaking engagements at summer camps in Arizona and Colorado and in churches in Phoenix, Tucson, Prescott and Globe, Arizona, presenting the work of the mission.

But, our construction work at the mission was not done by any means! All the masonry walls had to be laid up on all the slabs we had poured for the first three buildings. So, we then became mortar mixers, hod and block carriers and block layers. Harlan did most of the block laying with Bob assisting under his supervision. Andy and I did much of the "grunt" work since we were not block layers. Once the mortar was dry on each building we began building our own trusses and proceeded to sheath and shingle them in. Materials for all the trusses and sheathing etc. was supplied by Bill Parker Lumber Mill in Clay Springs, Arizona.

DIFFICULTIES AT THE MISSION
This phase of the building project and our good business dealings with Bill Parker and Parker Lumber, introduced a new chapter in the story of A.I.C.M. For some reason yet unknown to the crew and their families, the moneys for materials and living expenses, made available to us by Ellis Back the director, had dried up or had become spasmodic and insufficient. Our families needed money for food and necessities. The crew needed money for materials, lumber, nails, shingles, and roofing paper, etc. Our four families kept food on the table by sharing with each other. Mr. Parker, aware of our dilemma, came to the crew with an offer. If we would all come to his mill and spend about a week working with his crew building a roof over his saw rig, engine, and operators station, he would pay us with all the lumber we would need to close in the mission

buildings we had started. We accepted! I never did take the time to figure out what the dollar value would be, but with the loads of lumber he sent our way it seemed like he far exceeded his part of the deal with the mission! We easily built his roof system in one week and enjoyed great fellowship with his crew while doing it. He provided all the materials needed for the mission roofs and then some. We were able to complete all the buildings we had started. We were not about to sit around and twiddle our thumbs and wait for something to happen. We were men and women of faith and ability and ingenuity and we, with God's help, could make things happen! We believed that if God could feed the five thousand on five loaves and two fish, He would provide whatever we needed at the Mission. It was our responsibility to believe and act!

HOW TO DESTROY A GOOD CREW

But we were all in for a big surprise! Having been gone for several months, when the director finally arrived back at the mission, he quickly voiced his disappointment and disapproval with the progress we had made. "What right did we have to proceed without his approval and spend a week working at Parker Lumber?" And "Why did you build the buildings with such a simple architectural look?" His dream and plan was to use a "Georgian" architectural look with a brick veneer! But he had left me with no blueprints or plans. He had no explanation why he had sent no funds for the families or materials. The funds were there, he just didn't see to it that they were available for our use. The families had already become discouraged by his thoughtlessness and mismanagement. Now, with this negative reaction and verbal disapproval, they were deeply discouraged. So was I!

The result was the gradual loss of the crew. Andy and Kathy Cawalti and family were the first to resign and returned to Ventura, California. Harlan and Marge Kincade were next to resign, with Harlan not only taken back by Ellis's negative reactions to the work that we had done, but was also having suspicions that Ellis was keeping two sets of books. When Ellis had asked him to help with some of the accounting, he had observed some things that didn't seem quite right. Finally, there remained Bob and Vicky Adams and our family. Although Bob was serving as minister to our new congregation, he and Vicky were discouraged with the recent events at the mission and decided to move to Oregon and work with a congregation there. Betty and I and family were still with the mission, but after a face-to-face visit with Ellis, where he accused me of insubordination and changing everything, my response was to verbally resign—upon which his response was to say, "Well, I guess you should!" I later tendered a written letter of resignation but neither it nor any of the other family's resignations ever reached the AICM board of directors. It was a year later, while I was working at Parker Lumber, that the directors came to me after locating me at the saw mill, and with extreme shock, discovered neither I nor the rest of the crew had been working at the mission for the past year. Somehow, after all those months had passed, that information had not been passed on to them. I assumed everyone, the board members and supporting churches, all knew what had happened. Had I known otherwise, I would have told them myself.

PARKER LUMBER COMPANY

My involvement with Bill Parker and Parker Lumber came as a God send! The very next day after I resigned from the Mission, I drove out to Clay Springs to confer with Bill about the mission's dealings with his company. I wanted to make sure all our agreements had been met in full and there was nothing outstanding. He assured me everything was fair and square. And then another providential gift dropped right in my lap. Knowing of my resigning from the mission, he commented that "he wondered why it took me so long to leave, knowing what we were all struggling with?" And then he said, "I need you here at the mill— go to work for me—today! I've needed someone like you to supervise the guys on the green chain, wait on customers, load trucks, fall timber and drive the log truck. I know you can do all those things. I'll pay you well, buy your gas, give you a company pick-up to drive and you can help yourself to what lumber you need—OK?" I was flabbergasted! "YES!" And I did! I couldn't ask for a better man to work for or a better crew to work with—doing all the things a young man like me always dreams of doing—logging, lumbering—mountain peaks and meadows, wild life and forests—and driving a log truck!

So, I went to work the very next day for Bill Parker at Parker Lumber in Clay Springs, Arizona. Having grown up in the lumber business with my dad, it was a natural for me and fun in every way. I can honestly say that I do not remember one morning that I dreaded going to work. Every day was an adventure. Some of the work was dangerous, but I always worked with caution and Bill never pushed the crew to do things that were not safe. My jobs at the mill went in stages. After a big timber buy, the whole crew became "loggers". We all headed into the tall timber with chainsaws and would spend four to eight weeks falling trees that had been marked by the forestry dept. These prime mature Ponderosas were huge! Sometimes I felt like I was cutting down Redwoods. I also learned an amazing thing about the way the forestry deptartment managed these forests. The crew would fall and haul out millions of board-feet of logs and yet, if you could view the area of the cut from an elevated vantage point, you couldn't tell one tree had been taken. The Apache-Sitgreaves National Forest, where we did most of our logging, was one of the healthiest I have ever seen. The selective cutting allowed for enormous new growth! Crews would be hired to actually thin out some of the new growth. The new "dog hair" pine thickets would grow so thick you couldn't walk through them.

While some of the crew skidded and bucked up the logs into twelve, fourteen and sixteen foot lengths, my job was to crank up the log truck and haul them to the mill. There were days when this was a real adrenaline rush! Some logging areas were so far back into the forest it would take all day just to get one load. The logging roads were more like dirt roller-coaster rides. I was amazed the truck held together. This was a one-man operation with a truck-mounted log loader and trailer. I would load the trailer first, then position the truck/tractor next to the log deck and load it as full as I could possibly get it. I would then swing the boom on top of the load, chain it down, then hook up to the loaded trailer and make my way back to the mill. Some hauls were as short as ten to fifteen miles, others could be as long as one hundred twenty miles one way, from the forest to the mill.

ADRENALINE RUSH!

There was never a dull moment in the logging industry. One day while coming down a very steep, dirt switchback logging road, the air brake's warning buzzer came on...I was losing air faster than the compressor could keep up. I mashed my foot on the air brake pedal and held it mashed. I didn't have enough air pressure to completely stop the truck, but slowed it up enough with the gears and what air I had left, to safely negotiate the curves in the twisting, turning road. Finally the road leveled off enough that the air I had left would stop the truck! Upon inspecting the airlines on the truck and trailer, I discovered that a tree limb had flipped its way up into the airlines between the truck and trailer and tore an air line loose. The trailer had no brakes and the broken airline was draining my air reserves on the truck. Since the worst part of the road was behind me, I simply shut off the air line valve to the trailer, let the compressor build the pressure back, and "eased" the load back to the mill on the truck brakes and lower gears in the transmissions.

SLIDING THROUGH THE MUD

On yet another occasion, after loading and making the return trip from the Mogollon Rim area of Heber Canyon, I got caught in a monsoon downpour while coming down the steepest section of switchbacks with one-hundred-foot-plus cliffs at every turn. The downpour turned the road into slime and I felt the truck picking up speed. The tack wasn't registering increased engine speed, but when I looked in the rear view mirrors, I could see the tandem drivers pushing walls of mud like a dozer blade. The loaded truck and trailer were "sliding" down the mountain like a runaway sled! To my right was a bottomless canyon, to my left was a steep cliff rising straight up, with a shallow drainage ditch at the bottom, running along the edge of the road. I quickly decided my last and best chance of surviving this ride would be to let the truck and trailer slide off the road into the ditch on the left and let the load simply lay up against the side of the cliff. Good decision! The rig gently "schmooshed" its way to a stop in the ditch, in the mud, with the load leaning gently against the muddy cliff. That brief ride was so gentle that I didn't even break my left side rear view mirror. I waited for the rain-storm to pass and walked the logging road to the main highway. Two forestry guys in a jeep picked me up on the way to the highway and phoned the mill to let Bill know what had happened and to send a ride out for me. All's well that ends well! By the next day, the logging road had firmed-up and a log skidder was sent out to pull the rig back up on the road. I finished the trip and returned for more loads.

HIGH VOLTAGE—ANOTHER BRUSH WITH DEATH

On another assignment my job was to haul cut logs from a new power line right-of-way. A new power plant had been built near Joseph City, Arizona and enormous new electric high-lines had been "strung" through the Heber Canyon area from Joseph City to Tucson. The logging company that had cut all the forest right-of-way had not finished hauling the thousands of logs out of the area and had forfeited it's performance bond. The Forestry Department turned this "windfall" job over to Parker Lumber. One day Bill gave me the go-ahead to start hauling logs in from this area, which was a long way out. I got to the logged area about lunchtime and "providentially" decided to eat my lunch first. I found this area to be an amazingly remote area with lots of awesome wildlife! While eating lunch, I caught a flash out of the corner of my eye and as I turned to look, there, just beyond the pile of logs, was a mountain lion! At about the same time I saw him, he saw me! He was gone in a flash and a cloud of dust. What a breath-taking moment!

Shortly after me and the mountain lion exchanged glances, I noticed a cloud of dust in the distance, back on the logging road I had just been on. As I watched, I could see the dust cloud was coming my way and coming fast! Then, out of this cloud of dust came a power company pickup. As it pulled up to where I was parked, a power company official jumped out and immediately wanted to know if I had been loading any logs from this site. I answered "No, not yet, but I would be—that I had decided to eat my lunch first".

"Great!" he responded. "That may have just saved your life!" He then informed me that the power company was testing the new lines periodically and anyone sitting on a machine with a high profile—like the boom of a log loader—would be in eminent danger of being hit by an enormous jolt of electricity from the induction off the high lines just overhead. I asked if the lines were charged at that moment. He said they were not, but someone could "hit the switch" at any moment. I asked if he could radio the plant and find out if they were planning to do so right then, and during the afternoon. Just as he grabbed the microphone to his CB, someone hit the switch at the plant and the air literally crackled and snapped with the enormous voltage hitting the lines. He immediately jumped down off the running board of his pick-up and warned me to not touch the truck or anything metal. I asked him what in the world was going on?! He explained to me that the particular location where I was, was a high spot, where the highlines swept closest to the ground and the danger of induction, the greatest. Although the dozen or so high lines overhead, each fatter than the thickness of a pop can, were over 200 feet or more above us, the danger of induction was extremely high. He informed me that the induction from high lines once followed down the rising smoke from a burning brush fire below and killed some fire fighters on the ground. He suggested I move to another location on down the road at a lower spot and warned me not to touch the truck while standing on the ground. I should jump on the running board or truck ladder and then into the cab or loader. I was to avoid being "grounded" at anytime while in close proximity to the lines. He cautioned against even touching the truck's radio antenna and informed me that had I been sitting on the seat of the loader, loading logs, I could have been fried to a crisp! Well that made my day! So, as I said, eating my lunch FIRST on that day was providential! I did set up at another, less dangerous spot, hauled in a load of logs and then, each day, before leaving the mill, phoned the power plant for clearance to each location along the power line right-of-way. Another lesson learned. Was my job exciting (hair-raising) or what?

A SIXTEEN FOOT JAVELIN

Other interesting things happened at the mill. One of Bill's timber buys was a forest "burn" on Porter Mountain. A forest fire had gone through the hundreds of acres around Porter Mountain and the charred timber could be bought, logged, and milled into excellent lumber. Through previous experience Bill discovered that trees that had been through a fire would yield the greatest number of board feet of top grade millwork. But, one of the stipulations of a "burn buy" was that he would have to take everything, the large choice trees, as well as the long, tall "tooth-picks" six inches, eight inches and ten inches thick. Skidding, loading and hauling all this blackened timber was not only a pain in the neck, it was like working in a coal mine. By the end of the day we were all black as coal miners from all the charred bark. Under this charred bark the wood was perfect and made great lumber, but handling it was a pain. The bigger logs yielded lots of great lumber, but the small stuff was a headache. Bill usually sawed the small stuff up into three inch by four inch by four foot boards for semi-truck dunnage.

While Bill was hurriedly sawing up some smaller logs into dunnage, a sixteen foot by eight inch wide log had come loose from the hold down "dogs" that locked it to the carriage. As Bill was returning the carriage with the "loose" log past the spinning six foot saw blade, and not realizing it had come loose, the blade began undercutting the log, lifting it completely off the carriage, hurling it like a javelin right through the gable end of the new mill roof and over the office one hundred fifty feet away! It buried itself in the ground just beyond the office like a spear in a western movie. The sudden load hitting the full torque of the mill engine stalled it out and shut everything down. Bill was so startled and disgusted with what had happened, he simply walked to the remotest point in the yard and just stared at the horizon until he cooled down and got his wits about him. No one in the yard or around the saw rig nor in the office was injured. After a brief, collective sigh of relief and check of the saw rig, we restarted the old 6-71 Detroit and continued sawing lumber.

SAW BLADE ON THE RUN

More adrenaline! What was a normal quiet lunch hour, ended with what could have been an enormous disaster. One of my many jobs was to keep the big six foot saw blades sharp. I would touch up all the teeth with a portable grinder and replace any teeth that were too bad to sharpen. We would start the day with a fresh blade and then after the lunch break, replace that blade with another fresh blade. In the process of doing that very thing, two of the crew assigned to this task had just lowered the fresh blade down into the sawdust pit and slid it on the big two inch arbor. They were tightening the big nut that holds the blade caps and blade tight on the arbor shaft, when the person tightening down the nut was momentarily interrupted by someone needing some other tool he had with him. After passing that tool to the other person, he failed to finish tightening the arbor nut with the large socket wrench. Assuming he had completed his mission, he crawled out of the sawdust pit leaving the wrench and socket on the end of the arbor. Thinking things were all ready to go, Bill fired up the Detroit and engaged the saw arbor and blade. No one noticed the big socket wrench whirling around on the end of the arbor shaft and everything seemed normal until they began to run the first log through the saw. The handle of the socket wench slammed to a sudden halt on the end of the log and immediately torqued off the big nut on the end of the shaft and allowed the six foot spinning saw blade to drop off into the sawdust pit. As the unleashed blade whirled away in the concrete sawdust pit, it was throwing sparks and teeth, and cutting up lines and cables and terrorizing the whole crew! No one knew where the spinning blade was headed next. Bill and the saw rig crew scattered like rats to find cover behind the nearest pile of lumber! The giant blade finally ground to a halt, and the crew all came out of their hiding places. That was the end of making lumber for that day—and for the next few days. It would take a while to repair all the control cables and re-machine the saw arbor and "re-tooth" the blade. But again, there was another miracle with this incident—no one got hurt—not even scratched—just a few red faces and a frustrated boss! God was truly with us that day!

RED SAWDUST

Of a much calmer nature, was an unusual timber buy for Parker Lumber. It was a stand of inland fir located in a ponderosa pine forest between Payson and Winslow, a long haul from the sawmill. The buy was entirely inland fir. Bill bought it with a particular customer in mind. The customer was building a large mountain lodge, utilizing a large number of timber trusses and open beams and wanted all fir lumber. The crew logged it and skidded it and I hauled the logs to the mill. The interesting part of this job was getting used to working with fir lumber. Everything that went through our mill was white ponderosa pine and all around the mill were piles of white pine sawdust. As long as I had worked there, white sawdust rolled out of the sawdust pit. There was a mountain of white sawdust at the end of the conveyer chain and in piles all around the yard. Now, suddenly there was red sawdust coming out of the dust pit and cascading down the white piles of pine sawdust. Everyone at the mill stopped to look at this unusual sight—it looked like the big sawdust pile was bleeding. During the next few weeks all the sawdust piles turned red as we milled all the fir logs for this large order. Finally, we were finished with the sawing. Two or three flat bed semis arrived and we loaded all the fir timber beams and lumber on those trucks and then again, as they returned for more. Soon, the fir was all gone. Back to ponderosa pine.

BACK TO THE MIDWEST

During the three years we lived in Show Low, we became very comfortable with the community. Sherry and Cindy were involved in the Show Low schools. Sherry had been chosen to be on the cheerleading squad. With better income, we were able to afford to buy our own, newer house in a relatively new neighborhood near the high school. We enjoyed our new neighbors on all sides. The girls made lots of friends. The church was doing fine. We were settling in with the Show Low community. Then, as was so often the case through the years, either the telephone or the mail box would bring major changes in our life.

One day we found a letter in our mail box from a Glen and Sharon Moreland in Rochester, Minnesota. It was in a light blue envelope like one you would send a greeting card in or—an invitation! It was an invitation alright—an invitation to consider coming to Minnesota and minister to their congregation, the Marion Church of Christ. My first thoughts were, how did they find me clear out here in Show Low, Arizona, working in the lumber/logging industry? My next inclination was to pitch it in the trash. I hadn't been in the pulpit for ten years. I had been involved with some church work and some teaching, but not full-time pastoral ministry. This was a very scary proposition for me at this time and place in my life and for our family. Could I do it again? Should I upset their lives with another move clear across the country?

But as was always the case, the call of God was always very loud in the ears of my heart! I simply could not dismiss this invitation, this "call". I called the Moreland's to get the particulars and what they were planning as the next step. They and the congregation wanted to meet us—they would pay for our travel to Marion. My next major hurdle was to decide what to do about my position and my work at Parker Lumber. How would I break the news to Bill Parker? What would be his reaction to what I was considering doing?

It didn't take long to find out. The very next day after the call to the Morelands, I asked for a meeting with him in his office. I told him about the call to go back to church ministry and the very strong pull it was having on me to accept that call. I told him that I loved the lumber and logging industry and enjoyed working for him very much; that he had treated me very well—one of the best men I had ever worked for. It was a very difficult decision for me to consider. Bill took it very well. Some bosses would have fired me right on the spot. But Bill made the decision even harder. To my surprise, he began offering me generous incentives to stay with mill. His first offer at that very moment was a generous raise in pay plus a company pickup and all the gasoline for it. Each Friday evening after the mill was shut down, he wanted to talk with me more on that subject. It was to make new and bigger offers.

Next, reminding me of his first offer, he wanted to add to that—a partnership in Parker Lumber! Wow! Agony! It was so tempting! The next discussion a few days later, was to tell me that he knew I was one of the leaders of a growing church right there in Show Low which was considering buying property and building a new building. He was prepared to offer "all of the above" plus, all the lumber the congregation would need to build a new church building! I was torn! Talk about sleepless nights! A few days later the offer was "all of the above" plus, he would attend services with his family and consider becoming a member—in spite of the fact that he was Mormon. This was so extreme it was hardly believable! First, it was hard for me to understand that I was so valuable to anyone's business. This was very flattering! But it also occurred to me, that for a man to commit himself spiritually to a church on the basis of a business deal was not good, however well-meaning the person. The motivation for such a commitment must be because of Jesus Christ and not a business deal.

I was about to get another surprise. His last offer was for me to take a vacation of three or four weeks, go back to Minnesota and "meet with these people and get it out of my system". I did take him up on that offer. We packed our bags and made the trip back, meeting with the Marion congregation and also seeing some new scenery along the way. It was a great trip all the way and in every way. We saw some beautiful sights and some friends and had a wonderful meeting with the church and church board. We were impressed!

The first church members we met were Glen and Sharon Moreland and their children. We were to stay at their home during our visit, so we made that our primary destination. As we pulled up to their house, they met us coming down their driveway with greetings and a big welcome. Immediately we were greeted with new "nick names". I was greeted as Beuford, as in "Beuford Pusser", from the main character roll in the movie *Walking Tall*.

Beuford Pusser was the "town tamer sheriff" who hammered all the bad guys into line with an oak stick or baseball bat. I didn't exactly see that as my main role with this congregation, but they later confessed that as they saw us walking up the drive, Beuford was the first name that came to mind. Betty became "Betty Boops", from the cartoon pinup on the Old Maid cards. Her name was later changed to "Bumps" and mine became "Hoss", as in "Hoss Cartwright", on the TV program *Bonanza*. The year was 1978. It has been thirty years since that first meeting—we are still "Hoss" and "Bumps" and remain great friends!

We had planned that visit over a weekend so I could give them a sample of my preaching ability, such as it was and have the opportunity to meet the whole congregation. There was a fellowship dinner and a meeting with the church board. They offered an acceptable living wage and a parsonage, plus, something churches in Minnesota were just beginning to consider—fringe benefits. We had never been in ministry for the money and fringe benefits, so what they offered seemed generous enough for us to comfortably live on. Everything seemed to be a good match, so we accepted the call and then made the trip back to Arizona to pack again and move.

FROM LUMBER, BACK TO BIBLE TEXTS

After our return, I first had to break the news to Bill Parker, then begin packing, and arrange for a rental truck for the move to Minnesota. Bill took the news very well. He hated to see me leave, but understood my first commitment to ministry and desire to answer God's call to service. We got everything packed, said goodbye to the Parkers and crew all of our church friends in the Show Low area and made our way back to the land of the Danes, Norwegians and Swedes. I've discovered later that the girls hated this move, not because we were leaving our new home and their friends, but because we were leaving the family cat with friends in Show Low rather than deal with a berserk cat while traveling. Cats do not travel well! We could get another cat in Minnesota—and did!

A humorous event that still brings a chuckle from the family has to do with the very last moments of loading the Ryder truck. The truck was full to the roof and wall to wall. Betty came to the back of the truck with "one more thing"—a lamp shade that she could find no room for anywhere. "Have you got room for this?" she inquired. I opened the cargo door. There was not a single square inch of space for a lamp shade. When she then inquired "what are we going to do with it?", I took the shade, placed it up against the last box and slammed the door! We wouldn't know what that did to the shade until we got to Minnesota and unloaded the truck.

It probably wouldn't be good—it wasn't!

Again, my folks came out from California to help us drive one of the three vehicles. My brother Gary put them on the train at Pomona, California and I met them at the depot in Holbrook, Arizona. Betty drove our Datson station wagon with the girls. I drove the Ryder truck and my folks drove our loaded pick-up. We made our way east by first going north through Cortez, Montrose, and Grand Junction, Colorado and then east on I-70 through Denver. Dad didn't like the thought of going this way through the mountains. It was not the usual "safer" route in his estimation, but far more scenic! He later admitted the route was easier than he imagined, and they did enjoy the exceptional beauty of the Colorado Rockies! We continued east through Nebraska and Iowa, and then north to Minnesota on I-35. In Minnesota we took highway I-90 east to State Hwy-52. We exited off onto M-52 and then south a half mile to a corner with a convenience store/gas station, a motor cycle shop, and K.O.A. campground. From there we could see the parsonage and church building one block east. We turned left, went that one block and turned into the driveway of our new home. Having been in contact with the congregation about our progress, there was a crew of volunteers ready to help with the unloading. We then spent the next several hours setting up beds, placing furniture and doing all the basic unpacking. Also, the lamp shade didn't make it! We returned the Ryder truck and took Mom and Dad to the Minneapolis International Airport for the trip back home. Gary picked them up at the terminal in Ontario, California.

Show Low, AZ

Our first, two bedroom
home, no grass.

Taking VBS to the Hopi Reservation, AZ

Taking VBS to the Navajo Reservation, AZ

American Indian Christian Mission,
Building the bridge

A finished project

Outdoor worship,
Show Low, AZ

Parker Saw Mill
Clay Spring, AZ

Gordon operating
a logging truck in
the Arizona forest

CHAPTER 23

THE MARION
CHURCH OF CHRIST

It didn't take long to get back into the "groove" of ministry. There were soon sermons and lessons to prepare and deliver. There were new people to meet and new names to learn, names to add to the long list of names from previous ministries and associations—names like Predmores, Newells, the Campbells and the Allens. The Winters and the Pattersons also became a weekly part of our life. There were the Flurrys, the Eddies, the Willies, the Morelands, the Bjerkies, the Sparrows and—Carmela Castelana. There were many other names that slip my mind. Through the intervening years, we have felt especially close to Glen and Sharon Moreland. Glen was an elder with whom I served and Betty and Sharon worked together as banquet waitresses at the Rochester Holiday Inn. Every week there were stories and laughs. We maintain our friendship with them to this day through an annual fishing trip and contact with Sharon at Crossroads College where she serves as Coordinator of Alumni and Church Relations.

Once again, as a pastor, there were people to call on in the hospital and shut-ins to call on in their homes and nursing homes and communion to take. There were youth meetings to plan, board meetings to attend, and camp board meetings to attend. There was Daily Vacation Bible Schools to plan and conduct in the summer and at least two weeks of church camp at Pine Haven Christian Assembly on Long Lake, Park Rapids, Minnesota.

But the most important task was to get our girls settled into school and work. Cindy, who was finished with high school and not interested in college, found herself a job at Barlow's Super Market in Rochester, now known as HyVee and has worked there some twenty-seven years. She started out as a checker and has since become the Head Scanning Coordinator. Shannon was not school age when we moved to Marion. When that day came, we enrolled her in kindergarten at Pinewood Elementary School on the southeast edge of Rochester. Shannon did well at Pinewood except for one particular teacher who, to reprimanded her for counting on her fingers, would shake her by the shoulders. From then on Shannon saw her as a teacher to be feared. In spite of this negative experience, she did well and completed three and one half years at Pinewood School. She later finished third grade through the 12th after we moved to the Hancock, Michigan. She soon made friends both at school and in our local neighborhood at Marion.

Sherry became a student at Kellogg Junior High and suffered the frustration of being the new teenage kid in school. She later graduated to Mayo High School and there, experienced the sting of being rejected from the cheerleader squad (she was robbed). We reassured her that she should take heart, that maybe God had something much better in store for her. God did have something better for her. Her friends and teachers at school began to see her great talent in art and graphic design. She was an excellent student, but her ability in art was outstanding. Her art instructor encouraged her to enter her art in a statewide contest sponsored by the Printing Industry of the Twin Cities. She did and won a first place in the state of Minnesota for her collection of art work. We had the pleasure of accompanying her to the awards banquet in Minneapolis and see her presented with a seventy-five dollar prize and much recognition.

The next step for Sherry was college. We began researching colleges and universities and the scholarships and grants available to her. By graduation, she had decided on Drake University in Des Moines, Iowa. Drake would be expensive and we wondered where we would find the money for her to go there. At a parents orientation on the Drake campus, they assured us they would find scholarships, grants, and loans that would allow Sherry to attend Drake. Their claims were proven true. The Student Aid Department at Drake was excellent in uncovering every dollar available in grants, scholarships etc., some I'd never heard of. Sherry attended Drake for four years, majoring in Graphic Design. We had the privilege of seeing her graduate with her BA degree in the Spring of 1986. Her last two years at Drake she worked as a Resident Assistant in her dorm, contributing to her room and board. She now has her own graphic design business, "Paavola Design" at her residence in Minneapolis.

LIFE WITH THE MARION CONGREGATION

Very early in our ministry at Marion an unfortunate incident unfolded. I have always been attentive to welcoming visitors to the services and making new-comers feel noticed and welcome. It is imperative to church growth. One Sunday I noticed a couple near the front that I had not seen before. Assuming they were new, I asked if they were visitors and welcomed them. Suddenly there was a roll of laughter through the congregation and an angry scowl on the faces of the couple. Bad move on my part! I paid for that mistake the rest of my ministry there. Other members informed me that this couple were long-time members of the church. They may have been long on membership, but were certainly short on grace and forgiveness. Instead of seeing it as an innocent mistake by a new minister and laughing along, they saw it as an unforgivable insult and vowed revenge, which came nearly three years later. It had to do with our "bus".

Betty and I bought a large, used "pusher" (rear engine) school bus from the Strain's Bus Company for whom I drove. We took out half of the seats and converted it into a part time motor home for family camping and part time as a church bus for hauling kids to church camp. We took all the seats out for camping and installed moveable partitions for the bath, bedroom, and living room, with moveable cabinets. During the church camping season we would remove our living quarters and reinstall the seats in the front half of the bus. This would allow for a large number of campers in the seats and the empty back half for the mountain of luggage they would bring. Immediately following Sunday services, we would load up our own kids from Marion and the neighboring churches of Pleasant Grove and Stewartville. We would then pick up more campers at the Meadow Park church in Rochester and the churches at Concord, Owatonna, and Faribault. In the Minneapolis area we took on kids from Bloomington and Coon Rapids. As we left the Coon Rapids church parking lot, we were fully loaded with kids and luggage—stuffed in every available corner. The families in all these churches appreciated this service to their campers. It saved cars, gas and time and was a fun trip for all the variety of kids. It was "camp", before camp—a time to really get acquainted.

WHEN YOUR WORST ENEMIES ARE CHURCH MEMBERS

The wife of the disgruntled couple saw this as a time for revenge. After several round trips to Pine Haven with campers and having just arrived with another load, I received an urgent call from Betty who was at home in Marion. She told me I had been "turned in" to the State Highway Patrol under the charge of operating a bus charter service without an ICC permit. "What?"—I was astonished! "Who would have done this? Was it a bus company?"

"No," she replied.

"Was it some other churches and camping program?"

"No". I just couldn't imagine who would do this?

Betty then revealed that it was one of our own church members! With the help of an Elder, Glen Moreland, who had some "friends in high places" with the Department of Transportation we discovered it was the disgruntled wife, who just happen to work in that local state office, issuing various load and use permits. She saw her opportunity! Learning we were a church group, the State Patrol officer assured us that they would never have bothered us in our service to the campers. They were aware of the law regarding "charter service", but ignored it when it involved churches. But in this case, due to the fact that somebody reported it, they would have to enforce the law. I would be allowed to return the campers to their churches at the close of the camp week, but would not be allowed to continue the service in the future, except for our own church campers.

The revenge action by that one person ended the camper service for all these churches, the color-tours we hosted for our own senior citizens and almost ended our family's use of the bus as a motor home. We were advised that the only way we could use it for personal travel was if we painted the whole bus a completely different color and remove all the warning lights. I had already removed the lights and blanked out the "School Bus" signs with yellow paint. Not good enough! I had to completely change the whole paint scheme. How would I be able to do that over a week-end. We were planning a vacation to see my folks in

California with it the next Monday.

The congregation, realizing our dilemma, did a wonderful thing. They formed a volunteer paint crew to sand and scrape the bus and mask the windows to spray on a new blue and white paint job. We got the kids home from camp on Friday; the crew sanded and masked and bought the paint and started painting on Saturday. They finished the job on Sunday afternoon, after outrunning a thunder storm to Jim Newell's machine shed. We will be ever appreciative for the efforts of Jim and Maureen Newell and all the others on that paint crew! We left the next day after installing our living quarters. Later that summer, after returning home, we sold it to a nursing home, since we didn't feel we could justify the expense of just letting it sit idle except for one or two weeks a year.

A THRIVING CONGREGATION

On a more happy note, there were many more wonderful experiences while at Marion and even many more wonderful people. And the congregation grew! The attendance, when we arrived, was in the fifties and sixties. Soon it was running in the nineties and one hundreds. New people from the area were attending and staying. Students and faculty from Minnesota Bible College (now Crossroads College located in Rochester, MN) were coming out to our services and offering their talents and gifts in teaching and music. Besides the lasting friendships we've had with fellow alumni from our own years at M.B.C. in the fifties and sixties, we began lasting relationships with these new students and faculty from late seventies and eighties. We still connect for visits with these younger grads when traveling near their areas and at college events.

Yet, there were times I had mixed emotions about all this growth and the presence in our services of young theologians and professors who were "experts" at homiletics and theology. Having been out of practice for some ten years, I was again burning the midnight oil and sweating out my weekly sermon manuscripts. Although I felt very much inadequate and like Moses when he told God at the burning bush, "I cannot speak", nevertheless, I did speak, and the numerical and personal growth of the congregation reassured me that I could indeed do what God had called me to do at Marion. On one occasion, one of the professors who attended, who was considered very bright and articulate in his field of theology, confessed to me that he was envious of my ability to "connect" with the people with sound Biblical exposition. I was flabbergasted! What a wonderful compliment, and coming from an "expert"!

ONE NEW BUILDING/ONE OLD BUILDING

After we began averaging one hundred-twenty, there was substantial conversation about a new building. There had been discussions through the years about the inadequacy of the old one hundred-fifty year old building, but not the will to do anything about it. But now the old building was being "maxed-out" every Sunday with the need for folding chairs. The main sanctuary was full with folding chairs. The annex or "sheep shed" as they called it, was full also with folding chairs. The guys ushering were getting frustrated trying to find places to seat people. It was time! The church board gave it the thumbs up. Architects and contractors were hired; excavating began; concrete was poured; blocks were laid up; and the walls and roof were nailed into place. Sometime during 1980–81 the congregation moved into the new building. With all the new excitement and new space, the congregation grew even more. We filled up the new building too!

But, what to do with the old one hundred-fifty year old building? At first, a developer was interested in it. He had developed a new private cemetery between Rochester and Marion and wanted the old historic building for a cemetery chapel. He even sent out a crew to jack the building up off the foundation and set steel beams under it for transporting it to the new location. I never knew what happened to that deal, but it fell through. He couldn't move the building, it was still ours, but he just let the old building set their on the steel girders. Now what?

I got tired of seeing the building just sitting there with no action from either the contractor or the church board, so volunteered to dismantle the building myself for the lumber. I knew that some of the finest lumber in the country went to building those old buildings and it would make great material for our retirement cottage. I got the approval from the church board and went to work. Like skinning out a giant whale, I started at the top of the roof and pealed off the shingles and sheathing right down to the rafters and perimeter walls. The roof sheathing boards were amazing. I found many to be twenty-four inches wide, by sixteen, eighteen and twenty feet long, and without a knot. Fantastic lumber! I salvaged large stacks of clear two by sixes, eighths, tens, and twelve's. I was ready for the walls but thought, why struggle working off a ladder? Why not get the walls on the ground and tear them apart? I took my chain saw and sawed the front wall and bell tower/foyer away from the side walls. Baam! Down it came in a cloud of dust. Then I sawed the back wall loose from the two side walls and the old building opened up, exploding like the petals of a flower in the morning sun. Everything was now flat on the ground, making it easy to finish salvaging the rest of the usable lumber. I stored the lumber in some sheds on a large lot Betty and I had purchased a block south, on the edge of a creek. Soon, all that was left was for a dozer to come and push the trash into the basement and cover it with some fill dirt. With the fill and gravel in place and leveled, we doubled the size of our parking lot. And I now had the start of a lumber yard.

BACK TO THE GREAT OUT OF DOORS

There were many great experiences with the Marion church family. Several of the guys planned annual fishing trips to the Canadian side of the Boundary waters, to a place called Lac Des Mille Lacs, where there were thousands of acres of great fishing waters. There were bays and arms and inlets and large expanses of open water. I took it upon myself to serve as map reader and compass watcher. There were many times we could have gotten lost in the thousands of bays and arms of the lake. But it was a great fishing lake. Some of the biggest northern and walleye I've ever seen were caught in that lake. These were great times of fellowship and camaraderie for the men of the congregation.

There were other great times of fellowship for the teens as well. On one occasion I took a group of our teenage kids on a two week canoe trip in the American Boundary waters, out of Ely, Minnesota. The group was made up of a few high schoolers, our daughter Sherry, our Iranian son, Rob plus some college students. In our six canoes we paddled and fished and camped and portaged from camp site to camp site. It was a great time of fellowship and working together, and fishing and swatting mosquitoes and surviving in the rugged *Great White North*!

One of my more harrowing experiences happened on this trip. We started the day with calm waters and blue skies. At mid afternoon we broke camp and began paddling for the next camp on an island a mile or two away. The six canoes set out for the island which we could easily see in the distance. But soon, we could see something else on the horizon—

storm clouds! The horizon was black, with an incoming roller cloud with high winds and lightning, straight to the ground. Would we make it to shore before the onslaught began? Hardly! The storm did catch us four to five hundred yards from shore, but the kids were up to it. Maybe it was fear, maybe it was me screaming "paddle, paddle, paddle as hard as you can", or maybe a built-in sense of survival. Whatever it was, I have never seen teenagers paddle like they did in those few minutes—except for Sherry. She was busy putting on her rain gear so she wouldn't get wet. There were whitecaps and lake spray everywhere, but the kids blocked it out and charged straight ahead into the white caps. We all made it safely ashore, all in the same place, all heads and canoes accounted for. We beached the canoes and secured them and proceeded to set up camp in this new location.

Then, what was ironic, was that after this heroic, life threatening experience in the canoes, arguments broke out over tent sites and which ones were the driest and "which one saw it first"—like a bunch of grade school kids! We solved that problem and settled into fixing our evening meal of fresh fish and readying ourselves for an evening around a camp fire and bed. Over all, the days we experienced on the water were wonderful and scenic and awesome, as we fished and swam and fellowshipped together. It then came time to make our way back to the pick-up spot and return to the outfitters base camp.

THE BEARD

It was good to get out of the canoes and mosquitoes and dirty clothes and into the showers and then, into a clean comfortable bed. Arriving at the base camp, I announced to several how good the shower was going to feel and shaving off my two weeks of beard. Immediately, I heard this collective "NO!" No what? "No—don't shave off the beard", they said! "It looks great!" So, I've had a beard ever since. I was a little concerned about what the congregation would say. There were some humorous comments, but no objections.

A few years later, while living in Indianapolis, I decided to shave the beard off to look a little younger and take Betty out for dinner the evening of our anniversary. She thought I had been in the bathroom a little too long and looked in to see what I was doing. There I stood with exactly half a beard. I had decided to take it off one side at a time. It took twice as long as I expected, so was only half done. She took one look and began laughing. She laughed after I had the whole beard off. She laughed that evening at dinner. She laughed every time she looked at me. She laughed for a month! Shannon, our youngest was flying into Indy for a visit. She had arrived at the airport and was waiting for us in the boarding area. Betty got to her first. I got hung up at security removing my shoes and my belt and arrived at the boarding area a minute later. She saw me from a distance coming down the corridor and began screaming and covering her eyes. She had never seen her dad without a beard and mustache. Later, the grandchildren saw me and had the same reaction. They would cover their eyes and plead with me, "grandpa—grandpa—please, grow it back!" So, I did, before the world came to and end!

THE GREAT 1981 FAMILY BIKE TRIP

One of the summer vacations we planned while at Marion was a week long bike trip on the Sparta – Elroy, Wisconsin bike trail. Shannon was too small to manage a bike of her own, so I made a "nifty" bike trailer, using two narrow, ten-speed bike wheels, some oak slats, electrical conduit and nylon clothesline rope. The trailer easily carried Shannon, the tents, and two sleeping bags. It was so easy to pull behind my bike, I hardly knew she was back there. The plan was to haul the four bikes and bike trailer on top of our pop-up camper, set up camp at the camp ground at Sparta and bike the seventy miles to Elroy and back, staying in the bike campgrounds available in the small towns along the way. The Sparta trail had been a railroad bed, complete with bridges, trestles, tunnels, and depots. This railroad/bike trail is one of the most scenic and exciting in the tri-state area. The trail winds around through steep, hardwood covered hills and white-water streams. The main feature are the three tunnels on the trail. Railroad tunnels are rare in the Midwest, but the mountain-like hills in this area required the railroads to tunnel through. Of the three tunnels on this section of the trail, two are half a mile long, with the main tunnel stretching an entire mile. All the rails and ties are gone and there are no lights. It is so dark in the tunnel that bikers need to carry flash lights and walk their bikes through to the other end. We would not see light again until more than half way through.

There were two or three small towns between Sparta and Elroy with campgrounds, restrooms, and water fountains located by the depots in each town. There were cafes and restaurants available as well, so we could get a break from our "campfire" food. We got lots of exercise setting up and breaking camp each day and pedaling to the next depot. We met many other families on the trail doing just as we were doing and enjoying it. The nice thing about railroad grades is that there was never more than a two percent incline on any hill. Yet, there were many times the girls did not like all the pedaling, so they did a great deal of complaining, if the road wasn't downhill or flat. Mid-way through the trek I gave them each a nick-name, "Bitch", "Gripe" and "Complain"! They've never forgotten that trip and those names. All in all, it was a wonderful experience and something they still talk about and share with their families. On that same vacation we also camped at St. Ignace, near the Mackinaw Straits and pedaled Mackinac Island. Travel on the island is entirely on foot or by bike or horse. We spent an easy and fascinating day there. Good food, good chocolate fudge, good "trinket" shops and good scenery...and Shannon let Dad do all the pedaling!

THE BANJO MAN

An important addition came into my life during our years at Marion. One Christmas morning while the family was opening their gifts, Betty and the girls asked me to close my eyes and not "peek". I was sitting on the living room floor cross-legged, with my eyes closed tight, as they had ask...with their checking on me every second to make sure I kept them closed. Betty disappeared somewhere and returned to lay a somewhat heavy item in my lap. As I spoke, asking questions and making comments, I could hear this "object" echoing back to me with melodic tones. When I opened my eyes I found a five stringed Bluegrass Banjo lying across my lap. "Neat, what am I supposed to do with this?" I asked.

They then presented me with the "rest" of my Christmas gift...a "how to" book of instructions, and eight lessons at Schmidt Music in Rochester. Well, that sparked some interest in a new direction. I took the lessons, enjoyed the banjo and the music that it produced, and have been moving onward and upward ever since.

After a few years on the "beginner" banjo, I had an opportunity to upgrade to a better banjo and began teaching myself the Flatts and Scruggs style of three finger Bluegrass pickin. It has become a major source of enjoyment for me, playing with the family, playing for church services, for church camps, for Prime Timers on Campus at M.B.C. and for our home Bible study group. I've also developed an avid interest in Bluegrass concerts. To me, Bluegrass music is exciting, it is moving, it has a great classic sound, and lots of energy and life. It is music uniquely American. Long live Bluegrass! Their Christmas gift to Dad was the gift that kept on giving...and keeps on giving...for some thirty years now.

OUR IRANIAN SON

Probably one of the most wonderful and spiritually far-reaching events happen to us while ministering at Marion. The year was 1979 or '80 during the student revolt and take over of the US Embassy in Tehran, Iran. I happened to be watching the breaking news that evening around the dinner hour. At the very moment I was watching the TV news and pictures of Iranian students leading our US Embassy people blindfolded down the steps of the building, the phone rang. I picked up the receiver and couldn't believe my ears! On the other end of the line was an Iranian student, asking in very broken English, "if I could help him!" My mind was spinning. Who was this and where was he—in Tehran or the USA? Was this some terrorist plot to invade our homes here in America? He then told me he was a student from Tehran, Iran, had just arrived in this country, had been assigned to Rochester Community College, but was having difficulty getting his money and some of his things out of customs. He was living with several other students in a small apartment near St. Mary's Hospital in Rochester.

Big decision! What do I do with this? Meet him face to face and offer help or hang up the phone? In a huge step of faith, I told him I would call one of our elders and in a few minutes we would be there to meet him. Elder Steve Winters consented to go with me. We found him and found his situation just as he had said. After visiting with him and his fellow Iranian roommates for a few moments, I offered to have him come and live with our family at the parsonage. We could tell from the outset of our visit that he was much more afraid of us, because of what he knew we knew about the Embassy takeover, than we were of him. But he grabbed the few personal possessions he had and came with us to our home. We put him up in the family room downstairs. This would be his room for the next year or two.

We made Sohrab (now Rob), a part of our family life. He ate with us and began meeting friends and neighbors and members of the church. We helped him with his English and translated some of the terms in his text books. We helped him understand some of the slang used in our culture and the irregular usage of the language. We helped him through his difficult times when relationships with girlfriends failed. We also had the pleasure of being present for his college graduation. Being a Muslim, he did have one request, the permission to say his daily prayers to Allah. We did not object and each evening he would wash his hands and feet in the bathroom then return to his room to say his prayers. As the days passed he became interested in what went on in the church building next door on Sundays. We told him he would be welcome to come with us to worship and see for himself. He seemed surprised that he would be welcome to a Christian service. He did attend with us and immediately fit-in with the congregation. The acceptance by the congregation really impressed him. He began to feel the presence of Christ through the love of our family, and the congregation. One Sunday, following a worship service, as we returned to the parsonage, he shared how much he loved the morning worship and one of the songs we had sung that morning. When I asked him which song, he said, *Jesus Is Coming Again*. It appeared to me that faith in Jesus was beginning to take root in his heart.

Marion Church of Christ, Marion, MN

The Church Parsonage

Cynthia, Sherry me
and Shannon on the
Sparta-Elroy bike trail

A homemade Burley

CHAPTER 24

ANOTHER CHANGE IS IN THE AIR

The growth of the Marion congregation had reached a plateau. We were filling the new building every Sunday and once again, needed more room. There were discussions at board meetings about what to do. A few board members and I suggested two services. This did not appeal to the majority of the board. Next, I suggested doubling the size of our new building. That suggestion did not fly at all. They complained they had just finished a building program, why do another building project? Then came a suggestion from one board member that just "floored" me. His suggestion was, "Gordie—stop with the evangelism!" I couldn't believe what I was hearing and also what I was not hearing. As those words echoed around the room, allowing the board members to "chew" on what he had said, I waited for someone to step up and give a rebuttal. Nothing! There was this long deafening silence! As a responsible minister and servant of God, I began to see that perhaps my tenure with this congregation was coming to a close. How could I conduct a ministry of outreach, fulfilling the Great Commission, yet at the same time, discourage possible new converts because there was not enough seating in the building. Cut out with the evangelism? How long could I do that?

I PULLED A "JONAH"

God always has a way of answering those kinds of questions. Not long after this, I began getting contacts from some of my ministry friends at the Bible College and churches in Wisconsin, wanting to tell me about a new start-up congregation in Hancock, Michigan. The new congregation was being supported by the Wisconsin State Evangelizing Association and they were looking for a preacher who would be willing to move up into the far-away north woods to lead this congregation. No other possible candidate wanted to go this far into the wilderness. Everyone who knew about this congregation felt I would be perfect for the job, since I had been a logger and an outdoors man and carpenter, as well as a preacher. But I had a hard time with this call to ministry. As I looked at the maps, I saw the remoteness of the area and wondered how there could possibly be any people living there to minister to. Then when I discovered the severe and lengthy winters and the amount of annual snowfall (three hundred to four hundred inches), I lost my desire to answer this call!

But it would not go away. Almost grudgingly, I sent my resume and waited for an answer. About the time their affirmative answer came, we got a call from a local girl's home in Rochester, needing house parents. "That's the call for me!" I thought! A short move, no four hundred inches of snow in the winter and Betty and I can minister to the needs of troubled teenagers. We took the job. I sent a reply to the congregation in Michigan about my change of mind and resigned from the Marion ministry. They were very disappointed—both the Marion Church and the new Church in Michigan. And I was very stupid! Just a side note, we have remained good friends with the Marion congregation since that time.

After two months into this girl's home job it was beginning to eat me alive! We had been assigned troubled girls that should not have been in a residential care unit. We had big troubles twenty-four hours a day. I was feeling depression closing in! Shannon, who was now in second grade, sat by me on the couch one day and asked, "Daddy, do you think you will ever be happy again?" It showed that much?! The insight of a child! That revealing comment made me realize I had pulled a "Jonah", running the opposite way from God's call. The ministry call in Michigan, which I had rejected, was haunting me everyday. It would not go away. What had I done? What was up there in the Upper Peninsula of Michigan that was so important to God that He had to bug me everyday about it? Finally, I told Betty, "Lets drive up to Hancock and sneak in on them. Lets see what's going on there!" She was surprised I was still agonizing over that call to ministry. Yet, it did not surprise her. I think she knew as well as I, that that was maybe where we belonged.

OCTOBER, 1983, HANCOCK MICHIGAN...HERE WE COME!

We had just bought a new station wagon and thought a trip to Hancock would be a good way to get away and try out the new car. We packed our bags and left on a Saturday morning. We had a beautiful drive to the Houghton/Hancock "twin cities". We had never experienced being so deep into the northern wilderness of the U.S. We arrived late afternoon and arranged for a room at the Copper Crown Motel which, we later discovered, was the very place this congregation was meeting on Sunday mornings. The next morning, Sunday morning, the congregation would be meeting there in their conference room.

I had not planned on telling the congregation we were in town but had a change of heart. I decided to call Jim Wheeler, the only phone contact I had had. He was surprised we were in town! "Are you the one who sent the resume and then turned us down?" he asked.

"Yes", I admitted—that's me!" I told him of the struggle I had been having since I had turned down their call. "The Lord has me in a hammer lock and won't let me go, in considering this call to ministry," I confessed. I asked if they needed someone to deliver the sermon in the morning.

Jim said "Yes", and asked if I would be willing.

"I would be delighted!"

As we drove into town the day before, I was amazed at the beauty and scenery. I was amazed at the size and the activity of this remote twin town. Michigan Tech University was located here—college students! (We would inherit one of those Tech students as a son-in-law a few years later). Detroit and Northern Savings Bank's corporate headquarters was located here, in a ten story high-rise office building. Suomi College was located here—more students! The DNR had headquarters in Houghton, which serviced Isle Royal National Park with a transport ship and float plane services! Amazing—what they don't tell you in the maps and brochures.

What was most amazing was the young, energized, personable, talented, and visionary congregation which met that Sunday morning! We had a delightful first meeting! I delivered a message based on Ephesians, about the nature and mission of the Church. At the close of the service no one left for their cars. They all wanted to talk. One of their key members, Mary Carroll, immediately zeroed in on the main issue. "Now, Mr. Sorenson, are you sure you are not interested in serving this congregation?" she asked—so that everyone around could listen (like in the famous E.F. Hutton commercial). "No, I am NOT sure I am NOT interested. As a matter of fact, I am sure that I am ready to accept the call to serve this congregation as your minister, if you are ready for me", I responded.

Nobody went home. Mary invited everyone to stop at the store, buy some "take out" food, and come to her house—an instant fellowship dinner. She and the leadership wanted to nail things down right then and there, before we left town. We discussed the specifics of their vision for the direction of this new congregation. We looked the twin towns over, as well as a few houses that might be available for our new residence. The next day we drove back to Rochester, relieved that we had found our way again. There would be a congregational vote on our coming and a phone call Wednesday evening next, informing us of the results. The results were affirmative. The pay package and benefits were affirmative—I was amazed at what they offered! This would be the best pay package I had ever been offered by a church and that, from a new start up congregation.

A few weeks later we made a return trip to Hancock to preach for the congregation and to locate a house for us to live in. We stayed with Jack and Mary Carrel, who lived on Summit Street in Hancock. In our travels through their neighborhood we had noticed a two-story house with a for sale sign on it just around the corner from the Carrels. The address was 505 Elevation Street. On our first visit we had stopped there to look around and peek in the windows (it was vacant). On our second visit we looked again at that house, this time with the help of a realtor. We discovered the old two story Victorian had real hardwood maple floors through-out, even in the attic, and a garage across the street. We decided that was the one! The house had more than enough room, was in a central location and at a price we could afford—$45,000. The congregation loaned us the down payment of $4,000 which, five years later they forgave. So, the Lord had us right where He wanted us, ministering to a new congregation in Hancock, Michigan. We had work to do, a congregation to love and a home to live in. What's next?

As we had done what seemed like a hundred times before, we began doing again—we started packing the boxes. I think this time we even filled the boxes we had used and saved from the last move.

HERE WE GO—ON THE ROAD AGAIN

On Friday December 16, 1983, we made the four hundred mile journey to the Copper Country by way of Duluth, Minnesota/Superior, Wisconsin. I remember that date because it was again, on my birthday and as usual, the weather in mid-December was terrible! We drove in pretty much a blizzard the whole way, with temperatures between minus ten and minus twenty. What was normally an eight hour trip, turned into a fourteen hour trip. We will always feel a sense of deep gratitude to Dale and Marge Patterson of the Marion church for not only helping us box up our things, but for also taking the time, effort and expense to drive their loaded van with our things up to Hancock. They also did not just immediately turn around and head back to Marion. They devoted the next week to helping us unpack and get settled into our new home. By the end of that week, I needed to return to Marion to get our Jeep Renegade and Sherry, who would be on her way home from Drake University. She would be needing a ride to Hancock from Marion for the Christmas break. It all worked out great! I "bummed" a ride back to Marion with the Pattersons in minus thirty-five degree weather. It was so cold even in Des Moines, Iowa that Sherry's ride to the Marion area couldn't get her car started, so I borrowed our daughter Cindy's car to make the late night round-trip to Des Moines to pick her up.

SHERRY MEETS THE "COPPER COUNTRY"

We arrived back at the Patterson's in the middle of the night and awakened early for the final leg to Hancock. We loaded her things in the rag top Jeep and headed north. As the hours and miles crept by, Sherry made the comment, "Dad, I go away to college and my family moves away on me to some God forsaken place in the tundra! Where on earth are we going?" It was still minus twenty degrees—bone chilling cold! With the heater going full blast, we could still see our breath in the Jeep. It grew dark and the hours and miles went by as we went through one little town after another. Everytime we entered a small village, Sherry would ask, "Is this it?" Each time, my answer would be the same—"No, this is not 'it.'" I assured her we did have a home and it wouldn't be long. Finally, we topped the hill by the Copper Country Mall at Houghton-Hancock and saw all the beautiful lights of the twin towns spread across the valley below us. We were home! She was relieved and pleasantly surprised with what she saw—actual civilization and a beautiful winter scene!

Christmas, 1983 was just a few days away, so the next day we went out to buy a Christmas tree. The tree lots were empty. Someone gave us directions to a saw mill east of Lake Linden. The four of us drove out there to see what we could find. The mill was closed due to all the snow, but the owner of the mill, doing some work inside, saw us and came out to see what we needed. When we asked about buying a Christmas tree, he directed us out to a spot in the mill yard where there stood one lonely tree. The gentleman told us that that was the last one and we could have it "for free". We carried that last Christmas tree in the Copper Country to the Jeep, tied it to the top and made our way home. All in all, it was beginning to be a wonderful Christmas. The kids would all be with us at our new home, including Cindy and Sohrab, our Iranian son! Life was good!

But the snow did not stop! A week earlier, on the horrible day we moved in, we could barely find enough room at the edge of the street to shovel a place to park the truck. That night, we stayed at the motel and began unloading the truck the next day. Members of the congregation were there to help us carry boxes and furniture to their various places in our new home. We had to enlist little Shannon's help with a push broom to keep the metal walk plank on the truck and front steps to the house swept off so we wouldn't slip. It seemed like she made that trip up and down the walk plank with the broom every minute. We were beginning to experience what three hundred to four hundred inches of snow would be like. That winter we received three hundred seventy-eight inches of snow. It seemed like most of it fell on that day we were moving in! That night we stayed at the motel again and held church there the next day. The snow did not stop! We soon settled into life in the "great white north"—and the snow did not stop!

ROB—THE CULMINATION OF A GROWING FAITH—THE STORY CONTINUES

Earlier, before the move to Hancock, while still living in Marion, we announced to Sohrab, that we were moving to a new ministry in the Upper Peninsula of Michigan. He was very disappointed—disappointed that we were moving so far away! We assured him that he would always be our Iranian son and we would be back to the Rochester area because Cindy, our oldest, would still be living there. And, he could come to see us in Hancock and enjoy the beauty of this vast north country anytime he wanted. Good highways ran both ways.

After a few weeks passed, we got a call from Sohrab. He wanted to talk to me. He had a favor to ask of me. "Sure", I said, "What can I do for you?" I was stunned by his reply.

"Dad, would you baptize me? I want to become a Christian!"

"Would I baptize you? Yes! Yes! Yes! I would be delighted—honored to baptize you!" I replied! The only event greater than this would be the births and doing the baptisms of our three daughters. That next Sunday, at the close of the service, he made his public confession of faith and I baptized him into Jesus Christ for the remission of his sins. Since then, he has become an American citizen with a new name—Rob, married Saeda, has two sons and a business in Eagan, Minnesota. Actually, I should say businesses. In his small strip mall shop, he rents formal wear, makes keys, repairs shoes, sharpens ice skates, and does alterations. He also owns and manages condos and apartments and buys, details and resells used cars. I joke with him about doing heart surgeries on his days off!

They are now members of the Apple Valley Christian Church and are becoming supportive of an Iranian convert/evangelist doing TV and internet evangelism in Tehran, their home city. I asked Saeda what she felt about Rob's becoming a Christian. She thought it was wonderful and wanted to become a Christian herself. Recently, she also made that same public confession and was baptized and as well, one of their sons. I will never forget her response when I asked her how she viewed Christianity. Her words were, "Jesus is so wonderful! Jesus is so loving! Being a Christian is so positive! Islam is sad, and hard, and negative. There is no comparison!" She recently returned to Iran to visit her mother and family. Her mother also wants to become a Christian—wants Saeda to baptize her. In discussions with Rob about this, he tells me that if Iran could get rid of Mahmoud Ahmadinejad and his hit squads, many in Iran and Tehran would accept Jesus as savior. The general public is tired of the violence and the brutality and lack of freedom. They are tired of a negative, graceless, harsh, legalistic religion that forces compliance out of the barrel of a gun. Isn't it amazing how God works in ways we would never dream of!

I should mention here that like with Rob and young Jon Mathiason, we have always had our home open to ministry. We always viewed our home as something to share. Through the years we have had foster kids living with us, stray kids off the street and foreign students like Rob and foreign exchange students. Two Japanese students lived with us at different times, Kyoko Takahashi and Yuka Yamamoto; then Maja Haertner from East Germany and Jane Soares from Brazil. These young people were a blessing to our family, especially our girls, giving them a window on the customs, languages, and cultures of other lands and peoples. We hope we were a blessing to them also and a window on what a Christian family is like. Maybe a seed of faith was sown.

Sohrab Kavoosi, professing his faith on the day of his baptism

Rob & Saeda

CHAPTER 25

1983 TO 1996
THE COPPER COUNTRY
AN AMAZING THIRTEEN YEAR MINISTRY

From day one, the congregation began to grow. Many new people from every walk of life came to visit our services at the Copper Crown Motel, with many staying. We began having baptisms in the motel swimming pool. We always made arrangements for them in advance. We did not want to disrupt the use of the pool by motel guests. To my surprise, this was never a problem. It seemed as though the management gave us preference in using the pool for baptisms. There were times when the guests wanted to witness this wonderful "new birth" even though they had no idea who the candidate was. I've often wondered how witnessing those baptisms may have affected new faith in those guests.

Soon, we were running out of room. We were holding children's classes wherever we could find a corner—even by the sauna. There was no more room to even set up folding chairs. We knew we had to do something. But what? We seemed too small to do a major move as a congregation, (or so we thought). The congregation advised me to look around Hancock and Houghton to see if I could locate a bigger building to lease that would be suitable for church services. I spent many days "beating the bushes", looking for something suitable that we could afford. Nothing! The only building available that even came close to what we would need, would cost more than we could afford—$1,200 a month. Besides, we would have the cost of remodeling the interior to meet our needs. On to plan "B"—whatever plan "B" was.

WE WILL BUILD!

In mid 1984, after a congregational meeting, at which time I reported the sad details of finding nothing suitable to rent or lease, I was in for a great surprise. After a short discussion, they announced to me plan B—"Then we will build! See what good, suitable land in a good location might be available to purchase". The congregation had approximately $1,200 in a building fund, not nearly enough to buy land, but this group had an enormous reserve of faith. I had not witnessed the kind of faith and determination this little congregation demonstrated. It would be interesting to see how God would reward their faith.

One of the first places I stopped was at one of the local banks. I wanted to see if a building loan might be available. The banker I talked to was Gary Fynweaver, whose wife was an instructor at Michigan Tech and whose daughter and son were finished or had nearly finished high school. Gary was very gracious and helpful. First, he regretted that he could not recommend our congregation for any kind of a loan. We were too new; we were too small; we were too unproven and we had no collateral. He recommended we give ourselves a few years establishing a "history" in the community, building our building fund/bank account, and building our membership. "Then," he said, "come back and present your progress and need and I will push for a loan." There was nothing available for us at the money lending institutions. In reality God was saying "I already have a plan for you —I am going to be the banker! Watch this!"

So, I went to work as the congregation had asked, looking at prime pieces of land on the main streets and highways central to the Houghton/Hancock communities. I met with many different realtors who could give direction to my search. Not many weeks went by before I located an eight acre parcel on highway M-26, just three miles east of Hancock and less than a mile from Dollar Bay. It was a partially wooded hillside overlooking the Portage Canal—a very beautiful location. The selling price was $8,000—$1,000 per acre—not bad for prime property in that area. I informed the congregation and after looking the site over a quick business meeting was called. It was agreed to pay $500 in earnest money toward it's final purchase. We then had $700 left in the building fund. We had $7,500 remaining to be raised in sixty days when we were to complete the purchase. In the intervening weeks, we had another congregational meeting to discuss what funds had been contributed and how we might raise the rest of the money. No one seemed worried about the balance due. So much so, that when someone raised the personal financial needs of one of our families, no one flinched! The problem revealed was the possible loss of their family home due to unpaid back taxes. That problem had developed due to critical health problems in the family and enormous medical bills at Mayo Clinic in Rochester, Minnesota. I should not have been surprised, that quickly, someone in the group moved we pay the outstanding eight hundred dollar tax bill. With no further discussion a vote was called for. It was unanimous, a total affirmative! But let's see, that leaves a negative $100 in the building fund! They knew God would provide! What amazing faith! They did mentioned one plan they had up their sleeve. If necessary, each family would take out a personal bank loan for $1,000 or more and complete the deal. These Christians had guts!

MONEY FROM HEAVEN

A few days before the closing, not much had happened. I wondered what God would do. The congregation needed to come up with the rest of the money and close the deal. I recalled in the Old Testament, that before Abraham was about to sacrifice his only son, God provided a ram in the thicket. And in the New Testament, when the multitudes were hungry, Jesus fed the crowd of five thousand plus, with five loaves and two fish and had twelve baskets full left over. He also turned the water into wine. What would He do with our faith? We didn't have to wait long. One morning I went as usual on my walk to the post office to get the church's mail. I noticed, as I quickly thumbed through the handful of envelopes, one addressed to the Peninsula Christian Church from a bank drawer number in Marquette, Michigan. I had never seen a return address like that and I wondered as I walked, what it could be. I arrived at our home and immediately began opening the mail, starting with that envelope. I could not believe my eyes! As I tore it open, out dropped a bank draft for $8,000! My first thought was, "This had to be some kind of "scam"—this could not be real!" I immediately took the check back downtown to the Detroit and Northern Bank building, located our church members who worked there and showed them the anonymous bank gift of $8,000. I asked if it could be valid. They too were shocked! They all examined the bank draft and concluded that it was indeed valid! They had no idea who would have sent such a generous gift. It had to be God—money from heaven! We were ecstatic! We could now close on the eight acre building site and pay for it in full. What could be next?

POUR THE CONCRETE

The little congregation was pumped! God was rewarding our faith! We felt it was God's will that we proceed and He would continue to bless our efforts and our faith. So, hearing about an excellent excavating contractor who also happened to be a fine Christian and member of one of the Apostolic Lutheran Churches in the area, we contracted with him to clear the driveway area, parking lot and building site for the new church building. The only trees that needed clearing were a few along the highway on the slight rise to the parking lot where the driveway would go. The site for the building and parking had previously been a level four to five acre hay field and needed little excavating. The remaining four acres were a wooded hillside rising up behind the building site. What a beautiful and perfect spot for a church building! We had enough new money in the building fund by then to pay John Hendrickson the contractor, and then proceed with the building.

We could hardly keep up with God! We needed to quickly decide on a building layout and footprint and get a slab poured. But, you don't just do something that formidable on a piece of scratch paper or dinner napkin. The congregation proceeded with all haste to design an efficient, versatile, attractive church building. I had developed a close friendship with the director and staff of a Catholic sponsored service agency known as Little Brothers To The Elderly. This program and staff did an excellent job of ministering to the elderly of the Copper Country. Mike Aten, the director and I had become good friends, and he was aware of our congregation and what we were attempting to do. Through our conversations, he became aware of our need for an architect who could provide detailed scaled drawings of the walls, plumbing, and electrical layouts and dimensions. Aware that we had not hired one, Mike shared with me that he had been an architect for several years and knew just what we needed. He then offered, "Give me your rough drawings and I'll produce your blueprints for you—for free!" Again, I was amazed! God was at it again! He would not only be the banker, He would also provide the architect!

Our sister congregation in Marquette had all the moveable concrete forms they had used to pour the floor for their new building and offered them free of charge for our use. At the earliest opportunity, we hauled the forms over from Marquette and proceeded to find a concrete contractor. The building season was coming to a close due to the always-early and severe winters. But miraculously, we found a contractor available and hungry for one last job. In no time, he was setting the forms and getting things ready for concrete. Before the concrete could be poured, we needed to get all the plumbing and underground electrical lines installed. Again, miraculously it seemed, Manderfield Plumbing and Electric was ready and willing to do it—immediately. We were ready for the huge slab to be poured. As it turned out, the concrete workers had one perfect day left that November 1984, to do the whole pour, which they accomplished. They suggested we allow them to cover the fresh slab with plastic and a layer of straw—they were concerned about a change in the weather. They finished spreading the straw in the dark that evening—as the snow flakes began to fall. And the snow came and it came and it came! We didn't see the slab again until the first of May the following spring, 1985.

GOD PAYS THE BILL—AGAIN

As the winter of November and December 1984 buried us, we had a $10,000 bill to pay for all the preliminary plumbing, electrical and a concrete work. Within the thirty day billing period, when the payment would be due, I had again picked up the church's mail at the post office, and Betty had collected our personal mail from our own house box. We were sitting in the living room opening the mail when simultaneously, a $5,000 personal check dropped out of an envelope along with a letter from our friends, my old hitch-hiking buddy Dr. Phil Davis and wife Ella, in Bakersfield, California! Another check for $5,000 dropped out of a letter from a supporting family in down state Michigan! They were potato farmers there, who had a son–in–law and daughter at Michigan Tech University who were attending our church services. Dr. Davis commented that he had had a very good year delivering babies and had "too much" in his checking account and wanted to help us with our work!

The farm family revealed that they too had had a good year for potatoes and wanted to send a gift for the new building. The bill was paid! We had purchased the land, did the necessary excavating and architectural work and poured the slab. No need yet for a loan—and all the bills were being paid! We truly had a good Banker!

PUT UP THE WALLS AND COVER IT WITH A ROOF

The bills were all paid, but we couldn't find the slab! It was still buried under four feet of snow! At the end of April, 1985, spring finally came. The plastic and straw-covered concrete and forms finally peaked out through the snow. At my suggestion, the congregation considered building a beautiful, authentic, "real log" building that would compliment the wooded wilderness that surrounded us. "Who would do the work?" they wondered.

"I would!" I volunteered.

"You could do that?"

"Sure!" "OK!—lets go for it!" I had already been serving as the general contractor, why not just keep right on—serving as the head carpenter.

I hired a Michigan Tech student and church member, Bob Emmert, to help lay up the log walls. I ordered 38,000 thousand lineal feet of 8 x 8 northern pine timbers from the sawmill in Dollar Bay. The mill delivered portions of the order week by week and we began cutting and fitting and assembling walls. What a blast that was! It was a lot of work, but a lot of fun! We both felt like kids again, with a new set of gigantic Lincoln Logs!!!

Next, came the roof. We ordered extra heavy-duty stressed trusses for the roof, to handle the snow load. Three of us set all the trusses in one day with the help of a small truck mounted crane and operator. We braced it and partially sheathed it and then, with a whole crew of volunteers available on Saturday, finished the major remaining portion of the sheathing. We also black-papered and shingled it all on that following weekend, with volunteers from the Marquette congregation, joining our own church workers.

We didn't stop there! We continued right on, by hiring a sheet-rock crew and a "blow in" insulation contractor and Manderfield's again, for plumbing, heating, and electrical systems. We were on a roll! We hired a well drilling outfit for our water supply and a septic system contractor for our sewer system. Since I was also a finish carpenter, I busied myself with installing all the windows and doors and trim. Scott McConnell helped by setting all the cupboards and counter tops and installing all the hardware. We were almost ready for services! Ah, but there was one remaining, very large hurdle to jump—somehow, we'd have to pay for all of this and still finish the building. Amazingly, $30,000 more had come to the congregation from church supporters in Wisconsin and down-state Michigan. But that still wouldn't cover the remaining costs. But again, God was about to do something totally amazing!

Downtown Hancock, MI

Our home in Hancock, MI

Elevation Street

Bob Emmert and I are setting timber for the church walls

Building the walls

Peninsula Christian Church has a building!

CHAPTER 26

A BIGGER MIRACLE THAN A BUILDING

I knew that hardly a year had passed since I had visited with Gary Fynweaver the banker, but I would meet with him again anyway. He was surprised to see me. He wanted to know why I was back so soon. He wanted to know how we were doing with the list of things he had given us to accomplish, like growth, more money in the building fund, etc. I explained we were doing well. We had bought and paid for our land; had excavated and poured the concrete foundation and floor; erected the building and roofed it; installed the doors and windows; paved the parking lot; dug the well and installed the septic system; and that many of those things had been paid for! We needed to finish paying the bills and needed a loan of approximately $150,000 to finish the interior and equip it for services. His mouth dropped open in astonishment! He stood to close his office door and sitting back down, asked in all earnestness, "How on earth are you doing all of this?!" I wanted to tell him that "We already had a pretty good banker", but I didn't. Instead, I said, "To be honest, it was truly a "God thing—God was rewarding the amazing faith of this congregation—God was doing it all, with gifts of labor and love and money from His people!" He was amazed! He suddenly realized that he was looking at an organization so solid he would have no problem approaching bank officials for the whole $150,000 we needed to finish and pay off everything. Our building loan payments would be about that of a small home mortgage, easily affordable by our congregation. He did and we got our building loan! But the most remarkable thing was seeing Gary and his family begin attending services; even more amazing, a few months later I had the privilege of baptizing him and his wife into Christ. They became members of Christ's church in Hancock, Michigan. What wonderful and amazing chain of events! How amazing when God moves!

The original core group when I first met them in 1983, meeting in the Copper Crown Motel, consisted of John and Therese Blissett and their two children; Jim and Cindy Wheeler and their four kids; Jack and Mary Carroll and their son Jackie; Vern and Patti Perfetti and their four children; Paul and Sharon Halkola; Bob Emmert, a student at Tech, and his wife Holly; Kathy McConnell; and Debby McDowell. The group numbered approximately 16 adults plus a number of children. It wasn't long before many others joined us, including several students and Professors from Michigan Tech University.

We became involved with the local Christ-centered substance abuse treatment center "New Creations", also with "Little Brothers To The Elderly" and I became involved in a jail ministry at the local county jail, which led to the conversion and baptism of a young college graduate who was serving jail-time there for an attempted rape. His wife had separated from him and she had counseled and studied with me concerning her dilemma. I had the privilege of baptizing them both on the same evening. They renewed their wedding vows and were reunited in marriage. That also was a miracle! Earlier, Deb McDowell had asked me, "If I send a Bible to this neighbor who attempted this rape, would you follow it up with a visit?" I would—and I did, and in my visits with him discovered that at the very moment the jailer delivered the Bible to his cell, he was about to commit suicide by hanging himself. He was stopped by seeing the Bible in the jailers hand extended through the bars of his cell. He said that seeing that hand with a Bible in it extended through his cell bars, was like seeing the hand of God! He is now a brother in Christ!

All of this involvement by our members in areas of practical ministry brought an ever increasing number of seekers to our fellowship. It seemed as though first, the "swimming pool", and then later our new church baptistry, was in use on a regular basis. Our church family soon grew to a steady one hundred twenty in attendance, spiking higher at one hundred fifty on Easter Sundays. The original core members began asking me where I was finding all these people. I told them I didn't find them, they found us. I began asking all the newcomers why they chose to come to Peninsula Christian. The response was usually, "After moving to town" or "When we began hunting for a church, we asked others in the community where there was a church that cared about people?" They usually said, "Well, you want to go to Peninsula Christian". Compassionate, caring ministry always attracts people.

Another significant factor in this growth, was my involvement with students at Michigan Tech University. When Art Krieger and Dan Farrier, transfer students to Tech from other colleges, found Peninsula Christian Church active in the community, they began to attend. Art had been involved with His House campus ministry in Marquette, Michigan and Dan, at his home church, the Christian Church in Kalkaska, Michigan. We were delighted to have them! We were even more delighted when they asked me if I would lead a campus Bible study/ministry on the Tech campus. YES! YES! What else would I say! This was another God-send! We would have between ten and twenty students meeting each week at the Wesley House, on campus. From that start came many more students to our church services, thanks to Dan and Art. We began having Dan and some of the others to our home for Sunday dinner. Dan and our Shannon became good friends, like "big" brother – "little" sister. A few years later this led to Dan becoming our son-in-law and a great relationship with his parents, Gene and Shirley. More about that later.

GREAT FAITH AND GREAT COMPASSION

One of the wonderful traits of this congregation, I am sure the result of its great faith, was its ability to see human need and to respond with compassion. At our weekly men's breakfast, someone reminded us of the terrible aftermath of the 1989 hurricane Hugo. Others spoke of seeing TV news reports on the mess in South Carolina due to the hurricane and the enormous human need that still existed. Crews were still working on power lines; thousands of homes were still without power; people were still living in tents and garages and dealing with mountains of wreckage and trash piling up everywhere. Someone made the comment, "Too bad we couldn't do something to help!" Having some past experience in tornado cleanup in Iowa, I spoke up and said, "We can!" They were all ears. They wanted to know how and where we would begin. I assured them that if they would commit themselves to taking the time off and making the trip to Charleston with their tools, I would begin making the arrangements. They all agreed. I immediately got on the phone

With the help of our brotherhood church directory, I proceeded to make calls to our churches in the Charleston area. After speaking with representatives of both First Christian Church in Charleston and Pastor Allen Brown at Monks Corner Christian Church, I was assured of specific work sites helping people with critical needs and places to stay with local support from the congregations for meals. We were excited to get going!

HUGO, WATCH OUT, HERE WE COME!

First, we needed to raise money—and fast! The congregation was as excited to support the mission as we were to go. The money began to come in. Later, on the very Sunday afternoon we were about to leave, a car load of members from Zion Apostolic Lutheran Church in Hancock came rolling in our driveway, waving an envelope in the air. The envelope contained a $400-dollar freewill offering received that morning during their worship service. What can I say!! Next, we would need some means of transporting eight men and all their tools 1,400 miles from Hancock, Michigan to Charleston and Monks Corner, South Carolina. I noticed a bus for sale near the Michigan Tech campus. It had belonged to Michigan Tech, but had some minor roof damage just above the wind shield. The damage was not open to the elements and was hardly noticeable. The rest of the bus body was perfect and there were only 45,000 miles on the odometer. I inquired as to the price, took it for a test drive (it ran perfect), conferred with the guys about the price, which was $1,200 and all agreed to making the purchase. We took most of the back seats out and found it perfect for eight guys, their personal gear and a ton of ladders and tools. We were on our way!

On October 22, 1989, some six weeks after Hugo hit, eight of us in a 44 passenger bus, headed for Chicago; Indianapolis; Knoxville, Tennessee and Charleston, South Carolina. Switching driving duties with two other drivers, we drove straight through to Charleston.

After getting settled in the fellowship hall of the church building, and enjoying a nights rest, an elder of the First Christian congregation escorted our crew out to the Isle of Palms for our first job. A single woman with a teenage son lost a few shingles from numerous places on her roof. She was very lucky, as she had very little other house damage. It took less than a day to repair her roof. The crew was a bit perturbed when she began hinting that she wanted us to do a complete tear off and re-roof. It did not need a complete re-roof at all, only replacing shingles here and there where a tree limb had pierced the roof. At lunchtime the guys were grumbling about wasting our time on a house that was left in almost perfect condition. I asked how many of them had ever shingled a roof before. We had started the day, by taking time to show several of them how to apply three tab shingles. Most of the crew admitted they had never shingled a roof. I then suggested, "Well there you go—you just practiced shingling on a $160,000 house!" The whole crew broke out in laughter. The tension lifted and in a few hours we had easily fixed her roof as good as new. We loaded our gear and made our way to the Christian Church at Monks Corner and Pastor Allen Brown.

Allen Brown was great! He had already scouted out his community and had located those with the worst need. As he led us to a neighborhood in the Lake Moultrie area, he took the time to stop at random homes along the route to ask how they were doing and if they needed help. Many of these families were black and I am sure, as is often the case in the South, often passed over by white work crews. They were very appreciative that we would stop. They assured us that they were fine and had help on the way. I couldn't help but notice the day before, that when we were led through Charleston to the Isle of Palms by the church elder, we sped right past devastated black neighborhoods and homes. The elder never looked to the right or the left. It was straight ahead—to the middle and upper class white neighborhoods. The crew immediately noticed this disparity by church members and an elder who ought to know better.

Lake Moultrie was our destination and Allen warned us that the home he was taking us to was in very bad shape. A gigantic oak tree had blown down on Ruby Ray's home and smashed the entire roof down into the rooms below, as well as the north wall. Ruby was now living in her garage, with her pictures, keep sakes and furniture floating around in the rain soaked house. If we should decide that this was too big a job for us, we were to just say so and we would be given another, less difficult job to conquer. We took a look at the huge mess and this elderly lady's plight and decided to a man, that God called us down to South Carolina to do a job and not necessarily the easiest job. "We'll take it", we said! And immediately went to work.

GOD IS AT WORK, AGAIN

The first job was to get the enormous oak tree off what was left of her home. How would we do that? The one thing we were not equipped to do was cut up a tree that was four to five feet thick and seventy feet tall. I had brought my chain saw but how would we handle the huge sections of tree once we got it cut up? We had no crane or power-loader to remove it. Suddenly we heard a tractor and chain saws coming down the street. We went to see what was coming, and walking up the street toward us was a crew of guys with chain saws and a large front-end loader from a Baptist church somewhere. They were there on a mercy mission just as we were. Their specialty was tree removal. Immediately their leader approached us and asked if there was anything they could do for us. Was this a God thing or what? We said, "affirmative—could you remove that big oak tree?" He asked, "where do you want it?" We told his crew to pile it by the street. In thirty minutes the tree was gone! We then began our work of dismantling the broken sections of roof and piling the pieces with the sections of oak tree. The city clean up crew did the rest.

As the guys were working and cleaning the debris away, I was busy measuring and figuring the quickest way we could replace the roof. I found the dimensions were perfect for a set of twenty-four foot garage trusses. A truss company a few mile north of Monks Corner said they would fill the order and even though it meant the crew working the week-end, they would do so and have the trusses to us by Monday morning. Their crew had volunteered to do this for us. Wow! What a blessing! Sure enough, Monday morning the truck rounded the corner to Ruby's place—we had our trusses. We made a run to the local lumber yard for plywood sheathing, black paper and shingles which they delivered later that day, just as we finished setting the truss rafters. By Wednesday, the roof was shingled and we busied ourselves with re-wiring the house, trimming out the soffits, repairing the north wall and re-setting doors and windows. By Friday morning early, we were ready for the trip home.

MENDING FENCES AND MAKING FRIENDS

The story does not simply end with the repair of a house. First, there was the positive impact made on Ruby Ray. She had revealed to me the first day we arrived, "That she just didn't understand how God could be so good to her since she was not a church goer or even a church member. Why would we do this for her, she wondered with tears in her eyes? She was amazed we would come 3,600 miles round trip to fix her house!

Then there were the local "redneck" neighbors. All around us, they were looking over their fences and glaring at "these Yankees from Michigan". Having noticed our Michigan license plates, one of them must have called the police and city hall. In no time there was a black and white patrol car and a black City Inspector's car pulling up in front of Ruby's house. As these officials were making their way across the lawn, I began to wonder what kind of trouble we were in and "how much time we were going to serve". We didn't have to wonder long. Immediately, the inspector demanded to know who the contractor was. "That would be me." I said. He then wanted to see my contractors license—which I did not have. He then proceeded to chew us out for scamming the elderly lady we were working for. The audience of neighborhood red necks was taking it all in.

When he finally gave me a chance to respond, I informed the listening crowd and officials, that we were not charging her a thing for the work. Eyes brows raised, jaws dropped, and voices became silent, as I revealed that we were a church group from Hancock, Michigan, and at our own expense, we were fixing Ruby's house at no cost to her except for what materials she could afford! "This is a mission of compassion to her and the community" I said. Suddenly the inspector hung his head, placed his hand on my shoulder and apologized for the aggravation he had caused us and for interfering with our work. He then turned to the officer and others watching and exclaimed, "Too bad the TV cameras aren't here to report this! Ya'all have a good day men! And thank you!" The irony of this incident was that as the end of our time approached we could see we would not have time to finish patching the few holes in the sheet rock ceilings. We were assured by locals that a sheet rocker who lived in the neighborhood would gladly hire out to her to finish the job for a minimal amount. We later heard that the local "neighborhood" sheet-rocker charged her $3,500 to patch a few holes, but took her money and skipped town. I believe they call that hypocrisy, stealing, and fraud do they not?

Remarkably, as that day went on, some of the "rednecks" who had been glaring at us over the fence were now coming to us to invite us to their porches for lunch on following days. They told us to not bother fixing lunches, that they would be having "Chicken Bog" for us at one place, grilled chicken at another, and grilled burgers and brats at yet another. We had made friends of the whole neighborhood! Also, the ladies of the Monks Corner congregation volunteered to fix our evening meals and wash our clothes. We were to give them two men's dirty laundry each day, and they would bring back our clothes clean and folded. Each day we were bone weary tired, but spiritually lifted! What an exceptional week that was for people-to-people relationships and Christian witness! On Friday morning early, as we were headed home with the bus radio blaring, urgent news reports were describing a devastating earthquake in San Francisco. Instantly, the guys began shouting, "Head this bus west to San Francisco! We've got more work to do!" More than a "house repair" experience had happened to the guys that week! I reminded the guys they had wives and families waiting for them back in the U.P., expecting them home on Saturday. They would hang me if I didn't deliver them back home on time. San Francisco will have to wait!

THE CROWNING MOMENT OF THE HUGO TRIP

After returning from South Carolina, we hugged our kids and wives, put away our tools, washed our clothes and ourselves, and got back to business as usual. Tom Litzenberger had volunteered to serve as our treasurer for the trip, keeping track of monies coming in and being spent. The day we left for South Carolina he told the guys we had $2,300 to spend for gas, food, and building supplies. We kept that figure in mind, being careful not to be careless with our purchases, using it mainly for gas and oil for the bus and a few meals which were really fixed items. We all knew that if necessary, we could use our own credit cards for purchases over the $2,300. Things went well with expenditures on the way down. But, with having to buy some building materials and supplies for Ruby's house, the money was disappearing fast. Tom spoke to me about the problem and his concern that we might be running out of money before we got home. I assured him that God had provided for our church before and He would certainly do it now. He agreed.

AND THERE HE GOES AGAIN!

On the Thursday before we were to return home from Monks Corner, Allan Brown came to see how our work was going and to deliver our mail, which had that day caught up to us. There were personal letters for the guys from family and friends, but also several money gifts enclosed from groups and individuals who wanted to "join" us in support of our mission. I don't remember Tom saying how much had come in the mail that day, but I do know he was relieved that we had enough to get ourselves home. Then, a few days after arriving back in Hancock, I was in the church office going through church mail, checking the calendar for appointments, studying for my next sermon etc, when Tom stopped by the office for a visit. He looked like he had seen Jesus face to face! Seeing the look on his face, I asked him what had happened. His reply was, "Gordie, you not going to believe this, but after checking and rechecking every cent of money in the "bag", we have exactly $2,300 left over!" I was as shocked as he was! It was another "God thing", like the feeding of the 5,000! God was replenishing the money as fast as we could spend it! Gee! I thought things like that only happened in the Bible. We sent the money back to the Monks Corner church. And oh yes, I forgot to mention at the beginning of this story, that when the men went to their employers to ask for time off for this Hugo mission, each one was told he would be given paid time off as their contribution to the mission. God was blessing our mission even before we left town!

A MISSION TRIP TO VIENNA, AUSTRIA

Sometime in 1992 Betty and I received a call from our close friend John Mark Read, wondering if we would consider joining him and his wife Darlene and Howie and Sandy Ganong, on a three week mission trip to work at House Edelweiss outside of Vienna, Austria. House Edelweiss is a mission school that serves as a Bible college to European and Eastern Bloc converts wanting to prepare themselves for ministry in their home countries. We agreed, raised some money and vacation time and packed our bags for Austria. After the longest plane ride I've ever endured, we landed at London's Heathrow, then flew on to Vienna. Our mission was not to teach, but to serve as support staff for the house operation. Our jobs would be working in the kitchen, cleaning restrooms, doing laundry, cleaning student's rooms and doing yard work. Our commitment was for two weeks, and we would be serving the house while a group of Romanians, Czechs, and Russians would be there studying. We enjoyed the work, but even more, the fellowship with these devoted Christian students. Many of them had endured severe persecution, living as Christians in the Eastern Bloc's brutal totalitarian cultures. We admired their dedication and extraordinary effort in preparing for ministry to their people. Our German-English interpreter, who did an exceptional job communicating for us, and in English to German for the American Bible professors, had experienced the Communist secret police invading his home and arresting his wife. Day and night, he stood outside the Romanian jail with his Christian friends in minus ten degree temps and prayed for her while she was being tortured and interrogated. He and they, kept their vigil until she was released. These eastern bloc Christian students had all paid the price for their faith. We were in awe of their dedication and faith. It was an honor to fix their meals, clean their rooms and toilets!

An extra treat we enjoyed the first week before our duty at the house began, was a road trip through Czechoslovakia into East Germany. We were there to visit Maja, our foreign exchange student. Maja lived with us for a year and attended Hancock High with Shannon. While the Reads and Ganongs went on to West Germany to visit friends and places they knew there, we enjoyed a wonderful week with Maja, visiting her home, her high school, and some of the historic cities like Dresden, the Saxony Alps, and places around her city of Riesa. At her high school we had the privilege of meeting her school principal and speaking to two of their English classes. The students were allowed to ask Betty and me any questions they wanted. They were shocked at our openness. In the eastern bloc countries, you keep your head down, your eyes straight ahead and your mouth shut! The week with Maja, her sister, mother and grandmother was exceptional.

The Hugo Crew

Ruby Ray's
crushed home

Rebuilding Ruby's home
after Hurricane Hugo

Ruby and the guys

Eastern bloc converts/students and our crew

House Edelweise, Vienna, Austria

CHAPTER 29

SHANNON CROWNED

One of the major events in Shannon's life happened while we were in Europe. She was chosen to be crowned Miss Houghton County at the County Fair. We missed it! We were traipsing around Europe. We did not deliberately plan it that way, it's just the way things turned out. We had the Europe trip planned months in advance. At that time we didn't know for sure she would even be a candidate, let alone be picked Queen. On the evening of the Houghton County Fair, we all, the Reads, the Ganongs, and Betty and me, were in Maja's living room visiting with her, her mother and grandmother. We had been visiting late into the evening—after midnight—when a call came from Shannon in the States. She was phoning to announce that she had just been crowned Miss Houghton County! We were all ecstatic! We regretted we weren't there to see it all—a major disappointment for Betty and me! Thankfully, Sherry and Boyd were there to share the event with Shannon, and we do have a video tape of the ceremony, but it certainly doesn't compare to being there.

SHANNON CROWNED MISS MINNESOTA BIBLE COLLEGE

On that same subject, our youngest daughter certainly is a winner. Each year the students of MBC (now Crossroads College), where she was a student, would select one of the female students to represent the college as "Miss MBC". She was the one selected for the honor. One thing for sure, WE WERE PRESENT FOR THIS ONE! We have been proud of all three or our beautiful and talented daughters, and we were proud again to see Shannon receive this honor. An interesting feature of that years's presentation was the announcement, that by unanimous decision on the part of the student body and with Shannon's approval, the Miss MBC pageant was to be discontinued. Shannon and her fellow students felt that at a Christian college no one person should be singled out above the others, and that the money spent for the pageant would be better spent on some mission. Needless to say, we are proud of her and the students of MBC!

RIDING THE ORIENT EXPRESS

Back to our story in Austria and Germany. One of the great experiences of our visit was taking the Orient Express back to Vienna. Betty and I had made the trip with the Reads and Ganongs to Riesa, GDR, by a rented van. Since they were taking the van on to former West Germany, we agreed to make the return trip to Vienna by train. Maja took us to the huge train station in Dresden. From there, we bid her a tearful good-bye and made our return. The many highlights of this train trip include not only the beautiful scenery along the Elbe and Danube, but the beautiful people we shared our compartment with. One young college woman, Radka, who boarded the train at Prague, with whom we visited, continued writing to us after our return to the states. Soon, our mission stint was finished, and we, along with the Reads and Ganongs, made the long flight home. Those memories will last forever. God is good!

Shannon is crowned Miss
Houton County

Shannon is crowned
Miss M.B.C.

CHAPTER 28

AND THE BEAT GOES ON

Nine of the thirteen years we ministered in the U.P., I also served as a trustee for Minnesota Bible College. Sometime in 1995, during one of my visits to the Rochester campus, I was approached by Tay Shields (now Tay Odor), the college recruiter, about accompanying her, other staff and twenty prospective M.B.C. students from the surrounding four state area on a mission trip to Mexico to build a home for a homeless family. She thought I would like to be involved since I was a trustee and experienced at carpentry. I told her I was indeed interested—I would do it! The program was called "God's Hands Across The Border", and the mission was to build a house for a family in one week, as well as organize recreation and Bible classes for the kids in the neighborhood. The destination was Juarez, Mexico, just across the border from El Paso, Texas. This was going to be a major ten day marathon of hard work, heat, sandstorms and sleeping on the ground in tents. As always, I was ready for another challenge!

My question to Tay was how she planned to get all these people and tools and supplies to Juarez. She confessed she didn't have it all figured out yet, but had one fifteen passenger van ready, and was working on two others. She did not know how she would get the tools and supplies hauled down there. I then mentioned that I owned a "Greyhound Bus". A twinkle came to her eye and a grin, and a look that said, "Yeah, Gordie, and I suppose you also own a Holiday Inn in Juarez!" I assured her I was not joking, that I really did own a Greyhound bus. We had purchased the bus months before, to convert into a motor home. Most of the seats were out of it except for a few old couches and chairs and card tables. I had not yet converted it into a motor home. It also had two huge luggage bays below, each one larger than the back of a pick up truck. I told her that it was not air conditioned but would easily haul the kids, the tools and supplies down and back. If the college would pay the fuel costs I would be glad to use it for the trip. Tay was ecstatic!

A MISSION TO JUAREZ

In the meantime, the thoughts of the teenagers and parents in our congregation at Hancock were focusing on this mission trip as well. As plans developed, I discovered I had six of our own teens ready to commit to the trip. This action by these teens does not seem unusual, knowing their parents and their commitment to missions. On my end, there was more to do than service the bus. I needed to locate hammers and saws, mixing troughs and hoes, shovels and rakes and saw horses, and step ladders. Tay was finalizing the overnight stops and accommodations for our travel. Departure day arrived, and six pairs of concerned parents left their teenagers in my charge to get them to Mexico and back safely. After the hugs and kisses, I cranked up the big Detroit engine and made the 400 mile drive to the college campus in Rochester where we would pick up the other teens and staff.

We arrived at the college campus in good time and without incident except to learn that the bus's fuel pump, feeding the injectors was leaking. With the help of Berdine Strain, a friend of mine and owner of Strain School Bus Service, I easily located a new one and changed it in short order. We stayed a day on campus to allow for orientation classes and some time for team building. There were kids from South Dakota, Iowa, Wisconsin, and Minnesota, plus six staff. We all needed to get acquainted and on the same page. After a very busy and productive day we were ready to travel.

The next day, with Tay and a few students and staff in the school van, and the rest of us in the bus, we left for our first stop, Council Bluffs, Iowa, where we stayed the night in the church building. The next day we visited Boy's Town in Omaha, Nebraska, and then pushed on to Denver and Los Alamos, New Mexico, where we again stayed the night in the church building. The next day we finished the trip into Juarez, with one major glitch. Tay got too far ahead of us, and out of CB range north of Las Cruces— just when I needed to find a station to refill my diesel tank. I was so low I could feel the engine falter, so pulled off the freeway and into the first station we saw. Unaware I was no longer behind her, she sped on to El Paso.

After filling up with diesel fuel, we were on our way again, but without Tay and staff, and now with a severely ill teenage girl onboard. We had been enduring 105 degree temperatures on the trip with no air conditioning. The girl was having an asthma attack, and had lost her inhaler. She was losing consciousness and the nurse was riding somewhere ahead with Tay—and we were in big trouble! I could see two of the girls working with her, cooling her with wet towels, but I noticed the rest of the kids were clear at the back of the bus. At first, I wondered what they were doing, but then I could see in the rear-view mirror, they were holding hands and praying. Suddenly, as we approached El Paso, we saw a large blue and white H hospital sign and darted for the off ramp and to the hospital emergency entrance. She was immediately hospitalized, and in expert hands. Prayers answered! The one young staff member we had with us volunteered to stay with her so we could link up again with Tay and make our way to the Amor Ministry base camp south of Juarez. Someone would return for them at the hospital later.

We still could not reach Tay for directions. She was too far out of range. Later, we discovered she had returned to Las Cruces to find us. Unaware of this, we felt we had no choice but to make our way into downtown El Paso to see if we could get close enough for radio contact with someone, anyone, perhaps with the Amor team. As we made our way down the freeway, suddenly we saw staff member Chris Brooks standing on the shoulder of the freeway watching for us. With cars streaking by, we slammed to a stop to pick him up. He was wasted! He was thrilled! He was hot and wind blown, but he had all the information we needed to get connected up again. He led us to a McDonalds, where we met with the Amor ministry team. They led us across the border through the government border station and on through the narrow streets of Juarez to the mission base station. Whew! What a relief! But where was Tay?

Our task that evening was to set up camp, fix dinner, and unwind.

Tay did not make it to the mission base until near midnight. She had reconnected by radio with the Amor team and they informed her of connecting up with us, and was appraised of the girl and staff member at the hospital. She checked on the girl at the hospital and found they were ready to release her. She had mainly been dehydrated and with plenty of liquids and an inhaler, was soon doing fine. Tay arrived at the base camp with the girl and staff members late that evening. We were all relieved to be back together and all in one piece. We slept good that night—except for a dust storm! My sleep was interrupted by calls for help. I spent an hour in the middle of the night capturing blowing tents and re-staking them back to the ground in the blowing sandstorm and darkness. Wow, I thought, what a day, this had been! What a night this was turning out to be! Was this a taste of what lie ahead? We all did some praying that night, prayers of thanksgiving and prayers for God's help!

ON THE STREETS OF JUAREZ

The next day we were directed to the neighborhood and home site where we would be working. We broke out the tools, met the family, and began work, leveling the building site and forming up the slab. We had no power tools, requiring all work to be done by hand. All concrete had to be mixed in mixing boxes with hoes, and then worked into the forms, leveled and troweled by hand. We then began assembling the walls and roof system for the 11 feet by 22 feet two-room house. All cuts were made with hand saws, all nails driven by claw hammers. After assembling the sections on the ground, they were raised into place and fastened at the corners. The roof system was then constructed, and lifted in one piece by the entire crew, and set in place on the walls. Sheathing was nailed in place on the rafters, and covered with black paper and roll roofing. Black paper was then stapled to all outside wall studs and over-laid with chicken wire. The gravel we used for the concrete, was sifted into fine sand, and mixed into stucco cement and troweled on to the outside walls. This standard house came with one partition, two doors (one inside, one entrance) and four windows, all of which could be placed wherever the new owners preferred them. In the U.S.A., this structure would be considered a tool shed or chicken coop. In the barrios of Juarez this was considered a mansion.

One day, as we were working, a nearby neighbor asked if he could have some leftover scraps of the black tar paper we were using. We asked what he wanted the paper for, and he said he needed it to patch the holes in his refrigerator box "house" he and his ailing mother were living in. The Amor team investigated his situation, and immediately put him on the list for a new home. The family of four we were building the home for, whom we had met on our arrival, had been driven off their farm by drought and successive crop failures. They were living in a small four room house next door with twelve other adult and child family relatives. They were delighted and blessed to get their new home.

Each work day, we divided the crew into three teams and rotated them between water/rest breaks, working on the house, and playing with the neighborhood kids in the street. The team in the street would play organized games with the kids and teach Bible lessons. This was a big hit with the children. The water/rest breaks were a hit with the crews and very much needed. The climate was very dry and temperatures were usually around 105 to 110 degrees. Yet, even with all our care and caution, we had to send a few to the hospital. We almost had to force the kids to drink water. The bottled water we had carried with us was good and safe, but they liked the Coke and Pepsi they could buy at the little neighborhood store much better. We warned them about dehydration and that Coke and Pepsi only made the situation worse. As we all know from experience, you can tell teenagers many things, but you can't tell them much. It would take a visit to the hospital to get the point across.

WORSHIP IN A BARIO CHURCH

Being there over the week-end, we were invited to worship with the local congregation. What an amazing contrast to our American churches. All the families walk to the services and filled the little building to more than overflowing. The building was so full that many had to stand outside. Everyone sang and prayed. They would sing at the top of their lungs with tears running down their cheeks. The pastor prayed, but so did everyone else, as well. Their worship band consisted of one guitar and amplifier, played by the pastor and a beat-up drum set, played by one of the teens, using sticks whittled out of tree limbs. The music that arose from that gathering was amazing! Our kids were amazed! They were so in awe that they were still talking about it that evening around our campfire. The comments were, "These people really know how to pray! These people know how to sing! They really feel what they're doing!" One of the guys, with tears in his eyes confessed that he had been badgering his parents to buy him the latest set of drum sticks on the market, that he felt his "old" ones were just not good enough. After seeing the young drummer at that service play as he did on sticks made from tree limbs, he was going to go home and shut his mouth!

COMIN' HOME TO AMERICA

Soon, our work was done. We presented the new house to the family and shared a dedication service with them, asking God to bless their new home. It was time to pack our tents and tools and head back up the highway and home. As we drove north across the border through El Paso, Tay announced to us on the CB that she had a treat for everyone—we would be staying in a motel that evening. A collective cheer went up! It was just what we all needed, clean beds to sleep in and flush toilets and modern showers to use. For showers at the work camp, we had crude, open-to-the-sky partitions—blue plastic tarps draped over two-inch P.V.C pipe standards—and one gallon plastic jugs with one gallon of cold water each, which we poured over our heads and down over our bodies. In the outhouse toilets, we were advised to "save" the toilet paper we used, and put it in a bucket by the door. It would be disposed of some other way. Ugh! That was just the way they did things in Mexico. Using the shower and toilet was almost more than some could stand. Some of us were old enough to remember the "outhouse". It was not pleasant, but no problem, once we got used to it. But now—a MOTEL! We would be enjoying all the amenities, plus a swimming pool!

After a good night's rest, we hit the trail for home, making it to Security, Colorado by evening. Again, we used the church building of our sister congregation there for housing and breakfast. The next day was a big day on the road. I was well rested, well fed and ready to cover some miles home. We drove all the way from Security, Colorado to Rochester, Minnesota, stopping only for food, fuel and potty breaks. It was good to be "almost home". I say almost, because those of us from Hancock, Michigan had yet another 400 miles to travel. We spent the day on campus sorting out all the back packs and luggage, having debriefing sessions and group worship. After tearful good-byes, our Peninsula Christian crew cranked up the old Detroit engine again and headed north through Wisconsin to our home in Hancock. After an uneventful, but tiring eight hour trip, we were back with family and friends. It had been a wonderful, rewarding, and eye opening mission! It will be an experience none of us will ever forget!

M.B.C. group headed for Mexico. God's hands aross the border

Building a house.

Worshipping in a Bario church

The group from M.B.C. in front of "The Hummer"

CHAPTER 39

BACK HOME WITH FAMILY AND FRIENDS

For the kids, it was being back with families, and story telling about what they had experienced on the Mexico trip, and back to school again in the fall. For me, it was back to the office and studying to prepare sermons and lessons; back to house and hospital calls; back to enjoying Betty's and the girl's company and our friends at church. It was back to family drives in our open Toyota Landcruiser on Brockway Mountain Drive and around the tip of the Peninsula on a logging road to Beta Grise. We enjoyed other excursions to places like Freda, Douglas-Houghton Falls, Lac La Belle, McLain's State Park, and hiking the Porcupine Mountains, all, some of the most beautiful scenic spots in the country. We camped several times at McLain's State Park. Many of the camping sites were right at the edge of the Lake Superior shoreline. The water was usually too cold to swim in unless you were a polar bear, but the views and sunsets were breathtaking.

We enjoyed other great excursions while living in Michigan's U.P. Our church friends, Russ and Duffy Lepisto, took us sailing on their 28-foot Catalina sailing boat on several occasions. These were some of the most relaxing afternoons and evenings we have ever enjoyed. There were trips to Tahquamenon Falls, Pictured Rocks Lake Shore Drive, Whitefish Point where the Edmund Fitzgerald went down, and Sault Ste. Marie. At Sault Ste. Marie, we visited Bill and Marsha Ward, Marsha being an old Bible College friend, and of course, the Soo Locks, where we would see 1,000 foot ore boats and ocean freighters from all over the world making their way through the Locks. On one occasion, when my folks were visiting, we crossed to the Canadian side of Sault Ste. Marie and took the Agawa Canyon Rail Trip to Agawa Canyon and Falls. Again, the scenery was beautiful, with high cliffs and whitewater rivers and waterfalls. But, even more exciting for two old railroad buffs, was to be riding the train again, as it snaked its way through the hills and across the high trestles.

SALMON FISHING ON THE GRAND TRAVERSE

In our growing relationship with Tech student, Dan Farrier, we became friends with Gene and Shirley Farrier his parents, which led to visits at their home in Kalkaska. Those visits led to some great fishing trips with them on Grand Traverse Bay. A close friend of theirs offered his excursion fishing boat and guide service for a day of fishing on the Bay. This was a new kind of fishing for Betty and me. We were using steel line and dragging lures and bait over 100 feet behind the boat, fishing for lake Salmon. It was a great day! We caught the biggest fish we had ever caught. These were not Crappies and Blue Gills, these were 10 to 20-pounders. I caught a 9-pound lake Salmon and Betty caught a 26-pounder! She worked long and hard to reel that monster in. But when the guys offered to help her, she exclaimed, "You just leave me alone. I'm gonna do this myself!" We had caught others, but these were the best. They were cleaned and iced and taken home to provide us terrific fish dinners for many months. We've had the privilege of fishing with the Farriers and their friends other times since. We have always been very appreciative of these great fishing experiences. We are thankful for all the times of fellowship we've had with the Farriers in the past, and are hopeful God provides more in the future!

PENINSULA CHRISTIAN YOUTH ACTIVITIES

In the 80's and 90's we began to see a change in the youth activities in churches. I noticed a trend away from the traditional youth rally, which amounted to teens from the churches of a particular geographical area gathering on a Saturday or Sunday afternoon to sing a few choruses and hear someone preach a sermon. We wanted to try something different, to again attract many more teens to larger group gatherings. For us, at Peninsula Christian, we had the added disadvantage of being long distances from sister congregations. The closest was over 100 miles away.

WINTERFEST

We decided on a new format. First: we would have the kids arrive Friday evening. By leaving right after school, most could arrive for an evening songfest and get acquainted session. Second: we enlisted the help of students and student teams from Minnesota Bible College to lead the kids in special games, special music, and drama presentations. Third: we arranged for the teens to stay overnight with families in the congregation. This was great for involving the parents and church families in the rally. Fourth: we set the dates for the rally to coincide with the Winter Carnival at Michigan Tech. One of the features of Winter Carnival was the creation of large ice statues by students and student organizations all over campus. The statues were carved out of ice in full scale. The scenes were elaborate, and amazingly detailed, such as a full scale ice layout of "The Gunfight At OK Corral", with the "main street" buildings, horses, cowboys, and blazing guns! Of course there were many more similar type sculptures all over the campus. People would drive for miles, even from down state, to enjoy the amazing work of the students. So, built into our church youth rally was an afternoon of touring the campus in groups, to view this amazing ice statuary. Also on the program, was a Saturday afternoon of enjoying exercise, games, and group recreation at the Tech Recreation Center. We even offered downhill skiing on Mt. Ripley, a Tech-managed ski hill a mile down the road from the church building.

It was a daunting task, coordinating food, people, events, and host homes for the weekend. However, it proved to be worth all the effort. Each year we filled every seat, every home, nook, and cranny with teenagers. The "Winterfest" event, as we called it, was a huge success. It was great for the kids and parents, great for the MBC teams who came to help, and great for the churches and leaders. Thus, it became an annual feature of the Peninsula Christian Church.

THE GREAT KEWEENAW BIKE TRIP

Another big, one-time-event planned for the youth of the area churches, was a week- long bike trek from the church building in Hancock, to the tip of the Keweenaw Peninsula and back. Most of this trip would take us along the scenic south shore of Lake Superior. The churches were to bring their teens, along with their bikes and tenting gear. We would provide the trek guide—ME—along with the food and a "sag wagon" (support vehicle), to follow the group with bikes, bike parts, tires, and tools. The church building was our base camp. After their arrival, we led the some 100+ bikers through Hancock and along the twisting, turning County Road 203 to McLain's State Park, our first encampment. We enjoyed the remainder of the day and evening setting up tents, preparing an evening meal and enjoying fun and fellowship. After a good night's rest, we had breakfast, broke camp and continued on 203, along the shore of Lake Superior and then up a long grade to the town of Calumet, Michigan, stopping there for lunch. We then pedaled north a short distance on State Highway M-41, turned left to the lakeshore and descended a long downhill run to Eagle River, where we set up our next camp. The weather was perfect, the scenery was spectacular and we were off to a great start!

The next day we followed the shoreline highway to Brockway Mountain, and attacked the long Brockway Mountain Drive to the breathtaking summit. After the long up-hill climb the kids were exhausted, but seeing this view of Lake Superior with the big Ore boats steaming along out in the distance, and the awesome cliffs behind us down to the valley below, they were reinvigorated! After resting for a while, we made our way back down the steep, twisting east decent into Copper Harbor. We had to closely watch these young bikers. They weren't used to a road this steep and turns so severe, and some thought they could "turn it all loose" and fly down the hill. Thankfully, we had no spills. Everyone made it down safely.

We turned the kids loose with their group leaders, to shop and see the sights of Copper Harbor, Michigan, a one-time busy fishing village with a classic light house. We set up camp at Fort Wilkins State Historical Park to rest, eat, tour the fort and spend the night. The next day, we made the trek to the beautiful sand beaches of Beta Grise, a once small copper mining "location" on the southeast shore of the peninsula. The kids enjoyed swimming in the clean water and vacant white-sand beaches, and then camped again in that state park. From there, we made the long but scenic road to Lake Linden and back to the church building. We were one tired bunch of bikers but amazed at what we had seen and experienced. "I can't believe we did that!"

Gordon's proud catch.

Betty hits the mother load! Is it any wonder that she loves to fish?

CHAPTER 30

JUST BETTY AND ME

Through the years of raising three daughters, I hardly ever remember a time for just the two of us to simply enjoy time together by ourselves. To take a bike trip or a hike without a youth group or a number of kids tagging along seldom happened. We were always either with our own three or church kids. But Shannon came to us one day to tell us about an invitation from her sister Sherry and husband Boyd Paavola, to accompany them to Europe and pedal around Belgium and Holland on their bikes. At first, I rejected the idea, but Betty saw no reason why not to let her go. As the days passed, I began to rethink my position. I must admit, I had a "selfish" twist in my thinking. I thought, if I let her go with her sister for this lengthy period of time, it will allow Betty and me to be free to "do our own thing"! Think of it—for the first time, just the two of us doing what we want to do, going where we want to go. Cool! "Shannon, you go girl!" Excited about these new adventures, they planned their trip, and we planned ours.

FOOTLOOSE! LIKE KIDS AGAIN.

At first, we were thinking "Harley Davidson"—lets buy a big bike to tour the country. But after visiting with several veteran bikers, and learning the cost of these big bikes, we scrapped that plan. Beside the cost, they all pretty much agreed that a long trip out west on a Harley, covering many miles, would beat us to death. We agreed. We also scaled down the area we would tour. We finally decided we would go west/

northwest, starting at Rapid City, South Dakota and then proceed west through Missoula, Montana and Glacier National Park, always one our favorites spots. Then, we planned to go on to Spokane, Washington. From Spokane, we wanted to see some new country and new sites. We would go on to visit the Grand Coulee Dam and then find a good place to hike the trails of the Cascades.

But first, what would be an enjoyable, economical car to make this trip in? We wanted something affordable, something fun, something sporty. One day as I was walking past a car dealership, I noticed a little red Pontiac Fierro sports car sitting on the lot. I asked the dealer about it, and he filled me in on the particulars. It had low miles and an economical, four-cylinder motor and excellent handling qualities. It was sporty, bright red, and built low to the ground (at that time we could still get in and out of a car built low to the ground), with a price tag of $4,000. "We'll take it!" The one thing it was short on was cargo space. We would be forced to pack light and efficient and smart. We used light weight everything, tent, camping gear, cooking gear, and backpacks. Rather than pack in suitcases, we used the backpacks wrapped in plastic and strapped them to the little luggage-rack on the engine cover in the rear. This little car had a mid-engine arrangement, with the car's trunk in the front and hood in the rear. As it turned out, we had plenty of storage space for our gear.

We bid Boyd, Sherry, and Shannon good-bye as they were leaving for Europe with their bikes. We then packed the Ferro and headed west on I-90. What a joy! The little car was exciting to drive. It didn't know what a curve was, as it wheeled around the sharpest corners as flat as a pancake. It seemed that I hardly needed to let off the gas as we cruised the mountain roads. Mt Rushmore is always awesome. Glacier was, as always, spectacular and still one of our favorite places! We found our two-man tent and sleeping gear working just great. Our lightweight backpack cooking gear served us well. We were rested, relaxed, and well fed. We were having the time of our life! What a country! At Spokane we decided to get a motel. We had been sleeping on the ground several nights and had little opportunity to shower. A night in a comfortable bed and a shower was wonderful. While in Spokane, we visited Betty's niece Alisa.

From Spokane, we traveled west through the vast wheat country of eastern Washington. The Grand Coulee Dam was more awesome than we had imagined. What a marvelous engineering feat. Then, the map revealed something of a choice. We could drop back down to I-90 and go west through the Cascades, or we could take State Hwy-20 through extreme northern Washington and the Cascades. Hwy-20 is a narrow, two lane highway that winds through the apple orchard country, through places like Twisp, Diablo, Mazama, and Winthrop. We took it—what else could we do! At dinner time we stopped in Winthrop. Winthrop was like stepping back a century into the Old West, with saloons, and saddle horses tied to a hitch rails out front. We just couldn't help ourselves, we ate some "cowboy" food, checked out the shops and enjoyed the local western scene. It was like being in a John Wayne movie.

MOUNTAIN CLIMBERS

That afternoon, we made our way to a place called Marblemount and turned left down Cascade River Road, a gravel logging road. Twenty-two miles down this logging road we came to a dense forest of some of the biggest fir trees I had ever seen outside of the Giant Red Woods! There, at a place called Mineral Park, we found a beautiful Forestry Service camp ground nestled at the base of some huge firs, with a whitewater stream and waterfall next to it. It was like camping inside of a majestic cathedral, with a cascading waterfall for an altar and pulpit. That camp site alone was an experience in itself, and only cost $2.00 per night. We were the only ones there, except for a Washington University geology student we seldom saw. We also discovered this campground and parking lot to be the trail head for two of the many Cascade hiking trails. We took full advantage of that! Each day we would head up the wonderfully groomed trails to see how far and how high we could go. We didn't think we wanted to be too gung-ho for a couple of aging novices, so rather than carry full backpacks and gear with us, we decided to go out (up) as far as we could during the first half of the day, and then make our way back down to camp the last half. We enjoyed the trail going up so much, we lost track of the time and found ourselves getting back into camp after dark. Those trails going to the top of the world were so spectacular, we will never forget our experiences there. The first day we made it all the way up the Cascade Pass Trail and to the Cascade Pass rest area, where we found an eighty-five year old "mountain man" making his way down from somewhere way up at the top. Amazing! We met several other hikers on that trail, many of them senior citizens. "You go geezers!"

The second day we took Hidden Lake Tail, ever as spectacular as the first. But we saw no other hikers on the way up that trail. That trail took us even higher than the day before. Suddenly, we found ourselves in snow. On either side of the trail was melting snow and little steams with waterfalls plunging their way down to some larger stream somewhere below. We saw Marmots and Bighorn Sheep. We heard what sounded like thunder, and saw enormous sections of glaciers breaking off and plunging to the canyons below. Awesome! Finally, we trekked to what looked like the very top of the mountain range, and rested. We were no longer looking up to the peaks around us—we were looking straight out or even down on the peaks around us. And there were few or no trees around. Were we above the timberline? Possibly, I don't recall an elevation sign. After enjoying the awesome scenery, we discovered that the time had flown, and it was mid afternoon, and past time to start back down to the campground. As we made our way down this switchback trail, we met the only other people on that trail that day, a young couple. They were making their way up with full packs. He was "chomping at the bit" to go faster. She was dying. We stopped to visit with them for a while, allowing her time to rest and catch her breath. We then parted company and made our way down, as they made their way higher. We arrived at our tent long past dark, but what a marvelous day we had experienced!

The next day we broke camp, packed the little Ferro and headed for Mount Vernon, Washington where my niece Pam Kelly lived. She had been expecting us and was thrilled when we arrived. We had a great visit with her, her two children and husband Jerry. Mom and Dad, in southern California were following our trip by map, and decided that when we arrived at Pam and Jerry's, they would take the train to Seattle and join us. We met them at an Amtrack station in the Seattle area and enjoyed a great family fellowship. While at Pam and Jerry's we took some side trips to Vancouver, B.C., visited Ken Bosworth from the Webster City, Iowa church and his family in Anacortes, and then headed for Olympic National Park by way of Whidbey Island and ferry boat to Port Townsend. We camped in view of Mt. Olympus. We proceeded on around the Olympic Peninsula to the Hoh Rain Forest to enjoy a hike through the giant moss-covered Firs.

We then traveled on to the Aberdeen/Hoquiam area to visit Jack and Lynn Adams, Betty's cousins, and then on through Portland, Oregon, to Bend, to spend a day or two with Bill and Jean Tollis, more longtime friends. After some sightseeing and fellowship with the Tollis's, we went due east through Burns, Oregon, and some of the most desolate desert range land in the country. We continued east through Boise, Twin Falls, Pocatello and Idaho Falls, Idaho. We traveled still eastward to Jackson Hole, Wyoming, where we camped with an awesome panoramic view of the majestic Grand Tetons right outside our tent door. Just experiencing this majestic scenery was, in itself, amazing.

We entered Yellowstone National Park through the South Gate and were greeted with the stark scene of a blackened forest, as far as the eye could see. It was the aftermath of the giant forest fire that hit in 1989-90, and this was years later. After seeing the famous sites of Yellowstone, it was pretty much a straight shot home to Hancock. This was probably the most extensive and exciting and yet, the least expensive vacation we had ever taken. We may be too old to do it again, but it would be very exciting to retrace our steps—in a sports car and a tent.

The red Fiero

The Cascades

CHAPTER 31

THREE DAUGHTERS, THREE WEDDINGS, THREE SONS-IN-LAW

THE BUEHLERS

The greatest and most important events for our family, while living in the Upper Peninsula, was the experience of seeing our three daughters marry. Our oldest, Cindy, dated and became engaged to a young dairy farmer near Concord, Minnesota, Jeff Buehler. The year was 1983, and at that time, Cindy was working at the then, Barlow's Super Market, in Rochester, Minnesota. They became acquainted through Merle, Jeff's roommate, who happened to be the Frozen Food Manager at Barlows. One day Cindy was working the Service Counter when Jeff came in to buy a pop from the Pepsi machine near-by. When he inserted his quarter, the machine began to "sing" the Pepsi jingle. He turned to Cindy and asked, "Does this machine sing for everyone like that?" She looked straight at him and responded with, "No, only for you!" It was love at first sight! That acquaintance led to a date, and that date led to more dates, and then trips to his farm home to meet his family. An amusing and ironic incident happened on one of those trips to the farm. It involved a dark, rundown, and deserted farm house, standing on a corner about a half mile from his family's farm. Cindy commented at the time, asking "Whose old house is that? Did anyone ever really live there?" And how "spooky" the place looked! She said that "It gave her the shivers—that somebody ought to tear it down!" Little did she know!

Meanwhile, Betty and I had accepted the call to Peninsula Christian Church in Hancock and were making preparations to move there. Jeff and Cindy had been dating for sometime but in Cindy's mind the relationship was not progressing. She finally decided to move things off dead-center. She gave him an ultimatum to make a decision about what he had in mind for their future or otherwise, she was making the move with her family to the U.P. of Michigan. Jeff proposed marriage! (No pressure there!) She accepted! They set a date for August 25, 1984. They arranged for the wedding to be held at the Zwingli Church of Christ, in the nearby village of Berne, Minnesota.

On one occasion, prior to the wedding, Cindy was discussing with Jeff where they would be living after the wedding. He then announced to her that they would be living in "that spooky old house on the corner!"— yes, the one that gave her the shivers! Today, you would never know it was the same house. Jeff, being a carpenter as well as a farmer, afforded himself the opportunity and ability to "upgrade" that spooky old house into one of the most impressive homes in that neighborhood. The most impressive feature is the "grand" front porch extending the length of the front of the house. It's a great place to just sit and swing and visit, or picnic or—just sit and play my banjo!

So, on August 25th, surrounded by his and her family and friends from the community, the Zwingli pastor, his family's pastor, and I, performed the wedding service. The service, being a bit more liturgical than I am use to, went well. It was a great celebration for the families of this rural dairy farm community. As of this writing, they have been married for 24 years and have one son and two daughters: Drew, a Senior, and history major at the University of Wisconsin, River Falls; Allison, a Junior and nursing major at Winona State University in Winona, Minnesota; and Abigail, a freshman at Triton High School, in Dodge Center, Minnesota—and all straight A students! While on that subject, when I consider the accomplishments and achievements of all three of our daughters and their children, I can't help but borrow a line from Garrison Keillor's assessment of all the good folks living down in his fictional Minnesota town of Lake Woebegone—"where all the women are strong, all the men are good looking, and all the children are above average!" That certainly describes the "Sorenson bunch"!

THE PAAVOLAS

Sherry, during the Summer of '84, while home between her sophomore and junior years at Drake University, frequented the beaches of Hancock, Michigan, where we were living. There she met "the lifeguard", Boyd Paavola (sounds like a page from her parent's past). Boyd was a great guy, admired by his peers and respected by his coaches and instructors at Hancock High. He was an excellent athlete and hockey player, following in his father's footsteps. He life-guarded during the summers, while home from his own college program at Lake Superior State University in Sault Ste. Marie, Michigan. They became friends and hung out together with the other lifeguards during that summer. Sherry worked at Little Brothers Friends of Elderly, in Hancock. They "officially" dated during the summer of '85 and by August that year, were engaged to be married. In the fall, Sherry was back at Drake for her senior year. Boyd decided to check out the Canadian hockey league to possibly break into it professionally, and moved to Warroad, Minnesota. In order to spend some time together, during winter break, he flew Sherry to Warroad, which is about a "hundred yards" from Canada, and about 100 degrees below zero in the winter! She nearly froze to death!

In the spring of '86 Sherry graduated from Drake. Betty and I and Boyd were there to see her get her diploma and help her celebrate this major milestone. We have always been proud of the fact that she was the only one of all the Sorenson family "kin and cousins" to graduate with a four year bachelor's degree from a major university. "You go, girl!" After graduation, she moved back home to Hancock for the summer. Boyd served his last Summer as a lifeguard at the Hancock beach, and returned to The Sault and Lake Superior State for his senior year. Rather than try to carry on their relationship from long distance, Sherry also moved to The Sault and found a job at Maurices Clothing. She rented a room from our long-time friend, Marsha Greenly-Ward, sharing the house with Marsha's son Lance, and daughter Karen Greenly. She lived and worked there through the rest of '86, and then returned home to Hancock for Christmas.

Figuring that Minneapolis would offer the best job possibilities for them both after graduation, she decided to move there in January '87. She stayed with Bob and Marge Cash, our longtime ministry friends, and looked for work. She found a job in her field, and in April located an apartment (situated conveniently at the end of the Minneapolis International Airport's runway) that would be their first home after their wedding. That spring, Boyd graduated from Lake Superior State, and in May they knew it was time to get on with a wedding and settling down in Minneapolis. His degree was in Therapeutic Recreation, and there were jobs available to him in recovery and treatment centers there.

They planned for their wedding to be back home in Hancock at our log church building. Again, it was a beautiful wedding with Dad performing the ceremony. Many of our families were there, along with friends from Bible College and ministry friends. They had decided to have their wedding on June 6th, 1987, also the 28th anniversary of our own wedding. What we didn't know, was that our girls had decided to celebrate both. After their wedding and in the middle of their reception, while eating our cake and punch, the announcement was made by Bob Cash that the focus of the reception was changing. "We are now celebrating Gordon and Betty's 28th wedding anniversary!" We even renewed our vows with Bob "officiating". It took us totally by surprise but certainly made sense, why not do two for one? It was a wonderful double celebration!

Boyd and Sherry now have two children, Joshua and Chloe. Josh is now a ninth grader and being homeschooled. Chloe is in seventh grade doing an at-home, on-line computer school. Their permanent residence has been in the Crystal/New Hope suburbs of Minneapolis. Boyd has been a computer expert and communications installer for The Minneapolis Star Tribune for the past several years. Their church home during those years was the Bloomington Church of Christ, several miles away. They recently made a change, and now make New Hope Church their church home. It is only a mile away, and offers many youth activities. They love living in Minneapolis with its many lakes, bike trails and hiking paths. We love to visit them there.

THE FARRIERS

Last, but not least, is Shannon, our "baby". Having mentioned earlier our involvement with Dan Farrier and the student ministry at Tech, now let me tell you the rest of that story. Dan was a regular at Peninsula Christian Church. He became a regular at our home for Sunday dinners, along with other family, students, and friends. Shannon and Dan became quite good friends in spite of their age difference. Dan was well into his college program at Tech, but Shannon was still a senior at Hancock High. Dan would stop by to visit, and their relationship could best be characterized as a "big brother/little sister" relationship. Dan then graduated, and was grabbed up by the Shell Oil Company and sent to Atlanta, Georgia. A short time after his move, our family planned a vacation to the southeastern states. Betty, Shannon and I traveled to Nashville, Tennessee, taking in the sights and sounds of "Country". Then, after meeting our exchange student Kyoko Takahashi at the airport in Columbia, South Carolina, went on to Charleston to revisit Ruby Ray and others we met during the mission trip "Operation Hugo". From there we went to Florida and the Kennedy Space Center, and on to Disney World.

After Disney World, it was time to start heading back home, except for one more important stop. When Dan discovered we would be in Florida and Georgia, he insisted that we stop in Atlanta for a few days, so he could show us around his stomping grounds. He did show us a great time. He took us to Stone Mountain where we celebrated the 4th of July with what seemed like a crowd of millions. That evening the weather was perfect. The vast crowd sat in the open fields at the base of the huge stone carving on the side of the mountain and listened to bands, singers, and music groups, and then enjoyed a spectacular fire works display. Then, a phenomenal thing happened! In the dark, in that vast crowd, someone shouted my name. There with his family, was a friend from our sister congregation in Marquette, Michigan! Unknown to each of us, we had traveled all that distance, going different places in the southeast, visiting different people in different places, yet, on this evening of the 4th of July we ended up sitting on the grass in this huge crowd, almost next to each other. We were all in awe. "This had to be another God thing!" We all agreed!

Dan took us to several other great places, like CNN headquarters, the Cyclorama, the Coke Pavilion, and took care of housing us at his apartment during the two or three days we were there. Betty and I would drop off to sleep with the sound of pleasant conversation coming from the kitchen. Dan, Shannon, and Kyoko would sit on the kitchen floor until 3:00 a.m., deep in conversation. We had a great and very memorable visit with Dan. But it was time to be on our way back to Michigan.

A RELATIONSHIP CHANGES

Shannon graduated from high school and enrolled as a Freshman at Minnesota Bible College. During the year she would get calls from Dan saying he had to make a trip to the Shell facilities in Houston—he could get cheap air fares to Houston by flying via Minneapolis International. He also indicated he had some time to spend, and if she would pick him up at the airport, he could spend a day or two with her in Rochester, visiting her campus, meeting her friends and college staff, and spending some time together. "Well, SURE, she would be glad to do so! This interesting "airline connection" happened not once, but several times. At first, we were wondering what might be going on with these periodic trips to Houston via Minneapolis, but soon her mother and I were pretty sure what was happening. Then, as the months passed, there was an invitation to come to the Washington D.C. area, where Shell Oil had transferred him. He paid for her airfare out to Reston, Virginia to spend some time with him visiting D.C., the Kennedy Center taking in some performances, and then the historical sights. Hmmmm, I wonder what is developing here? Then there was a trip together to Seattle, Washington to enjoy Thanksgiving with his friend Dave Peterson and wife.

Soon there were invitations to visit his home and family in Kalkaska. He would pay her airfare to Grand Rapids where he would pick her up, then enjoy relaxing visits with his family, especially at Thanksgiving and Christmas. The amazing thing I began to realize was that she just wasn't getting it—that he was interested in being more than her "big brother". On a visit home during one of her school breaks, Shannon and I had a casual talk around the kitchen table. In our conversation she confessed that she couldn't figure out why he was so good to her, paying for all those trips, having her meet his family etc. "Why is he doing this for me?" she asked.

I then realized for sure, she wasn't getting it! I asked her directly, "You really don't know what's going on with Dan? You really don't know why he is doing all these nice things for you?" No—she just couldn't figure his motive. I responded, "Well, let your father explain the whole thing to you."—she was all ears. "Dan doesn't want to be your big brother anymore!" At that announcement her mouth dropped open, her eyes opened wide and the "light bulb" came on! Maybe a little confused, maybe more from shock, she was beginning to put the pieces of the puzzle in place. "He wants a RELATIONSHIP with you—a real boy/girl relationship!" I announced. "Dan wants a boy/girl relationship with me?" she exclaimed. She just couldn't believe it. She just couldn't believe that this bright, gentle, handsome, talented, well mannered, "Prince" of a man would want the company of the beautiful, young, talented, naïve, backwoods country girl. "ME?" she repeated. "Yes, you" I reassured her. And that was the amazing, humorous, delightful, beginning of Mr. and Mrs. Dan Farrier.

That was the beginning, but the relationship continued to unfold with phone calls and visits and then—"THE" phone call! It was Dan. He wanted my confidentiality and the answer to a huge question. He was asking my permission to marry Shannon. After a pleasant hour long visit asking questions and expressing any concerns we had with the age difference, we gave him our permission. We were delighted that he wanted to marry our Shannon! He had plans to invite her to his home again for a holiday, at which time he planned to formally propose to her. We assured him we would not tell. It wasn't but a day or two later that Shannon called us from college "just to talk". She was sharing about her classes and campus life and then—an interesting bit of news about several of her girlfriends.

"You just won't believe it" she exclaimed, "all of my girl friends have recently gotten engaged and are making wedding plans—WEDDING PLANS!—Can you believe that?—BUT NOT ME!" She continued, "I am just not ready for marriage!"

Suddenly, I am almost choking, afraid to say anything for fear of giving away "the secret". I couldn't help but think—honey, you are in for the biggest surprise of your life! I did make it through the rest of the conversation without giving an inkling of what was coming.

The rest is history. She made the trip to his home for Christmas, enjoyed a great time with Gene and Shirley, his parents, and then took a hike with Dan through the woods to his favorite spot. It had snowed a little and thawed some, but even though it was a bit sloppy, Dan got down on one knee, "popped the question" and slid the ring on her finger. Of course, she was in the clouds. When she returned to our home in Hancock, she was so excited, showing off her ring and telling how it all happened. Betty and I sat there and beamed with a special kind of pride and grins that looked like "the cat that ate the canary". She studied our faces for a moment and then suddenly put her hands on her hips and exclaimed, "You guys knew all the time, didn't you!?" We confessed that we had in fact, known all along! We then had a great time of hugs and laughter and confessing as to when we knew and what we knew. It will be a great story to tell the grandchildren.

So, on August 19, 1995 the big day arrived. Dan's family from Kalkaska, and friends from Tech came. Our own family from Minnesota, and friends from college and ministries we had served, had all arrived to witness Dan and Shannon exchange their vows of marriage. As before, with the two older daughters, I, her proud father conducted the service and tied the knot. As they left to go to the reception there was the customary "rain" of rice, and as a personal favor, a friend of the congregation with a prize winning 1930 Model A Ford coupe with a rumble seat, arrived to be their "chariot". On this beautiful afternoon, they were taken on a grand tour/ parade of both downtown Houghton and Hancock and the Michigan Tech campus, riding in the open rumble seat. Since we knew there would be a gathering larger than we could accommodate in our church building, we arranged for the fellowship hall at Mt. Zion Apostolic Lutheran Church. Having several friends and ministry friends in that congregation, they were very accommodating in allowing us the use of their building.

But the wedding wasn't over! His home congregation wanted to have another wedding for them in Kalkaska. So we loaded Shannon's clothes, furniture and other belongings into our motor home and drove to Dan's home for another reception/celebration and final send off. The day of the Kalkaska Church celebration Betty and I and Dan's parents loaded all of Dan's remaining personal furniture and clothing items into the RV with Shannon's. After the evening festivities at the church we turned in for the night. The next morning at 2:00 a.m. the two of them left for the airport in Grand Rapids, and their honeymoon in Hawaii. I had awakened about the time they were leaving and I had some difficult moments as I heard the car pull away. Our last one was leaving the nest.

Later that next day, Betty and I left for Reston, Virginia, with their things. At Dan's apartment, we met a crew of volunteers from the church he attended, who helped with the unloading. One of his friends made the humorous comment, "Gee, I've never seen anyone move in a Greyhound bus before!" Everything came together beautifully. We moved them in and spent some time in Washington, DC, sightseeing. This trip was great for them, and for us. We saw things and did things we had never experienced before, and will probably never do again. Their furniture and personal things had been delivered. And suddenly, we had an empty nest!

Cindy, Shannon, Sherry

Cindy & Jeff—August 25, 1984

Boyd & Sherry—June 6, 1987

Dan & Shannon—August 19, 1995

The Buehlers—Jeff, Cindy, Drew,
Abby, Allison Christmas 2007

The Paavolas
Boyd, Sherry, Josh,
Chloe & Finn
Christmas 2006

The Farriers
Coleman, Dan, Shannon,
Clay, Caleb —2007

CHAPTER 32

SUDDENLY, A MINISTRY ENDED!

Peninsula Christian Church continued to hum along, as strong as ever. Each Sunday the building was full of Bible classes, parents, students, kids in the nursery, coffee, and wall to wall worshippers in the auditorium. Through the years 1993 to 1996 we were maxing-out the new building every Sunday. The dilemma was a topic for discussion at every board meeting. Going to two services was suggested, but rejected because of the concern of creating two congregations. "Besides, we won't be able to know everybody," they said. I considered both arguments as unfounded. Nobody knows all the members, even in a small congregation. Nobody listened. I then suggested we consider a major addition to our building. We could turn the existing building completely into education rooms, plus a large gym/recreation room, and build a totally new worship auditorium with twice the seating capacity. The congregation voted that down. The vote was not unanimous, but the majority vote ruled.

Needless to say, with no additional room for growth, the growth stopped. It appeared the congregation was slipping into the comfort mode. With the size of the congregation and with a weekly campus ministry at Michigan Tech, and other local ministry commitments, my schedule and plate was getting full. The congregation felt that with me approaching age sixty, perhaps what was needed was an assistant. They authorized me to search for an associate minister who could take over the campus ministry, plus our youth programming, and some of the teaching responsibilities. In my search, one name among several kept popping up, Ed Gund. Several of my friends in ministry knew of this young man and highly recommended him. I met with him at his parent's home in north central Wisconsin and was impressed with his campus ministry background and his personality. In a meeting with the congregation, he again came across well; so well in fact, a "call" was extended to him, his wife and family. The congregation wanted them to be a part of the ministry team at Peninsula Christian.

UNDERMINED

All was well, until he actually arrived on the scene. From day one, his persona changed. The very first Sunday, we happened to arrive in the church parking lot at the same time. As we walked from our cars to the front entrance I extended a greeting to him and his family. It was as though I didn't exist. There was no response, no eye contact, nothing whatsoever. He and his family simply entered the building and went about their business. For the next several months his demeanor remained the same. I was totally confused. Had I done something to offend him? I decided to have a personal one-on-one meeting with him to find out what the problem was. He was unaware of any problem! He was surprised I would suggest that there was. But that something was wrong was evident to the men on the board. When they asked me if I knew what the problem was, I was at a loss for an explanation. It became one of the most stressful times of my years in ministry. He was of no help to me personally. It was obvious his intention was to take the ministry and program of the church where he wanted it to go. The board was concerned that I was losing control of my leadership over him. That was not the problem at all. There had been no cooperation, no teamwork from the first day. For many years I had been in leadership roles. I had never been one to hold a gun to the head of anyone under my leadership. It was evident that to have cooperation with Ed, I would have to do just that. What was really evident was that he wanted my job! The young "bull" was going to run off the "old silverback". I couldn't believe that something like that could be happening among supposedly Christian men. I was in for a big surprise!

He had evidently convinced the board that what was needed to get the church moving again was a younger minister. The fact there was no room left in the building to grow had never occurred to them. On a Sunday afternoon in August, 1996, I received a call from one of the elders to meet with them in the late afternoon. As I walked into the meeting I casually asked "Well, what do we need to discuss this afternoon?" Their immediate response was, "Well, we've decided we need a change of leadership, we're asking you to leave the ministry here within sixty days". I couldn't believe what I had just heard! I asked them to "run that last statement by one more time; I don't think I heard you correctly". So they repeated the statement. It was for real! I was floored! I had indeed heard correctly!

As the discussion proceeded, it was evident that because I was turning sixty, they wanted someone younger. Their actual excuse was, that they knew my heart was really with missions. My leaving would "free me up to pursue my heart's desire". I don't know how they could reason that at sixty years of age I would have the time and energy to organize and raise the financial support to go into full time mission work, and do it in sixty days! If that were true, then why didn't they propose to send us to the mission field and offer to be our main supporting church? Most people, even ministers and missionaries, are planning for retirement in their sixties. I was not planning on retirement at that point, but certainly not going to the mission field either! Up until that point I was still feeling strong enough and positive enough about the future of the congregation, that I was planning on another five to ten years at Peninsula Christian. It was not to be.

As my mind reeled with this news, and with what I knew lay ahead, I began asking them questions. I asked if the congregation had made this decision, and did they even know about it. To my surprise, they did not. This had been strictly the decision and action of the then three or four elders. I asked how and when they wanted "this action" announced. They said it was up to me. I could word it how-ever I wanted, and do it whenever I wanted. I don't remember if it was from a sense of reality or a feeling of anger, but I immediately responded that I would tell the congregation that very next Sunday and read my letter of resignation. I realized that to protest or fight their action was of no use. To fight it, and insist on staying would only polarize the congregation. The last thing I wanted was to create a fight, and split the membership. That thought had always been abhorrent to me. It never crossed my mind to do such a thing.

There was only one thing to do, announce it to the congregation and to our family and friends and start packing boxes and look somewhere else to serve God. Although I soon recovered from the initial shock, it has taken me years to forget the pain.

HOW TO DESTROY A CONGREGATION

Most of the pain has come from what happened after our leaving. They were successful in immediately getting a replacement. Mr. Gund thought for sure he had the position "in the bag". It was later revealed to me that they set a date for an interview with him, but he appeared at the interview late, and in his dirty, sweaty, muddy work clothes, and was ill prepared to answer their questions or state clearly what his vision and plan would be for leading the congregation. The board was so appalled, that much to my surprise, they did not offer him the job. They chose a young man who had been involved in campus ministry in southwestern Michigan. He had been dealing with incoming high school and college students. He had been in a position to call all the shots and develop the program himself. He was not used to working with adult church board members and teachers and worker volunteers. Through our contacts with friends in the church, we heard that after three years of forcing his plans and ideas on the congregation, he had polarized the members into warring factions. Long-time members were walking out, fleeing to other churches, and the membership had been cut in half or deeper. After a short three year ministry, it seems he felt he had done all he could do—he was moving on. Wow! A three year ministry to tear a congregation apart! That's got to be some sort of record!

GOING TO PLAN "B"

Going back to that infamous August 1996 board meeting, and the original shock of being asked to leave, we called our daughters to tell them we would be leaving Hancock, and moving somewhere—where, we didn't know, but somewhere. We also called our closest friends in ministry, Howie and Sandy Ganong and John and Darlene Read in Indianapolis. And wouldn't you know it—God was already at work—way ahead of us. I called Reads first, because I also needed the new telephone number for the Ganong's. Darlene answered the office phone as though she was expecting my call at that very moment. Before I could get a word out of my mouth about our new circumstances, she exclaimed, "Oh, its you Gordie, the guys were just talking about you, discussing how much they could use your help right now with the remodeling business—Oh, John and Howie just walked in—let me put John on."

Hearing it was me on the other end of the line, John immediately begins kidding me about "hitting him up for a job". When I immediately said that I would indeed be looking for a job, he began to realize I wasn't joking around. There was a pause, and then he began asking what was going on with me up in the UP. I explained to him what had just transpired with the board and that we would be moving somewhere else. Realizing that I really would be needing some kind of new employment or ministry, he responded by telling me to collect my wife, my stuff, and my tools, and get down to Indy as soon as I could—he actually needed me now, if not sooner! His remodeling business was booming, and he needed my help. It was another "God thing". I was going to become a carpenter! That's not bad—Jesus was!

A CONGREGATION IN SHOCK

The Sunday following the board meeting, I gave the morning message and then asked the congregation to stay for a minute more, that I had something important to share with them. I began reading my letter of resignation. I have never seen such shock on the faces of a crowd before. I explained that my resignation was in agreement with what the elders had requested, and I thanked them for the great thirteen years we had partnered together in the amazing growth and body life of the congregation. I could hear gasps, and see tears flowing down faces, aghast with what they had just heard. When I finished, I closed with the benediction, after which no one moved. Everyone just sat there in stunned silence. I told them they would be alright, that I was alright, and it was OK for them to leave. They didn't know what to do. They just sat there. Gradually, they got their wits about them and made their ways to the doors and their cars and home. Later, it didn't take long for them to figure out what they wanted to do. They demanded a congregational meeting. They did meet. Betty and I were not there; we were busy with packing and moving plans. But they did meet—they wanted to "hang" the elders! "Hang" might be a bit of an exaggeration, but it was close to that. Part of the shock was that the elders had decided to fire me without any discussion with the congregation. This was just the beginning of three years of troubled times for that church, i.e.. a new minister, church in-fighting, and a split, and then another new minister. The latest and current minister appears to be a good fit for them. Some new life and vitality has come back to the church, and they are growing again! But sadly, many of the old members are gone, and attending elsewhere. We just received a note today, 2008, from Karen Fay, that the church was growing again, the building was full of new young couples with children every Sunday! Betty and I are ecstatic!

READ BUILDERS: FROM MINISTRY TO CARPENTRY

I accepted John Read's invitation to join his remodeling business in Indianapolis. After all, there was more than just hammers and nails and boards and a pay check tying us all together. We were all graduates of Minnesota Bible College (Crossroads College) and closer than family. During the next sixty days we busied ourselves with packing boxes again and loading the motor home. I even made a two week visit to Indy to look for a place to live and help with the carpenter work. I then returned to Hancock to help finish packing and to make the move Since I had found no suitable house we could afford, John and Darlene invited us to stay in their front bedroom and share their facilities. Betty fit right in, serving as housekeeper and cook. We actually had a great nine months staying with them, at which time we were able to purchase our own home. We almost regretted moving to our own place. Who else could successfully pull off something like that, but a bunch of old Bible College alumni? Our Bible College years were hard times for all of us students, and many of us wouldn't have made it without each other's help. We shared the joy and laughter, but we also shared the struggles, and the hard times. We were always there for each other. We are still there for each other.

CHAPTER 33

NEW WORK,
A NEW CHURCH AND
ANOTHER MISSION

While living in Indianapolis, we placed our church membership with the Oaklandon Christian Church, and developed many more wonderful friendships. Of course we became involved in several church mission projects. One of those projects was joining a large mission group from that congregation going to Rosarita, Mexico, south of Tijuana. We flew into San Diego, California to linked up with the lead team from AMOR Ministries based there. They took us to an outlying barrio where in seven days, we built three houses for three different families. It was a very ambitious undertaking but very rewarding.

The one couple, I remember, had two children. Her kitchen was in a rickety shed the size of a mid-western outhouse, and their house consisted of a U shaped row of cement blocks about the size of a queen size bed. It stood about four feet tall and was covered with a few tree limbs and a blue plastic tarp. At first I mistook it for a stack of building materials. They had a nasty, snarling dog tethered at the open side for protection, and as I saw the family crawling in and out at various times of the day, I realized that the "stack of cement blocks" was really their home. In seven days we were able to present this family and two others, each with a new two room house with a concrete floor and eight foot ceilings. As with all AMOR ministry homes, it was a about 22-feet long by about 11-feet wide with two doors and three or four windows. These AMOR homes were mansions compared to most other structures in the neighborhood. All the work, from pouring of concrete to the sawing and nailing of boards was done by hand. There were no power tools, thus, there was no chance for cutting off fingers and toes by novices. And, no need for bulky generators and air compressors and all the gas cans and hoses that go with them. Speaking for myself and the teens and adult team leaders, all in all, there is nothing that gives as much personal satisfaction as presenting to a homeless family a new home that you helped build with your own two hands. Ten days after arriving in Mexico we were back on the plane headed home to Indianapolis—pleasantly tired.

A GOOD BUDDY, A GREAT LOSS

Also, while we lived in Indy, Betty and her good friend Sandy Ganong, worked together at the Oaklandon church, ministering to the children enrolled in "Mom's Day Out". But Sandy and Betty did more together than Mom's Day Out. They were joined at the hip, as they say! They coffee'd together, shopped together, went to thousands of "Cheap-day" movies together, garage saled together and enjoyed many church functions together. Wherever you saw one, you knew the other one was close by. But as is often the case, as our bodies age, sudden tragedies strike us down. On a day in January 2002, while on their annual visit with the Reads to their friends Bruce and Jan Burdick in Hot Springs, Arkansas, Sandy slumped over in her chair, the victim of a brain aneurysm. She died a few hours later in the hospital at Hot Springs. Within the next few days, many family and friends from around the country gathered at the Oaklandon church in Indianapolis to bid Sandy good-by. We were all in shock! She had been so healthy and happy and in good spirits. Suddenly—gone! But certainly not gone forever! One of these days soon, we will all enjoy her light-hearted and zany humor again as we fellowship with all who have gone on before us. Come Lord Jesus!

LIFE GOES ON IN INDY

While living in Indianapolis, we enjoyed Gaither concerts and week-ends at the Read's beautiful lake home on Sweetwater Lake south of Indy. Many wonderful afternoons were spent boating and skiing and going for relaxing cruises on their pontoon boat. It was here, at their lake home, that our own family twice celebrated family reunions, where we and all three daughters and families could enjoy a week together on the lake. We were either swimming on their beach, going off the diving board and water slide, or enjoying the paddleboats, and skiing behind the power boat. In the evening after dinner, the thing to do was feed the huge catfish off the deck above the boat garage.

The house was so big and well equipped that everyone had his own bed and/or bedroom, and his own bath and shower. There was a game room with a pool table, and card tables, and two TV rooms. There were also two kitchens if needed, as well as a grill and picnic tables out on the deck. Before our first family get-together there, our kids kept calling to ask where everyone was going to sleep—imagining that the lake home was just a small four or five room "cabin". We assured them that everything would be fine and adequate to house the sixteen of us. When they arrived, they were in awe! They could not believe the accommodations! Years later, as we reminisce over those two family vacations, they all agree that those weeks to be the best ever. We will probably never be able to repeat those days at the lake-house. John and Darlene are nearing retirement and have the lake home for sale. Bummer!

WORK, WORK, WORK

For John and Howie and the crew and me, it was putting in 40-hour (sometimes more) weeks, working on customers homes, remodeling, fixing and repairing baths, kitchens, family rooms and roofs. We had the privilege of developing long-lasting relationships with many of John's customers. We also had the fun of figuring out naughty house problems and creating solutions, like curing reoccurring roof leaks after repeated fixes by professional roofers. I was often busy creating custom cabinetry for special applications.

One of my jobs with one of our good customers, John and Martha Carmody, was designing a kitchen out of existing cabinets that would be more easily accessible for her. In her broom closet, I designed, built, and installed six roll-out shelves. She had been having a difficult time locating and reaching items stashed in the back. Her new ball-bearing glide full-extension shelves were an immediate hit! She couldn't get over how easy it was to pull the heavily loaded trays fully out! She ordered fourteen more for every cupboard and cabinet in her house. I made her a roll out waste-basket tray, a roll-out cookie sheet tray, a roll-out dish soap-cleanser- SOS pad scrubber tray for underneath the kitchen sink, even a concealed, roll-out silver and valuables tray. It has been eight or nine years since I did her custom kitchen, and have received several Christmas cards from the Carmodys, thanking me for the wonderful roll-out trays.

THE "EGRESS" MAN

Another project I did while working on a remodel job with the crew, was to create a window egress for a new bedroom being installed in a basement. This project would have nothing to do with cabinetry or finish carpentry. This job demanded brute force. Since the window egress was to be installed in a rear corner of the house where all the underground power lines and water lines and sewer lines entered the house, and since there was a bunch of landscaping i.e.. scrubs, bushes and trees in that corner as well—right where we needed to dig the hole for the egress, it required my digging by hand, a ten foot by ten foot by twelve foot deep hole alongside the foundation! "Holy cow", I thought. "What's next!"

At 12-foot deep, every spade full, every shovel full of dirt had to be staged up to ground level. I created a set of four giant steps from which to shovel the dirt to the next level and then into a waiting wheelbarrow. I then had to wheel each load to my waiting pick-up and haul it away to a new location. The hole was so deep, it tended to be darker at the bottom. One day the homeowner came out to locate me and to see my progress. He shaded his eyes, peered down into the hole and then, as if he had not seen me, began to look around the yard to see where I had gone. I yelled up out of the hole, "You lookin' for me?" I scared him half to death! He had not seen me. He couldn't believe I was that deep down. It had been necessary to dig that deep to get to the "pee gravel" and drain tile below the level of the foundation, for the window pit to have drainage. Finally, I was there!—I could stop digging!—and out of the hole came a Chinaman!

Next, with the help of Ron Horban, John's son-in-law, I had to cut a hole in the basement wall the size of the large double-hung window to be installed. The walls were one foot thick, steel-reinforced concrete. We had to rent a chain saw type power saw with a large concrete and steel cutting blade to get through the wall. We made a perimeter cut where the rough opening would be, then several vertical cuts through the wall where the window would go. We then took a sledge hammer and beat out the sections of concrete, making a rectangular hole in which the new window would fit. It worked great! I then laid six by six treated timbers around the three sides of the "pit" like a log cabin wall. I created flower bed steps at the back, to easily exit the window pit. The new window was beautiful and large enough for their high school age daughter to simply open the window in case of an emergency, and simply walk up the stepped flower bed to ground level and safety. The owners loved it. The crew was even impressed enough to give me a new name—*The Egress Man*! Somehow, word of it spread to my friends in Iowa and Minnesota. Even our daughter in Minneapolis heard of my egress work. My new name, "The Egress Man", has stuck with me. I've done a couple more egresses like that one, even our daughter in Minneapolis had me do one for her basement office. She loves it.! Actually, I began refusing to do anymore. They are too much work for an old man! Let the younger guys do them.

THE HUMMER

Previously, in my story, I spoke of our "motor home". Sometime in 1990 or '91, we purchased a 1957 Greyhound bus from ABC Bus Company in Faribault, Minnesota, with the dream of converting it to a motor home. I drove the bus the 400 miles home to Hancock, Michigan, with Betty following in the car. The bus ran well, but we noticed differential grease from the bus, all over the car's windshield. The first order of business was to replace the main differential grease seal. As the months passed, and as we had the money, we began making other improvements. First, were improvements in the steering, tires, and drive train. At first we made no improvements to the inside, just concentrated on the drive train. When we bought it, the seats had been removed and partitions had been installed, but there were few cabinets, no bathroom, beds, or other amenities. There were only a few old couches and card tables with folding chairs scattered around. We did use it on a few occasions for camping and for the big mission trip to Mexico. We also used it making our move to Indy and earlier, moving Dan and Shannon to Reston, Virginia.

Knowing that retirement was just a few years away, and with money and materials more readily available while working at Read Builders, we began to make major improvements. We finished the inside with new cabinets, closets and drawers; a bathroom vanity and sink, and a new shower and RV bathroom stool. I also installed new fresh-water and black-water holding tanks, along with all necessary plumbing and electrical lines. The last thing we did while living in Indy, was to have it stripped and a totally new paint job sprayed on, along with a new rear engine cover and headlight package. On the Indy west side, we located an automotive paint shop that specialized in painting Indy race cars and car haulers, who was hungry to do another big project. We worked a deal with "Christophers", and after picking colors and the paint scheme, two weeks later, she was a finished "one-of-a-kind" motor home!

As I drove into the parking lot to pick it up, I could see a bus just like mine sitting there, just out of the paint booth. It was just too beautiful! I just knew it couldn't be ours! I went in to pay the bill and look for my bus, at which time I was directed back out the door from whence I just come, and was told, "You just walked right by it! That's your bus!"

"That's my bus?" I exclaimed!

Indeed it was! I couldn't believe the transformation! It was beautiful! Where the blanked-out windows had been skinned over, we had their resident artist air brush a large ruby throated humming bird on each side, (hence, "The Hummer"). The Hummer was—is, a work of art. We get lots of thumbs up while driving down the freeways. We later had the Detroit Diesel engine overhauled, along with the air compressor, and a set of spring brakes installed on the rear axle. For (another) "old timer" she's in great shape.

John & Darlene Read

The Indy Gang—Betty, Sandy, Darlene, Gordon, Howy & John

CHAPTER 34

OH NO!
ANOTHER MOVE!

We never knew when God would call us to His next mission. We had been in Indy for three years. We loved our new home and neighborhood. We loved the congregation at Oaklandon. We had some money in the bank. We had settled in! We were healthy and feeling great. Life was good! We should have known something was coming. God, it seems, never wanted us to get too comfortable. When we did, He always had a new assignment for us.

One day our daughter Cindy called us from her home in Concord, Minnesota. There were the usual exchanges of greetings and the latest news about the family and friends. Then she informed us that the Concord Church of Christ, just down the road, was looking for someone to replace their present minister, who was planning to leave. She said that Roger Quartin, their minister, had spoken with her about the possibility of my being a candidate. He urged her to contact me and have me send a resume to the church board. The Concord church was not an unknown to me. A few years previously, the minister then, Steve Grice, had secured my services to preach a week of pre-Easter meetings there. It had been a very good experience, allowing me to become personally acquainted with many members of the congregation. Because of that experience and the fact that our ministering there would put Betty and me just three miles away from Cindy and her family, and only eighty miles away from Sherry and family in the Twin Cities, the idea was very appealing. I sent my resume.

WE'RE GOING TO CONCORD

It took a very short time to hear from the church board—they wanted us to come. We made a trip there to see Cindy and family, preach for a Sunday service, and meet with the board to discuss details and plan for the move. Once again, it was resume the usual routine—pack the clothes, pack the books, pack the kitchenware, pack the tools, and then finally, pack the truck. This time the truck would not be a rental truck—it would be a semi-truck. Rick Jones, a member of the Concord church, drives a dry goods semi for Hanson Trucking in West Concord. The congregation contracted with Hanson Trucking, and Rick to be in Indy on moving day—of course again on my birthday, December 16—this time 1999. What is it about my birthday? Rick and our Indy neighbors, and the crew from Read Builders helped load the semi. There was a new twist this time. With the assistance of a nearby ramp and loading dock we loaded our Mazda pick-up into the semi and stacked boxes and furniture around it. We also loaded our bus/motor-home with the remaining furniture and household items, and then made our way to Minnesota, caravaning behind Rick in the semi.

We made the entire distance to Concord in one day. It was around 7:30 p.m., and getting dark when we arrived at the little rural church building and parsonage. The congregation had a wonderful surprise awaiting us. As we crossed the bridge and looked to the left across a little valley, we could see that the members had lined the last hundred yards from the main highway to the Church's drive way with luminaries. It was a very beautiful and meaningful welcome for us, as hundreds of candles flickered in the night. Many volunteers were there to help unload. Many hands made quick work of a big job. The only thing left to unload was the pick-up. We did that the next morning at the Hanson Trucking loading ramp and dock.

WE COULD DO IT BLINDFOLDED

Again, it was time to—hang up the clothes, put away the dishes, unpack the books, organize the office, put away the kitchen tools and appliances, arrange the furniture, organize the garage, and once again get into the flow of small town U.S.A. Getting into the flow meant spending hours in the office again, preparing sermons and lessons. It also meant learning where to shop, where to have the car serviced, where to get a haircut, and where everyone lived. It was also back to attending committee meetings, and of course the inevitable "board meetings", where plans were discussed and dates were set, but far too often, little of significance accomplished. My memories of board meetings through the years, was that there were too few who were qualified to be board members, too many with little or no vision for the church's mission and future, and by far too much time and effort given to preserving the traditions and relics from the past. Too often board business was about maintaining the status quo. Board meetings were by far, the most frustrating hours spent in ministry. I thank God for those few who were Biblically literate and in tune with the Biblical mission of the church and who had a vision for what the church should be doing. The amazing thing is that in spite of these obstacles, the church miraculously survives, and in some cases even grows!

CHAPTER 35

ITS TIME TO RETIRE

We had, and still do have many dear friends in that congregation. There are many there, who are true servants, and continue to quietly pray and give of themselves and their time and resources in service to Christ. These we will not forget, servants like Dennis Dohrmann, our only elder, and wife Cindy, Barb Loquay, Rick and Wendy Jones, Bob and Karen Smith, Jason French, Jeff and Ann Franzen, Shirley Moe, and our own daughter Cindy Beuhler, and others.

We served this congregation for four years, with intentions of staying even longer if progress continued. But the last year, growth was stymied due to lack of space.

THIS JOB IS KILLING ME

At a frustrating board meeting I received a huge wake-up call. While sitting in the meeting, suddenly the left half of my body went numb! My first thought was, "I have heard about these kind of things—this is a mini-stroke or a stroke!" I didn't know if I should have the guys call 911, or just sit and see if it would go away. I waited, it began to go away! The feeling began returning to my arm, hand, leg, and face. As the meeting closed, I wondered if I would be able to stand and walk. After the chairman closed the meeting with prayer, I arose, stood steady on my feet, and walked out of the meeting and up the stairs. I crossed the parking lot to the parsonage and found everything normal again. But, I began to say to myself, "This ministry is going to kill me! I am 67, I don't need the frustration! I don't

Gordon & Betty in front of the Concord Church of Christ

The Concord Parsonage

need to continue doing this! They no longer need my leadership. It's time to retire and head for Texas!"

"WE'RE A HEADIN' FOR TEXAS!"

Months before these events, sometime in 2002, our daughter Shannon, and husband Dan in Texas, told us of their plans to build a new home in the Tomball area of Houston. They had purchased a one acre wooded lot and were working with a contractor and architect, and had settled on a plan. The plan included an extensive woodshop, since Dan was an avid woodworker. Knowing we were making plans to retire but as yet having no retirement home, they began thinking of providing a place for us to live on their new property. There had been discussions with the contractor about building a second floor apartment above the shop, but he didn't feel he could include it in the quoted price. We were thrilled they were willing to even consider doing this. The solution was to move the shop and bus port closer to the east property line, then add a ground floor apartment to the west end. When they took the idea to their contractor he saw no problem with including it in the plan. He would do it! We would have a five room apartment waiting for us whenever we were ready to retire.

As construction on the house proceeded, we resigned from our duties, effective as of October, 2003. And—once again, we packed our belongings for the move—this time to Texas. Fortunately, we were able to again contract with Rick Jones and Hansen Trucking to ship our things by semi to storage units in the Tomball area. We made that move on—you guessed it—December 16th, my birthday. Our things remained in storage there until our apartment was finished. While awaiting its completion, we lived for three months in the Hummer at an RV park a few miles away. Soon, the apartment was ready, and we transferred our things from the storage units to our new home. About that same time, Dan and Shannon's house was ready for their move, also. We then pitched in to move their things. At last, our new address, 12 Rolling Glen Lane, Tomball, Texas was a reality!

Tomball, Texas was not new to us. For several years, while living in Minnesota, we had been taking ourselves off the Concord church payroll for a month for income tax purposes. Our Social Security, plus church salary, put us in a penalty situation. We used those weeks off, usually in

January and February, to be "Snow Birds", to get a break from the bitter winter cold. We would drive the Hummer, towing our pick-up, to a great little RV park in Spring, Texas. From there, our home away from home was only three or four miles from Betty's sister Jill, and only eight miles from Dan and Shannon and the boys. It was a great way to enjoy our Texas families, great winter temperatures, a shortened winter and make lots of new friends. A couple of times, we included trips west, through Tucson, visiting my sister and friends there, and then to California to visit Mother and our family and friends in the Los Angeles area.

RETIREMENT IS NOT FOR THE FAINT OF HEART

Retiring is not as easy as it sounds. We had been physically active all our lives. I was also kept mentally active, with weekly studies and preparation for sermons and lessons. Now and then I had a funeral message, and even a Baccalaureate message to be delivered at the local high school. I had also been deeply involved with the members of these congregations as their leader/shepherd. They looked to me for comfort, for guidance, for spiritual food, and for direction through the difficult times in their life. Suddenly, it was mostly all gone. Emotionally, I found myself back to my frame of mind after graduating from high school, wondering what to do with the rest of my life? Days of depression would come and go, where I began to question my worth and my purpose, and even if God were really there. Couple those thoughts, with the fact of losing my hearing and some mobility, and I suddenly realized that now in retirement, after I had fought the major battles of life and won, I might be in for the real battle of my life! Retirement is not for the faint of heart.

As the months of retirement continued on, I began to realize that God is still there, working, supporting, and sustaining. His reassurance and healing touch comes through our many friends in the churches and ministries. Although there is no longer a regular routine schedule of events, as when in active full time ministry, nevertheless, new and serendipitous events and blessings come unexpectedly. All during the summer of '06, while summering in the Concord area, Sharon Moreland of Crossroads College kept me busy almost every weekend doing supply preaching for churches all over southern Minnesota and northern Iowa. I must confess, being back in the pulpit again and connecting the people with the Word was exhilarating, and recharged my batteries! When we

weren't doing that, we were doing volunteer work at Pine Haven Camp near Park Rapids, Minnesota. At Pine Haven, I did everything from cutting down dead, dying, and damaged trees to repairing screen doors on the cabins. I even had the pleasure of designing a mini RV park for other future volunteer retirees who would serve the camp, while living in their RVs. That mini RV park is now a reality and ready with full hook-ups. What fun!!!

KATRINA TRIP NUMBER ONE

In 2005, on one of our visits north to Minnesota, we decided to take a different route home. We would return by way of the U.P. of Michigan and visit our friends in Hancock, and Peninsula Christian Church. We parked the Hummer in Barry and Karen Fay's driveway, and had a wonderful visit with them and others from the church, before proceeding east to Marsha and Bill Ward's at the Sault. We visited the Ward's, then crossed the Mackinac Bridge, making our way to my cousin LeRoy Illium's and wife Millie in downstate Michigan. From Illiums we drove east to Midland for a visit with my brother's grand daughter Amber. From there we went south into Indiana to visit our dear friends Howie and Nancy Ganong and John and Darlene Read. While visiting there, we were approached about traveling with a group from the Oaklandon Church in Indianapolis, to Slidell, Louisiana , to help with the Katrina clean up. Since we were headed back that way to get home to Texas, we signed on. Because we didn't have an extra driver for the Hummer, we decided to leave a day ahead of the church crew. We arrived in Slidell with no problems, and made our way to the Christian Church parking lot. We backed into a spot next to the backside of the building near both water and electric hook ups. We settled in. The place was already a bustle of activity. First, they had cleaned the muck and silt from four feet of ocean water out of the building. A crew from Texas with four-wheel drive ATVs with push blades, made quick work of this. They removed the soggy carpet by cutting small holes in several places at the far corner of the auditorium. Then, hooking the carpet over the ATV ball hitches, they pulled it all loose and right out the double doors—all in one large, soggy, muddy mess.

My first, and main job upon arrival, was to hang the new doors! I hardly had time to strap on my tool belt!

"Please," they pled with me! "Please install the restroom doors—please!" All the wood trim, wood structures, wood doors, wood anything, had to be removed and replaced. The crews who had arrived early had done much of this, along with removing the carpet. Now, it was time to replace those things—*especially*, pled the women, *the restroom doors*! While the main crew from Indiana went to work building a new platform for the sanctuary, I began installing thirty complete new door systems—jambs and all. "Restroom doors first!" cried the women! So I did. Within an hour, the two restroom doors were on and in service! They were delighted! Some of the crew cleaned, some finished sheet rocking; some painted—I hung doors!

After a day or two, we decided to take a break from our work at the church building and go into the surrounding neighborhoods to do some cleanup work. I must say, I have seldom seen so much devastation by wind, and so much water. It was like the whole Gulf of Mexico washed up into Slidell—at depths of four to eight feet in some places. Everywhere, there were mountains of trash and tree limbs and trees and appliances and furniture and cars and clothes and bedding and kids' toys. We helped several families clean up the enormous mess in their home and yard and then returned to the church building to finish readying it for services the following Sunday. The church building was also to be used as a relief center for the surrounding neighborhoods. We then bid good-bye to the folks at Slidell and the team from Oaklandon, Indiana, and made our way back to our home in Texas. We were tired but rested, with a sense of great satisfaction and accomplishment. And the doors were all on!

KATRINA TRIP NUMBER TWO

A few months later, in March of 2006, I got a call from my friend John Read in Indianapolis, asking if I would be interested in meeting him and son-in-law Ron Horban, and a crew from John's congregation, to do some more Katrina repair work in New Orleans. I saw it as a great opportunity to do some more much needed carpentry relief work with friends, and enjoy seeing families returning to their homes. Again, I signed on. We met at the Crossroads Ministry Center just off I-10 near the southeast shore of Lake Pontchartrain. This is where we slept and were fed. I was amazed to find that eighteen months after Katrina had struck, there was still no electricity or heat in the building. Temperatures were in the thirties at night. We slept with our clothes and jackets on, along with any wool army blankets we could find—and still froze!

The Louisville Crossroads church ministry team had discovered the huge Faith Church building complex standing empty, and found it perfect for what they needed, and available for lease. I was amazed that such a new and large facility would be standing empty. I was told that the entire congregation of 1,700 members had moved away on the heels of Katrina, and only 70 of their members were returning. They no longer needed the building. That was part of the disturbing and eerie feeling we all felt while working and staying in those neighborhoods of New Orleans. It was a ghost town! We worked everyday in the Chalmette area, south of the Lower Ninth Ward. Everywhere we looked, there were whole subdivisions, whole neighborhoods, standing empty. There was just nobody home! Here and there were signs of life, with one family in one neighborhood, and then a block away in another neighborhood another family, cleaning and repairing and painting.

Although we had this strange feeling that we were the only ones there, yet another incident painted a different picture, one that reminded us that SOMEONE ELSE was there! On one of the first days, we were working in the yard of a home under repair. I had just cut down a mangled tree that was leaning over the front of the house. The crew was picking up the cut pieces when we heard an airplane circling overhead. Our crew, and others around the yard, stopped to look up at the plane. We noticed heavy "smoke" coming from the back of the plane. Some thought he was in trouble. My thought was that it was a "sky writer", something I hadn't seen in many years, something most people never see. Then, as we all stood in the yard looking up, the pilot, with a trail of smoke billowing from the back of his plane, began writing this huge message over the city of New Orleans. As we watched—the sky writer spelled out the words, JESUS LOVES YOU! A cheer went up. The whole neighborhood cheered! It made our day! The neighborhoods may have looked empty, but HE was there all the time!

BOBBY "TEX" GRANGER

On my way home from New Orleans, knowing I would be passing through Orange, Texas, and with a rumor of a Bible college friend living there, I decided to look him up. Just one surprising phone call, and easy directions, and quickly, there I stood, in Bobby "Tex" Granger's front yard. I had a great visit with Bobby. I hadn't seen him in 45 years. He is still preaching at the West Orange, Church of Christ, and sawing lumber harvested from his twenty acre wooded farm, to be shipped for the rebuilding of New Orleans. It was good to see him again. I also had the pleasure of meeting his wife and grand daughter. I am also very appreciative of his major contribution to the New Orleans rebuild. God was at work again through this old friend.

NOT THE LEAST OF BLESSINGS

Other blessings received in these later years of our lives would have to include the annual Ball Club Lake fishing trip with our dear friends from the Marion Church, Glen and Sharon Moreland, Steve and Joan Winter, Ron and Karen Piotrowicz, Lyle and Coleen Dietz, and Mike and Terry Blachek We spend a week together fishing, laughing, and camping, and then later, at the end of summer, gather together for a fish fry. Of course, also mixed into these summer activities is the fellowship we enjoy with our two daughters and husbands and grand children in Minnesota. We will continue to be snowbirds, as long as I can see the road, and reach the peddles on the Hummer.

Rebuilding after
Hurricane Katrina

CHAPTER 38

MOM'S FUNERAL

Mother was 94 and in failing health at a care facility in Azusa, California. She was suffering some from dementia and couldn't remember much. In the last days, she complained about having to live so long. She often asked, "Why can't I just go home and see Dad?" Last New Years holiday, she got to do just that. We laid her to rest on January 10, 2007. We rejoiced together that mother was through with the pain and frustrations of this life, and indeed at home with Dad. My siblings asked if I would officiate at her funeral. At first, I questioned such a request. "Isn't that expecting a lot of big brother?" Then I thought—no—I could do this. I could make it a victory celebration, and include personal stories and information that would be comforting and encouraging to all the family. I knew several weeks in advance that this day might be coming soon, so I set about putting together some thoughts and a message. I am glad I did.

When the word came from my brother Gary, that Mom had passed on, we packed the car, and headed west to Tucson, to pick up my sister Peggy. We drove on to California and to the home of my niece and her husband, Karen and Bill Ryczek, where we would be staying. The funeral went well, and as usual, God provided me the self-control I needed, and the right words to say to give Mom a proper "send off". We remained in California for a few days to visit Betty's family and then made the return trip home.

Peggy had earlier shared with me the need for some repair work on her home. Knowing something of this in advance, I brought carpenter tools with me to do this repair work. Having no room for us to stay at her home, we stayed a couple of nights in a close-by motel. We needed to stay longer but our reservation ran out, and there were no other motels available, due to lots of bad weather to the north. The resulting rush on available rooms left us "homeless!" I called an old high school friend, Gus Pappas, who lived in Tucson. I asked if he might know of some motel that might have a room available in a situation like this. He said, "Yes, I do know of one—it is called, The Gus Pappas Motel! Mary and I would like you and Betty to come and stay with us!" End of problem! We did stay with Gus and Mary, and enjoyed an exceptional time with them. It was good to renew a friendship from high school, share in our faith adventures, and their hospitality.

Their hospitality allowed us the extra time needed to fix Peggy's house. Betty and I were able to patch all the holes in the walls, repair the holes in the floor, and re-frame and hang four damaged doors. I also repaired and stabilized the front steps, hand rail and landing. We didn't get everything fixed, but at least the main things were repaired. We left the painting for her to do. She was excited to get her house fixed. I was glad to help her out. My main prayer for Peggy is for happiness and peace to come to her life and home.

Ahead of us, we still had the long trip home from Tucson to Houston. To make the trip even more difficult, New Mexico and Texas, were having some of the worst winter weather in several seasons. Cold winds, freezing rain and dropping temperatures, had driving conditions across west Texas deteriorating by the hour. We were receiving regular cell phone calls from our friends, the Metcalf's in Houston, who were following our progress, and warning us of storms and conditions ahead toward Austin and Brenham. They reminded us that they, and our friends at church were praying for us. That fact soon became very apparent. It seemed that as we traveled eastward the weather around us cleared enough to give us safe passage. When we reported our locations at various times of the day, they were surprised we were making such good progress. Of course, our years driving in the Minnesota and U.P. winters prepared us well for the freezing conditions we were experiencing in Texas. We returned home safe and sound, thanks to God and the prayers of our family and friends.

CHAPTER 36

THE LAST CHAPTER

The rest of 2007 was sprinkled with various other serendipitous blessings. As we snow- birds made our way back to Minnesota in April, we decided to visit Bible college friends along the way. We first visited John and Marsha Luther at their lake home at Lake Whitney, Texas. I brought my tools with me to do some little repair favors along the way. We had a great time with John and Marsha. I built them a new storage shed under their deck stairs, and then shared lots of great memories and good things to eat.

Next, on our way north through Kansas, we stopped in Wichita for a visit with George and Kay Bloomquist. Both George and I have lots of Scandinavian blood, so we spent most of the time sharing "Ole and Lena" and "Swen and Ole" jokes, and laughing our heads off. They took us north of Wichita to Lindsborg, Kansas, a thorough-going Swedish settlement. What a wonderful day, looking and learning and laughing. On our return that day we stopped at the little town of Galva, Kansas for a short surprise visit with Roy and Bev Peterson. They had been members of the Webster City Church of Christ in Iowa, and both George and Kay, and Betty and I had, at different times, served that congregation as associate ministers, and knew them and their family.

Later, making our way north to Iowa, we stopped in Omaha, Nebraska, to visit Virginia and Tom Mortenson. Virginia was another graduate of MBC, and a personal friend. While in Omaha, we also visited Jim and Bonnie Harmon. Jim was a "Timothy" of mine, along with his brother

Dave, through our ministry at Liscomb, Iowa. Jim and Bonnie had been serving a Disciples church in the Omaha area. His brother Dave and wife are now serving with Lincoln Christian College in Lincoln, Illinois. We also stopped in Storm Lake, Iowa, to visit my good buddy Jack Barber and his wife, Lucille. Jack is fighting cancer, and so far, winning. I wanted to check on his progress, and give him encouragement for his ongoing struggle. He also recently retired from the Storm Lake ministry and is now serving as a Chaplain with Tyson Meats in Storm Lake.

Jack Barber up-date: Before finishing my last editing of this book and on our 2008 return trip to Minnesota, we stopped in Storm Lake to visit Jack and his wife Lucille again. He was not doing well. His very first words to me after our greeting was, "Gordie, will you have my funeral?" I was stunned! "Yes Jack" I said. "But you're not done here yet!" But he knew. A week later we heard he had fallen, had severe brain damage and surgery and was finally recovering at a care center in Storm Lake. But on July 3, 2008, his battle was over—the Lord took him home. On July 7th I held his funeral at the Storm Lake Church of Christ where he had ministered and where we had shared so many great times in the youth fellowship. I made the occasion a celebration of Jack Barber!

ONE LAST WEDDING? OR MAYBE NOT.

Forty-four years ago I had my first wedding (mentioned earlier in the book), for our long time friends Bob and Arlene Eckman. Early in the spring of 2007, I received a call from Heather Eckman, their youngest. She reminded me, that I had performed her parents wedding back in '63, and "what a good tight knot I had tied". She then exclaimed, "And I want you to do mine and Rusty's!" I agreed! I was honored and delighted to do their wedding. So, I dusted off my old marriage ceremony, we packed our bags, and in June 2007, made our way to Montrose, Colorado. We flew to Denver, but discovered it was much cheaper to drive a rental car from Denver to Montrose than flying all the way. We were glad we did! It was a beautiful and scenic drive. As many times as we've been in Colorado, we still discover so many more wonderful scenes to see, and highways to drive.

All the Eckman clan and kin had traveled from Minnesota and South Dakota to Montrose for the wedding. Bob and Arlene's little ranch was crawling with folks. Our accommodations were wonderful. They had borrowed a friend's motor home, and parked it just outside their back door. The meals were bedlam, but the fellowship was great. The weather and scenery were perfect, with the snowcapped San Juans to the south. We had a rehearsal the next day, Friday, with the wedding the next day, Saturday. Except for a few minor glitches, the service went perfect. The music was excellent; the attendants did their thing; the nervous bride was beautiful! Within the hour, they became Mr. and Mrs. Rusty Stark. What an honor it was for Betty and me to be a part of their life, and once again, 44 years later, a part of her parent's life. By the way, the lights were on this time—everyone witnessed this wedding service seated!

Oh by the way, this will not be my last wedding—I've been requested to perform another wedding on October 17, 2008!

ABBY'S BAPTISM

Probably the best way to end this book is with a beginning. While back at our oldest daughter Cindy's home, she and the family informed me that their youngest, thirteen year old Abigail, had made a decision to accept Jesus into her life, and she wanted her Grandpa Sorenson to baptize her! I could not have been more thrilled! What an honor to baptize a grand daughter! It was 1952, I was fourteen when I made that decision and was baptized. We had Saturday afternoon to fill the baptistry and plug in the "tank" heater to take the chill off the water. The following Sunday morning she made her public confession of faith before her peers and the congregation, and immediately following, I baptized Abby "into the Father, and the Son, and the Holy Spirit"—just like her Grandpa did 55 years earlier! She, at that moment, started a new walk with Jesus Christ! She had always walked with him, but this experience in the water had made it complete! A new life in Christ!

And now, a close to this book about my life—or maybe not—who knows what God may yet have for me to do?

THE END...or maybe not!